Herink.

STRATEGIC VS. EVOLUTIONARY MANAGEMENT

A U.S. – Japan Comparison of Strategy and Organization

Advanced Series in Management Volume 10

Series Editors: **A. BENSOUSSAN** and **P. A. NAERT**

*University of Paris-Dauphine
and INRIA
Paris
France*

*INSEAD
Fontainebleau, France
and UFSIA,
University of Antwerp, Belgium*

NORTH-HOLLAND
AMSTERDAM · NEW YORK · OXFORD

STRATEGIC VS. EVOLUTIONARY MANAGEMENT

A U.S. – Japan Comparison of Strategy and Organization

Tadao KAGONO
Kobe University
Kobe, Japan

Ikujiro NONAKA
Hitotsubashi University
Tokyo, Japan

Kiyonori SAKAKIBARA
Hitotsubashi University
Tokyo, Japan

Akihiro OKUMURA
Keio University
Yokohama, Japan

in collaboration with:

Shiori SAKAMOTO
California State Polytechnic University
Pomona, California
U.S.A

Johny K. JOHANSSON
University of Washington
Seattle, Washington
U.S.A.

1985

NORTH-HOLLAND
AMSTERDAM · NEW YORK · OXFORD

HD
70
.U5
N513
1985

ISBN: 0 444 87754 1

Publishers:
ELSEVIER SCIENCE PUBLISHERS B.V.
P.O. Box 1991
1000 BZ Amsterdam
The Netherlands

Sole distributors for the U.S.A. and Canada:
ELSEVIER SCIENCE PUBLISHING COMPANY, INC.
52 Vanderbilt Avenue
New York, N.Y. 10017
U.S.A.

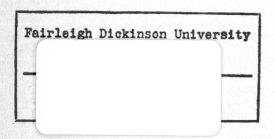
Library of Congress Cataloging in Publication Data

Nichi-Bei kigyō no keiei hikaku. English.
    Strategic vs. evolutionary management.

    (Advanced series in management ; v. 10)
    Translation of: Nichi-Bei kigyō no keiei hikaku.
    1. Industrial management--United States. 2. Industrial
management--Japan. 3. Strategic planning--United States.
4. Strategic planning--Japan. 5. Industrial organization
--United States. 6. Industrial organization--Japan.
I. Kagono, Tadao, 1947-   . II. Title. III. Title:
U.S.-Japan comparison of strategy and organization.
IV. Title: Strategic versus evolutionary management.
V. Series.
HD70.U5N513 1985   658.4'012'0952   85-6745
ISBN 0-444-87754-1

PRINTED IN THE NETHERLANDS

PREFACE

This book is a result of a long, evolutionary process of learning and unlearning. The original research project was started in 1976, when we began a large-scale empirical study of Japanese companies and their management practices. At that time, an international comparative study was only a dream to us all. Frankly speaking, we didn't have a clear-cut research plan then. But our dream has finally come true, partially through will power, persistence, and chance.

An opportunity for conducting an international comparison arose in 1979, when one of the authors, Kagono, visited the Harvard Business School for a one-year stay. We revised the 1976 questionnaire to enable us to conduct a comparative study of strategy and organization between U.S. and Japanese companies. We mailed the same questionnaire – in English and in Japanese – to the *Fortune 1,000* companies and to 1,031 Japanese companies listed on the Tokyo Stock Exchange in April, 1980.

We expected the response rate to be low, given the fact that the questionnaire was 13 pages long. But 227 companies in the U.S. and 291 companies in Japan completed and returned the questionnaire.

We conducted a statistical analysis of the questionnaire data, which we believe is the first systematic attempt to compare the strategy and organization of Japanese companies with U.S. companies. The findings of this analysis are included in Chapter 2 of this book.

Though the findings were interesting by themselves, we were not able to gain sufficient insight into actual differences and commonalities in management practices between the two countries. We, therefore, augmented the statistical analysis by conducting in-depth case studies with selected companies, thanks to the financial support of the Japan Economic Research Center in Tokyo and the cooperation of Mr. Akira Iio, a senior economist there. The findings of this intensive case analysis are found in Chapters 3 and 4 of this book.

Two of us visited the U.S. in 1981 and 1982 and interviewed several U.S. companies as well as subsidiaries of Japanese companies. At the same time, we interviewed executives of Japanese companies back home. As a result of this field work, we identified two contrasting orientations toward strategy and organization between the two countries. The Japanese strategy was labelled "operations orientation" and the U.S. as "production orientation". The Japanese organization was labelled "group dynamics" and the U.S. as "bureaucratic dynamics". These two orientations are discussed in Chapter 5.

Given the new insight we gained from these case studies, we then re-analyzed the questionnaire data. We wanted to test whether or not the quantitative data base confirmed the findings of the field study and to present new hypotheses concerning the strategy and organization of high-performing companies. These findings are included in Chapter 6.

We began this research with the integrative contingency theory, presented in Chapter 2, as our theoretical base. Stated simply, this theory takes an open, engineering view of organizations. During the three research phases (i.e., statistical analysis of questionnaire data, analysis of case studies, and re-analysis of questionnaire data), however, we confronted many cases and patterns that could not be explained by the open, engineering view alone. We, therefore, developed a new theoretical perspective and arrived at an "evolutionary" view of organizations. The theoretical and practical implications drawn out from our long research project are discussed in the final chapter.

We encountered many problems and challenges throughout our research. In hindsight, we feel as though they became the seeds of development for further inquiries. In pursuing these inquiries, we exchanged ideas with a large number of people. Without their timely and valuable assistance, we could not have completed our research.

Professor Michael Y. Yoshino at the Harvard Business School helped us send the questionnaire to U.S. companies in the first phase of the research. Professor Hirotaka Takeuchi, who was also at the Harvard Business School at the time, assisted us in developing the research design. The research funds provided by the Ministry of Education and the Japan Securities Research Foundation were instrumental in getting the project started in the first place.

We are indebted to the Japan Economic Research Center and the warm support of Mr. Takanobu Suzuki, the chief of its research planning department, in the second phase of the research.

Our colleagues Ken-ichi Imai, Hirotaka Takeuchi, Hiroyuki Itami, Hideki Yoshihara, Akinobu Sakashita, Yoichi Komatsu, Junzo Ishii, Tom Roehl, Takashi Nagata, among others, gave us critical but constructive comments on an earlier draft of this book. Professor Susumu Takamiya helped to arrange interviews with Japanese executives. Mr. Koichiro Aoyama, a director at the Nomura Research Institute (NRI), gave us access to the materials and records accumulated at NRI.

Numerous executives and managers in Japan and the U.S. generously spent a considerable amount of time in interviews. We would like to acknowledge their contributions by mentioning the names of their companies: Ajinomoto, Amada, Cincinnati Milacron, Du Pont Far East, Eli Lilly Japan, Fujitsu, Hitachi, Kao, Kyocera, Levi Strauss, Matsushita Electric, Mitsubishi Electric, Motorola, NEC, Renown, Seibu Group, Sumitomo Electric, Suntory, Takeda Chemical, Texas Instruments Asia, Toray, Toshiba, and Toyota.

This book was first published in Japanese by the Nihon Keizai Shimbun, Inc. Its editor, Mr. Akitake Kurosawa, was instrumental in organizing the divergent ideas we generated. Professors Shiori Sakamoto and Johny K. Johansson, our collaborators, gave us valuable comments and helped us translate the book into English. Dr. Carel van Houten, senior editor, and John Butterfield, technical editor, both at Elsevier Science Publishers B.V. (North-Holland), gave us continued encouragement and professional advice. All the members of the Institute of Business Research at Hitotsubashi University were helpful in putting this book into print. In particular, we thank Katsuhiro Umemoto, Takashi Yazaki, and Dan Trullinger for their editing and flexible administrative assistance and Harumi Seto for her assistance in typing and producing the manuscript.

Compared to the Japanese edition, which was awarded the best academic book of the year (1984) by the Academic Association for Organizational Science, several revisions are made in the English version. First, we further developed our theoretical framework (i.e., an evolutionary theory of organization) and proposed a self-organizing paradigm to explain our findings in the final chapter. Second, we added a more detailed description of Japanese companies for our non-Japanese readers and simplified our description of U.S. companies. Third, we re-organized and expanded Chapters 3 and 4 in the Japanese edition into three chapters.

In the course of developing our ideas and methodologies, we have been greatly enriched by the discipline given to us by our mentors: Professor Emeritus Kuniyoshi Urabe of Kobe University for Kagono; Dean E.T. Grether, Professors Francesco M. Nicosia and David A. Aaker of the University of California at Berkeley for Nonaka; Professor Moriyuki Tajima of Hitotsubashi University for Sakakibara; and Professor Robert B. Duncan of Northwestern University for Okumura.

Finally, it seems like a Western tradition to say something about our wives and children at the very end. Our male chauvinism, however, prevents us from conforming to that tradition. They know how we feel.

Tadao Kagono, Ikujiro Nonaka, Kiyonori Sakakibara, Akihiro Okumura

CONTENTS

xiiContents

7.3.3. Similarities and Differences between H and V Type Adaptation 250
7.3.4. An Evolutionary View of Organizations – The Self-Organizing
       Paradigm 255
7.4.   Practical Implications. 264
7.4.1. Japanese-Style Management and the H Type of Adaptation 265
7.4.2. S Type Adaptation and the American Firm 268
7.4.3. Toward a Symbiosis of Heterogeneous Types of Adaptation 270

Appendix A: Questionnaire (Japanese) 277
Appendix B: Questionnaire (English) 293
Appendix C: Japanese Company Descriptions. 307

CHAPTER 1   IN SEARCH OF A NEW PERSPECTIVE ON JAPANESE MANAGEMENT

1.1   Introduction

The performance of the Japanese economy (both before *and after* the oil crises) and the competitive strength of Japanese firms in a number of key industries are well-documented. The "successes" have led to much scholarly and professional interest by those in the West. In significant instances, the competitive strength of Japanese firms has come to be perceived as a menace and has caused international friction. This has created a climate of mixed feelings, one ripe for heated discussion, and into it a number of arguments have been precipitated about why the Japanese are so successful and whether the keys to success are transferable to other socio-cultural settings.

These "common sense arguments" have evolved during the last few years. Initial attempts to demonstrate the reasons for the Japanese successes invoked cooperative relationships between business and government, favorable industrial relations brought about by a company union system, and loyal workers with high morale due to the Japanese socio-cultural setting. Later attempts have included QC circles, long-term investment, intense competition within the domestic market, high quality and low cost made possible by recent investments in production processes, etc. And most recently the Japanese management practices, which used to be synonymous with inefficiency and backwardness, have come to be regarded as keys to high quality and competitive strength.

The common sense view argues that the above factors together are responsible for the Japanese successes. But this view is subject to a number of questions. The first and foremost question concerns the degree of success of Japanese companies. Are they really so successful? A comparison of performance should give a tentative answer to the question. Comparing the before-tax return on equity of the major U.S. and Japanese corporations (Table 1-1), it becomes readily evident that the American companies outperform Japanese firms in the majority of cases.

Table 1-1 Comparison of Return on Equity (Before-Tax, 1982)

Sector	Japan		U.S.	
Chemical	Toray	6%	26%	Du Pont
Semiconductor and Telecommunication	NEC	19%	13%	Motorola
Electric Machinery	Hitachi	26%	27%	GE
Computer	Fujitsu	22%	38%	IBM
Foods	Ajinomoto	22%	38%	General Foods
Automobile	Toyota	23%	4%	GM
Toiletries	Kao	16%	19%	P&G
Apparel	Renown	17%	26%	Levi Strauss
Industrial Materials	Sumitomo Electric	15%	29%	3M
Machinery	Amada	19%	4%	Cincinnati Milacron
Construction Machinery	Komatsu	22%	-5%	Caterpillar
Steel	Nippon Steel	7%	-6%	US Steel

Figure 1-1 shows the average ratios of operating profits to sales between the U.S. and Japan for ten different industries. Clearly, the U.S. outperforms Japan in most industries in terms of profitability, implying that the basic assumption of Japanese success may be an illusion. Of course profitability is only one of many criteria of success. It is, however, difficult to conclude that Japanese companies have generally been more successful than American firms. It seems more reasonable to begin with the working hypothesis that, however measured, the "degree of success" in a crosscultural comparison varies considerably from industry to industry and varies also in a comparison of industries within a given country. Moreover, there are generally more and less successful companies within any particular industry of a given country.

Figure 1-1   Comparison of Ratios of Operating Profits to Sales
of Major Industries
(For details of companies surveyed refer to appendix
1A at the end of this chapter)

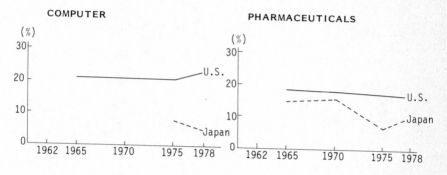

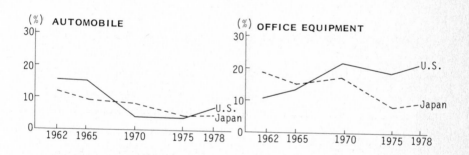

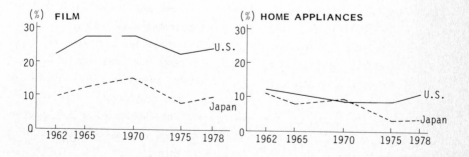

Figure 1-1   (continued) Comparison of Ratios of Operating Profits
to Sales of Major Industries

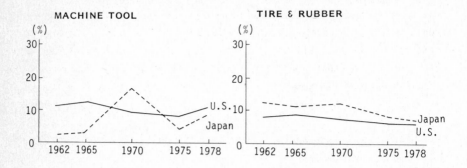

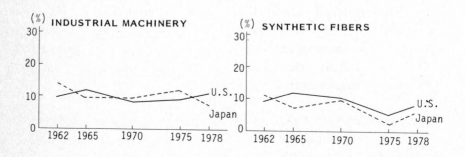

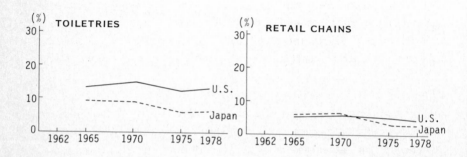

A second important question concerns the generalizability of certain of the common sense conclusions, for instance, the idea that participative management is a key of Japanese success.

We are aware of important exceptions to this management style in Japan; and there are major Japanese firms with highly autocratic, top-down mangement systems which are, in fact, also very successful. This points up that many stereotypical characteristics are not necessary and sufficient conditions for success. A given management system might produce high performance under certain environmental conditions, but not always. The vital point is that many stereotypical characteristics of Japanese organizations and management are not necessary and sufficient conditions for success, *even in Japan.*

Thus, there are *many* questions left unanswered. The principal purpose of this book is to provide answers to some relevant and basic questions concerning Japanese management: What *are* the general characteristics typical of Japanese management practices and to what degree do those characteristics differ within and between industries? How do these characteristics compare with those of U.S. management? What strengths and weaknesses do Japanese management practices have and *under what conditions*? What are the relevant historical, economic, and societal circumstances that fostered the development of these characteristics?

As the brief survey of the literature on Japanese management below shows, most of the previous published research have been either intensive studies of a relatively small number of firms *or* limited in the number and types of variables which could have explained the findings reported. It is not surprising, therefore, that there are still unresolved issues. In addressing the questions which motivated our research, a *broader framework* is employed as a way to integrate and build upon previous findings, and to help resolve apparent conflicts by adding new knowledge in a few places.

While this book is a scholarly undertaking, we hope, as its authors, that we have not lost sight of the common-sense dictum that *all* cultures can and must contribute much to each other. We hope that this modest contribution to better understanding of "western" and "eastern" managers, alike, might help reduce the friction between us. If it does only that, our effort will have been worthwhile.

1.2 A Brief Survey of Studies on Japanese Management

1.2.1 Traditional Foci on Japanese Management

The first modern treatment of Japanese management was written as a Ph.D. thesis at MIT by a Japanese-speaking American scholar, James Abegglen, in 1958. Using an anthropological approach, Abegglen identified life-time employment, the recruiting of new graduates directly from school, promotion from within, and the seniority-based wage system as the predominant characteristics of Japanese management. His findings strongly influenced subsequent studies which came to be dominated by two principal foci. The first was on those management characteristics unique to Japan; the second focus was on the socio-cultural orientation of the Japanese people, especially its "groupism."

The studies on the unique features such as life-time employment, company-union organization, seniority wage and promotion system, the organization of top executives, *ringi* decision system, etc. explained how those institutions function and why they were created and maintained. Yoshino (1968), in a thorough study, emphasized their effect upon the ability of Japanese management to respond to new environmental challenges. Hirschmeier and Yui (1977) analyzed the historical processes which created those systems and Urabe (1977, 1978) posited that most of the unique institutions were based upon the expectations of company and employee that equity of exchange between the two parties will be achieved in the long run. Koike (1977, 1981) questioned whether the "unique" institutions were really unique to Japan and argued that the pervasive building of skills and expertise through in-company training programs, on the job training, and long-term evaluation comprise the basic, distinguishing characteristics of Japanese companies.

Other major studies focused on the socio-cultural orientation of the Japanese people. Hazama (1971) shed light on the paternalistic aspect of

Japanese companies, and Tsuda (1976, 1977) saw an "emergent living community" in Japanese firms. Both authors characterized Japanese companies as clans rather than as modern "contractual" organizations. Iwata (1977) argued that the clans appear because of the psychological "groupism" -- the opposite of "individualism" -- of the Japanese people and Nishida (1982) asserted that such clanism is a consequence of a mode of social linkage unique to Japan. The common theoretical orientation of these authors is their emphasis upon the groupism observed among Japanese companies and people and their attempt to explain it in socio-cultural terms.

Ouchi (1981) and Pascale and Athos (1981), again emphasizing groupism, asserted that clans can also be observed among well-managed American firms. Ouchi called these American firms Type Z. The Type Z organizations, characterized by long term employment, slow promotion, long-term evaluation, group decision-making, and unique management styles, create a *clan* which contributes to employees' sense of belongingness and trust. Pascale and Athos (1981) shed light on the "soft" aspects of management, including, shared values, staffing, styles, and skills, which were seen as no less important than the "harder" aspects of management like strategies, structures, and systems. Although Ouchi, Pascale and Athos argue that groupism is hardly unique to Japan, their conclusions reinforce those cited earlier in their emphasis upon the importance of cohesive groups in successful management.

1.2.2 Limitations of the Dominant Perspective

This brief overview of a few key contributions to the Japanese management literature is sufficient to give the major outlines of what can be called the "dominant perspective."[1] Some of the limitations of this perspective can now be identified.

(1) Emphasis on socio-cultural uniqueness

The first limitation of most of these studies is their over-riding emphasis on socio-cultural uniqueness and failure to weigh the importance of other possibly very relevant factors. It is perhaps reasonable for the first stage of an international comparison to focus on socio-cultural differences. Culture does deeply influence management practices and the studies cited have succeeded in helping us to understand that many basic characteristics of Japanese companies are attributable to unique socio-cultural factors. But the socio-cultural perspective might be challenged on two points.

The first is its inherent theoretical limitation. The socio-cultural perspective seeks to explain the emergence and maintenance of unique social systems by reducing causal factors to certain of a country's cultural attributes, for example, its dominant values, norms, and psychological orientations. From the socio-cultural perspective, the cultural base provides the independent variables while management systems and practices are viewed as dependent variables. The problem derives from the tendency of those independent variables to be "elusive, diverse, and always changing" (Hamaguchi and Kumon, 1982).

Fundamentally true of modern societies, including Japan's, is that their cultures are comprised of diverse subcultures, and each subculture is continuously evolving in directions different from that of others. For example, entrepreneurs play innovative and major roles in cultural evolution (Schumpeter, 1934) by, in fact, creating diverse subcultures. It is, therefore, very difficult to accept that there would be just certain values, norms and beliefs which definitively constrain all of a society's management practices. Even the idea that the causal link between culture and management practices is necessarily unidirectional is questionable. We think that the rate of cultural change and the degree of cultural diversity facing organizations are more pertinent to a normative framework for management than an analysis based on the assumption of a stable "cultural base."

Another difficulty of the socio-cultural perspective relates to the vagueness of the implications which can be drawn from it. At least thus far, the socio-cultural perspective has failed to give definite answers to important practical questions, for example: Why are the Japanese successful in some industries and not in others? What are the strengths and weaknesses of the management practices observed among Japanese companies? Some new studies have recently emerged which in part address such issues. Hayes (1981) and Wheelwright (1981), focusing on operations management in Japanese companies, argue that the production process is a key factor in the success of some Japanese companies. Abernathy et al. (1981), comparing the production policies of U.S. and Japanese automobile companies, point out the centrality of production strategy to the success of Japanese automobile firms. Kohno (1976), Tsuchiya (1978), and Okamoto (1979) discuss the impact of Japanese decision-making processes and systems on the strategic behavior of Japanese corporations. Imai and Itami (1981) posit that loosely-coupled interorganizational networks contribute to the adaptability of Japanese companies. These studies are changing the dominant focus of observation from a socio-cultural to a less culturally-specific, managerial one (Kagono et al., 1981). A major consequence has been to shift the focus from necessarily culture-bound explanations for *existing* differences to a focus which, inclusive of cultural factors, seeks explanations which contribute to a general normative framework for managerial decision-making.

(2) A lack of empirical data

The second limitation of the bulk of studies on Japanese management practices originating both in the U.S. and Japan is the lack of empirical data satisfying accepted standards of scientific methodology.[2] While not necessarily "unscientific," many contributions are based more upon casual observation and incomplete data than upon sound empirical evidence. The absence of careful methodology and empirical data have contributed to the creation of stereotypical views and a lack of theoretical coherence.

It is not surprising, given these shortcomings, that many studies have presented findings supporting researchers' initial biases. The consequence has been misunderstanding, arbitrariness and confusion.[3] The root cause is the fact that, contrary to the dominant perspective, there is diversity in the management practices of Japan. Thus, casual observation of a few cases will not be sufficient for an accurate assessment of Japanese management. For a definitive assessment, several methodological criteria must be met. First, the populations of comparison should be identified explicitly so that it is clear which organizations we wish to draw

conclusions about. Second, scientific sampling techniques should be used
so that representativeness is ensured. And third, actual data should be
systematically gathered and analyzed.

(3) The lack of orientation toward a more general theory of management

The third limitation of the dominant studies to-date is that their
discussions do not lend to an extension of the theory of management. The
study of Japanese firms represents an important opportunity to test the
generalizability of existing theories and develop them further. The
principal orientation of the dominant studies to find and explain
uniqueness, precludes this possibility. We hope that this study of
Japanese companies sheds light on aspects of management which, indeed,
contribute to the existing theories of management and, thereby, assists in
the formulation of a general theory.

Considering these limitations, we need to study (1) managerial aspects of
Japanese companies, based on (2) the systematic collection of empirical
data, in order to (3) propose a more general theory of management. This
constitutes the basic mission of this book.

1.3 Theoretical Framework and Research Method

1.3.1 Contingency Theory

A starting point for this research project was the contingency theory of
organization. Contingency theory was proposed in the early 1960's by
British researchers (Burns and Stalker, 1961; Woodward, 1965) and more
fully developed by American researchers (Lawrence and Lorsch, 1967;
Perrow, 1967; Thompson,1967). The fundamental ideas of it can be
summarized as follows.

The environment surrounding an organization is always changing.[4] Changes
in industry structure, customers' preferences, technology, competitors'
behavior, legislation, and societal norms and expectations generate a
variety of opportunities and threats. This is called *environmental*

variety. The word "variety" is defined in cybernetics as the number of distinct elements relevant to choice of action or response (Ashby, 1956, p. 126).

An increase of environmental variety imposes information and decision burdens on firms. How effectively a firm copes with these information and decision burdens determines its degree of goal accomplishment, i.e. company performance. A firm must use a variety of resources (people, materials, money and knowledge) to deal with opportunities and threats. This is termed *organizational variety*. The pattern of matching resources with opportunities and threats over time represents the firm's strategy. To implement a chosen strategy, people's activities must be organized. Patterns of people's interactions within the firm comprise organization. Strategy and organization are constrained by the resources available. What constitutes requisite variety in strategy and structure depends on the nature and magnitude of environmental change. When good matching is achieved, firms can cope effectively with opportunities and threats, and attain high performance. Although reasonably good performance can be achieved with a misfit between environmental and organizational variety in the short run, a good fit is necessary for sustained high performance.

Based on these ideas, the aim of contingency theory is to construct normative propositions concerning the kinds of fit that are necessary between the firm's environment and its strategy and structure.[5]

Contingency theory is used as a starting point in this study for the following reasons:

(1) Contingency theory was developed through comparative empirical research. Consequently it is an appropriate framework for an international comparative study.
(2) The theory is a comprehensive framework which can account for interdependent relationships among an extensive variety of organizational phenomena.
(3) Contingency theory is wholly consistent with a number of analytical paradigms (such as the information processing model or the resource dependency model), and can incorporate many different empirical

findings and theoretical models.

(4) Contingency theory has provided measuring instruments for operational indicators of managerial phenomena.

We had previously been and still are developing an information processing paradigm (Nonaka, 1972, 1974; Kagono, 1980), but for the present purpose we regard the contingency framework to be superior. One of the aims of our study is to enrich organizational theory in the context of a wider ranging comparative study than reported heretofore, and in the process, perhaps provide theoretical extensions as well.

1.3.2 Method of Comparative Analysis

To fully understand the characteristics of Japanese management, it is necessary to compare its characteristics with those of management abroad. We have chosen U.S. firms for comparison. The United States is the undisputed forerunner of modern management and has produced most of management's current principles and theories. Also, Japanese firms have introduced many managerial techniques from the U.S. before adapting them to their own specific needs. For these reasons, U.S. firms seem most appropriate for comparison; such a comparison would seem to offer the most promise for substantive gains in theoretical and practical applications.[6]

The methods of comparative study often used in contingency theory are of two kinds: survey methods using large samples, and intensive case studies of a few firms.

These two methods have complementary advantages and disadvantages. Survey methods have the advantages of enabling us to (1) identify general population characteristics and formulate hypotheses from large-sample data, and (2) test hypotheses applying statistical analysis. They have the disadvantages of (1) tending to be superficial and (2) making it difficult to analyze dynamic phenomena.

The intensive case study method has the advantages of (1) making possible more in-depth analysis of a few cases, (2) more easily discerning causal relationships, and (3) better analysis of dynamic phenomena. Its disadvantages include (1) uncertainty in the generalizability of propositions and hypotheses derived, and (2) the greater likelihood of introducing researchers' selective perceptions and biases.

Survey methods are in general appropriate for hypothesis testing and intensive case methods are more useful for hypothesis generation. For the purposes of achieving greater insight and analytical soundness, in this research, both survey and intensive case study methods are used.

1.3.3 Structure of the Book

The order of the book's chapters follows the sequence of the research as it was conducted. We present the findings and results of analysis that were obtained at each stage of our process of inquiry. This should provide the reader with the understanding of Japanese management that is necessary for comprehension of the ensuing phase and should enable him or her to logically follow the development of our theoretical model.

Chapter 2 presents the results of a survey of the largest companies in the U.S. and Japan based on the holistic contingency framework. The aim of this analysis is to *clarify* the differences and similarities of U.S. and Japanese management. This analysis also clarifies on what characteristics more intensive research should be focused. The analysis in Chapter 2 reveals a difference in the adaptive patterns of U.S. and Japanese firms. Two consistent adaptive patterns (American and Japanese modes) are identified and their strengths and weaknesses are discussed.

In Chapters 3 and 4, intensive case analyses of management strategies and organizational structures in different forms of organizations are presented. The results are summarized in Chapter 5. Intra-country differences are also discussed in this chapter. This in-depth analysis is the basis for a new conceptualization of the empirical differences found in strategy and structure. The differences are described in terms of an *operations* orientation vs. *product* orientation (strategy), and in terms of *group* dynamics vs. *bureaucratic* dynamics (organization).

Returning to the survey data in Chapter 2, the impact of these strategy and structure variables upon firm performance is analyzed statistically in Chapter 6.

Finally in Chapter 7, hypotheses and propositions derived from the case research and statistical analysis are organized, and theoretical and practical implications are developed. An integration and generalization of the strategic orientation and organizational principles of U.S. and Japanese firms is proposed, a new typology of organizations is presented and a general theory of organizational adaptation underlying the typology is put forward.

Notes

1. Other than these, related to the internationalization of Japanese enterprises, we should not forget other useful researches which accurately described the characteristics of Japanese Management. In particular, Ishida (1976), Yoshihara (1979), Kobayashi (1980), and Yasumuro (1982) are worthy of mention.

2. The research on Japanese Management based on systematic data-collection has been mainly developed by social science researchers in such areas as sociology and cultural anthropology. These studies can be classified into those based on sociological survey data such as, Marsch & Mannari (1977), Azumi (1979, 1980), Pascale (1978), and those based on methodologies of cultural anthropology, such as Dore (1974), Rohlen (1974), Clark (1979). The former group employs research methods developed in Europe and America to specify the organizations of Japanese enterprises. This methodology is based on the idea that Japanese organizations do not possess any speciality. We are of the opinion that measuring instruments of the management discipline more appropriate for international comparison should be developed.

3. Sugimoto & Maoa (1982) indicated that the theories based on the uniqueness of "Japanese" and "Japanese Culture" to-date lack scientific methodology. Using the methodology of "grouping of episodes," the argument up untill now can lead to entirely opposite conclusions by mental experimentation. It can be said that the danger of the method based on grouping of episodes can be demonstrated by actual examples.

4. In addition to business enterprises, contingency theory can be used to explain adaptive patterns of all sorts of organizations in government, schools and hospitals. With the idea of business enterprises in mind, the major framework of this theory is explained here. For the details of contingency theory, one may refer to Lawrence & Lorsch (1967),

Nonaka (1974), Nonaka et al. (1978) and Kagono (1980).

5. On the main propositions of the theory, one may refer to Nonaka et al. (1978).

6. At present, more comparative analysis including European countries is in progress (Okumura, 1983).

References

Abernathy, W. J., K. B. Clark and A. M. Kantrow, "The New Industrial Competition," *Harvard Business Review*, September-October 1981, pp.68-81.

Ashby, W. R., *An Introduction to Cybernetics*, London: Methuen, 1956.

Azumi, K., "*Nihon no soshikikozo* (Japanese Organizational Structure)," Written in Japanese, *Soshiki Kagaku (Organizational Science)*, 12-4, 1979, pp.2-12.

Azumi, K., "*Soshkikoze no chikaku - Igirisu, Nippon, Sueden no hikaku* (Perceptions of Organizational Structure: A British, Japanese and Swedish Comparison)," Written in Japanese, *Soshiki Kagaku (Organizational Science)* 13-4, 1980, pp.26-36.

Burns, T. and G. M. Stalker, *The Management of Innovation*, London: Tavistock, 1961.

Clark, R., *The Japanese Company*, New Haven, Conn.: Yale University Press, 1979.

Dore, R., *British Factory - Japanese Factory*, Berkeley: University of California Press, 1974.

Hamaguchi, E. and S. Kumon (eds.), *Nihonteki shudanshugi* (Japanese collectivism), Written in Japanese, Tokyo: Yuhikaku, 1982.

Hayes, R. H., "Why Japanese Factories Work," *Harvard Business Review*, July-August, 1981, pp.56-66.

Hazama, H., *Nihonteki keiei* (Japanese Management), Written in Japanese, Tokyo: Nihon Keizai Shimbunsha, 1971.

Hirschmeier, J. and T. Yui, *Nihon no keieihatten* (Development of Management in Japan), Written in Japanese, Tokyo: Toyokeizai Shimposha, 1979.

Imai, K. and H. Itami, "*Nihon no kigyo to shijo* (Firms and Markets, the Japanese Case)," Written in Japanese, *Kikan Gendai Keizai*, 43, 1981, pp.14-27.

Ishida, H., *Nihon no roshikankei to chinginkettei* (Japanese Industrial-Relations and Setting of Wage Structure), Written in Japanese, Tokyo: Toyokeizai Shimposha, 1976.

Iwata, R., *Nihonteki keiei no hensei genri* (The Organizing Principles of Japanese Management), Written in Japanese, Tokyo: Bunshindo, 1977.

Kagono, T., *Keiei soshiki no kankyo tekio* (Organizational Adaptation to the Environment), Written in Japanese, Tokyo: Hakuto Shobo, 1980.

Kagono, T., I. Nonaka, K. Sakakibara and A. Okumura, "*Nihon kigyo no senryaku to soshiki* (Strategy and Structure of Japanese Firms)," Written in Japanese, *Soshiki Kagaku (Organizational Science)*, 15-2, 1981, pp.11-34.

Kobayashi, N., *Nihon no takokusekikigyo* (Japanese Multinational Enterprises), Written in Japanese, Tokyo: Chuokeizaisha, 1980.

Kohno, T., "*Nichi-bei no senryakuteki ishikettei no hikaku - Senryaku kozo chokikeikaku no hikaku* (A Comparative Study on Strategic Decision Making in Japan and U.S. - A Comparison of Strategy, Structure, and Long-Term Planning)," Written in Japanese, *Gakushuin Daigaku Keizai Ronshu*, 13-1, 1976, pp.81-115.

Koike, K., *Shokuba no rodo kumiai to sanka - Roshi kankei no nichi-bei hikaku* (Labor Unions and Worker Participation at the Workplace -- A Japan - U.S. Comparison of Industrial-Relations), Written in Japanese, Tokyo: Toyokeizai Shimposha, 1977.

Koike, K., *Nihon no jukuren* (Japan's Well-Trained Labor), Written in Japanese, Tokyo: Yuhikaku, 1981.

Lawrence, P. R. and J. W. Lorsch, *Organization and Environment: Managing Differentiation and Integration*, Boston: Harvard Business School, Division of Research, 1967.

Marsch, R. M. and H. Mannari, *Modernization and the Japanese Factory*, Princeton: Princeton University Press, 1977.

Nishida, K., *Nihon shakai to nihonteki keiei* (Japanese Society and Japanese Management), Written in Japanese, Tokyo: Bunshindo, 1982.

Nonaka, I., *Organization and Market: Exploratory Study of Centralization vs. Decentralization*, Ph.D. Dissertation, Graduate School of Business Administration, University of California, Berkeley, 1972.

Nonaka, I., *Soshiki to shijo* (Organization and Market), Written in Japanese, Tokyo: Chikura Shobo, 1974.

Nonaka, I., T. Kagono, Y. Komatsu, A. Okumura and A. Sakashita, *Soshiki gensho no riron to sokutei* (Theory and Measurement of Organizational Phenomena), Written in Japanese, Tokyo: Chikura Shobo, 1978.

Okamoto, Y., *Hitachi to Matsushita* (Hitachi and Matsushita), 2vols. Written in Japanese, Tokyo: Chuokoronsha, 1979.

Okumura, A., *"Yoropa kigyo no keiei* (Management of European Firms),"
Written in Japanese, *Keio Keiei Ronshu,* 4-3, 1983, pp.51-71.

Ouchi, W., *Theory Z: How American Business Can Meet the Japanese Challenge,* Reading, Mass.: Addison-Wesley, 1981.

Pascale, R. T., "Communication and Decision Making across Cultures: Japanese and American Comparisons," *Administrative Science Quarterly,* 23, 1978, pp.91-110.

Pascale, R. T. and A. G. Athos, *The Art of Japanese Management,* New York: Simon & Schuster, 1981.

Perrow, C., "A Framework for the Comparative Analysis of Organizations," *American Sociological Review,* 32, 1967, pp.194-208.

Rohlen, T. P., *For Harmoney and Strength,* Berkeley: University of California Press, 1974.

Schumpeter, J. A., *The Theory of Economic Development,* Cambridge, Mass.: Harvard University Press, 1934.

Sugimoto, Y. and Roth Maoa, *Nihonjin wa "nihonteki" ka* (Are the Japanese really "Japanese"?), Written in Japanese, Tokyo: Toyokeizai Shimposha, 1982.

Thompson, J. D., *Organization in Action,* New York: McGraw-Hill, 1967.

Tuchiya, M., *Nihonteki keiei no shinwa* (The Mythologies of Japanese Management), Written in Japanese, Tokyo: Nihon Keizai Shimbunsha, 1978.

Tsuda, M., *Nihonteki keiei no yogo* (The Case for Japanese Management), Written in Japanese, Tokyo: Toyokeizai Shimposha, 1976.

Tsuda, M., *Nihonteki keiei no ronri* (The Logic of Japanese Management), Written in Japanese, Tokyo: Chuokeizaisha, 1977.

Urabe, K., *Keieisanka to nihonteki roshi kankei* (Participation in Management and Japanese Industrial-Relations), Written in Japanese, Tokyo: Hakuto Shobo, 1977.

Urabe, K., *Nihonteki keiei o kangaeru* (Essays on Japanese Management), Written in Japanese, Tokyo: Chuokeizaisha, 1978.

Wheelwright, S. C., "Japan - Where Operations Really are Strategic," *Harvard Business Review,* July-August, 1981, pp.67-74.

Woodward, J., *Industrial Organization: Theory and Practice,* London: Oxford University Press, 1965.

Yasumuro, K., *Kokusai keiei kodoron* (Theory of International Managerial Behavior), Written in Japanese, Tokyo: Moriyama Shoten, 1982.

Yoshino, M. Y., *Japan's Managerial Systems*, Cambridge, Mass.: MIT Press, 1968.

Yoshihara, H., *Takokuseki keieiron* (Theory of Multinational Management), Written in Japanese, Tokyo: Hakuto Shobo, 1979.

Appendix 1A List of the Companies Surveyed for Figure 1-1

	1962 JAPAN	1962 U.S.	1965 JAPAN	1965 U.S.	1970 JAPAN	1970 U.S.	1975 JAPAN	1975 U.S.	1978 JAPAN	1978 U.S.
Computer				IBM CDC DEC NCR ICT Scientific Data		IBM CDC DEC NCR	Fujitsu	IBM CDC DEC NCR	Fujitsu	IBM CDC DEC NCR
Automobile	Nissan Toyota Toyo Kogyo Prince(Merged into Nissan in 1966)	GM Ford Chrysler AMC	Nissan Toyota	GM Ford Chrysler AMC	Nissan Toyota	GM Ford Chrysler	Nissan Toyota	GM Ford Chrysler	Nissan Toyota	GM Ford Chrysler
Film	Fuji Konishiroku	Kodak General Anilin	Fuji Konishiroku	Kodak General Anilin	Fuji Konishiroku	Kodak	Fuji Konishiroku	Kodak	Fuji Konishiroku	Kodak
Pharmaceuticals			Takeda Chemical Sankyo Tanabe Seiyaku	AHP Warner-Lambert Pfizer Merck Sterling Drug Rexall Drug	Takeda Chemical Sankyo Tanabe Seiyaku	AHP Warner-Lambert Pfizer Merck Sterling Drug Dart Industries	Takeda Chemical Sankyo Shionogi	AHP Warner-Lambert Pfizer Merck Sterling Drug Dart Industries	Takeda Chemical Sankyo Shionogi	AHP Warner-Lambert Pfizer Merck Dart Industries Johnson Bristol-Myers
Office Equipment	NCR Japan Tokyo Electric	NCR Xerox Burroughs Addressograph	NCR Japan Tokyo Electric	NCR Xerox Burroughs Addressograph	NCR Japan Tokyo Electric Casio	Xerox Burroughs Addressograph	Ricoh Tokyo Electric Casio	Xerox Burroughs Addressogragh	Ricoh Tokyo Electric Casio	Xerox Burroughs 3M
Home Appliances	Matsushita Sanyo Sharp Sony	Whirlpool Motorola Zenith Collins Admiral Sunbeam	Matsushita Sanyo Sharp Sony	Whirlpool Motorola Zenith Collins Admiral Sunbeam TI	Matsushita Sanyo Sharp Sony	Whirlpool Motorola Zenith Admiral Emerson	Matsushita Sanyo Sharp Sony	Whirlpool Motorola Zenith North American Emerson Sunbeam Studebaker	Matsushita Sanyo Sharp Sony	Whirlpool Motorola North American Emerson Gould Studebaker Carrier

Appendix 1A (continued) List of Companies Surveyed for Figure 1-1

	1962 JAPAN	1962 U.S.	1965 JAPAN	1965 U.S.	1970 JAPAN	1970 U.S.	1975 JAPAN	1975 U.S.	1978 JAPAN	1978 U.S.
Machine Tool	Toshiba Machine Hitachi Seiki Okuma Machinery	Norton Ex-Cell-O Cincinnati Sundstrand	Toshiba Machine Hitachi Seiki Okuma Machinery	Norton Ex-Cell-O Cincinnati Chicago Pneumatic	Toshiba Machine Hitachi Seiki Okuma Machinery	Norton Ex-Cell-O Cincinnati Chicago Pneumatic	Toshiba Machine Toyoda Machine Makino Milling	Norton Ex-Cell-O Cincinnati Chicago Pneumatic Warner & Swaysey	Toshiba Machine Toyoda Machine Makino Milling	Norton Ex-Cell-O Cincinnatti Warner & Swaysey
Industrial Machinery	Kubota Komatsu Sumitomo Machinery	Harvester Caterpiller Deere	Komatsu Sumitomo Machinery	Harvester Caterpiller Deere Allis-Chalmers Foster Wheeler	Komatsu	Harvester Caterpiller Deere Allis-Chalmers Kaiser ACF	Kubota Komatsu	Harvester Caterpiller Deere Allis-Chalmers Dresser ACF	Kubota Komatsu	Harvester Caterpiller Deere Dresser FMC Ingersoll-rand
Toiletries			Shiseido Kao Lion	P & G Colgate Bristol- Meyers Avon Kellogg Revlon Max Factor	Shiseido Kao Lion	P & G Colgate Bristol- Meyers Avon Revlon Max Factor	Shiseido Kao Lion	P & G Colgate Bristol- Meyers Avon Revlon Chesebrough	Shiseido Kao Lion	P & G Colgate Avon Revlon Chesebrough
Tire & Rubber	Bridgestone Yokohama Rubber	Goodyear Firestone General U.S. Rubber Goodrich	Bridgestone Yokohama Rubber	Goodyear Firestone General Uniroyal	Bridgestone Yokohama Rubber	Goodyear Firestone General Goodrich Uniroyal	Bridgestone Yokohama Rubber	Goodyear Firestone General Goodrich Uniroyal	Bridgestone Yokohama Rubber	Goodyear Firestone General Goodrich Uniroyal
Synthetic Fiber	Toray Teijin Asahi Chemical	Burlington Textron Celanese	Toray Teijin Asahi Chemical	Textron Celanese Akzona	Toray Teijin Asahi Chimical	Celanese Akzona Burlington	Toray Teijin Asahi Chemical	Celanese Akzona Burlington	Toray Teijin Asahi Chemical	Celanese
Retail Chains			Midoriya Marui Nagasakiya Jujiya	Sears Roebuck A & P Safeway J.C. Penney Montgomery Woolworth Kresge	Midoriya Marui Nagasakiya Jujiya	Sears Roebuck A & P Safeway J.C. Penney Woolworth Marcor Kresge	Daiei Seiyu Ito-Yokado Jusco	Sears Roebuck A & P Safeway J.C. Penney Woolworth Marcor K mart	Daiei Seiyu Ito-Yokado Jusco	Sears Roebuck A & P Safeway J.C. Penney Woolworth K mart Kroger

CHAPTER 2 A COMPARISON OF U.S. AND JAPANESE ORGANIZATIONS

This chapter identifies differences between the strategies and organizational characteristics of U.S. and Japanese firms through the statistical analysis of large-sample data.

Comparative studies to-date have focused on relatively few environmental and/or structural and/or process variables. We see the essence of management to be a striving toward an integrated "balance" between the many variables in a way that enhances organizational performance. This is why the present comparative analysis, while hardly purporting to be "the whole truth," includes consideration of all of the variables of an "Integrative Contingency Framework" described in the following section.

The analysis of this chapter seeks to discern broad and pervasive "difference profiles" between U.S. and Japanese organizations based upon survey responses from managers in each group. The extent of such differences would seem critical to the more detailed managerial comparisons of U.S. and Japanese firms which follow in the three subsequent chapters.

2.1 Conceptual Framework and Research Methodology

Conceptual Framework
We consider a business organization to be a unified whole. Its objectives, strategy, technology, organizational structure and process, as well as the personal predispositions of its members are interrelated and interdependent. If the organization is to cope effectively with its environment, it must develop an integral configuration among its components. This holistic perspective is an extention of the theory of organizations developed by contingency theorists (Burns and Stalker, 1961; Lawrence and Lorsch, 1967; Nonaka, 1972; Lorsch and Morse, 1974; Nonaka, 1974; Nonaka & Nicosia, 1979; Kagono, 1980), and may be termed an "integrative contingency theory" (Nonaka et al., 1978). It seeks to provide understanding of the interrelationships among the major components

of the organizational milieu as well as between the organization and its environment.

Figure 2-1 depicts the conceptual framework of the "integrative contingency theory." The figure shows various components that should be taken into account when organizational comparisons are made. Our purpose is not to "prove" or disprove the model but to provide a theoretically sound framework for approaching the study of organizations in a holistic way.

The first component includes environmental variables -- i.e., variables which describe the characteristics of various aspects of the external environment an organization faces. These include product markets, input markets and relationships with other organizations with which the organization interacts in its attempt to survive within a given domain.

The variables included in the second major component of this framework are named contextual variables. They are related to the objectives, strategy, technology, size and function of the organization. Although these might be considered among internal characteristics descriptive of the organization, we find it more explanatory to differentiate them from other internal characteristics because of their nature as "mediating" variables. For instance, the objectives and strategy of an organization clearly must reflect the opportunities and constraints imposed by its environment. At the same time, however, objectives and strategy serve to define and give meaning to relevant environmental opportunities and constraints. Furthermore, the objectives and strategy determine the required organizational characteristics which, in turn, influence further objective formation and strategy formulation within the organization. Thus these variables must be differentiated from the environment on the one hand and from organizational variables on the other.

The third component of the framework describes the internal characteristics of organizations. We have subdivided this component into three subsets of variables. The first subset describes the characteristics of an organization's structure, e.g., the pattern of division of labor and distribution of authority. The second subset

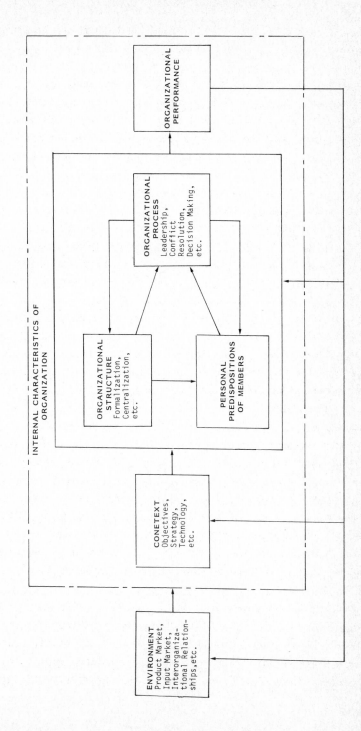

Figure 2-1 Conceptual Framework of the Integrative Contingency Theory

INTERNAL CHARACTERISTICS OF ORGANIZATION

ORGANIZATIONAL PERFORMANCE

ORGANIZATIONAL PROCESS
Leadership, Conflict Resolution, Decision Making, etc.

ORGANIZATIONAL STRUCTURE
Formalization, Centralization, etc.

PERSONAL PREDISPOSITIONS OF MEMBERS

CONETEXT
Objectives, Strategy, Technology, etc.

ENVIRONMENT
Product Market, Input Market, Interorganiza-tional Relation-ships,etc.

describes the managerial behavior and processes which activate and supplement the structure, such as leadership style, modes of decision making and conflict resolution, communication, etc. The third subset describes the personal predispositions of organizational members. These subsets are, of course, highly interrelated.

The fourth and final component describes the effectiveness of the organization itself. The arrows linking this component to the others indicate that organizational effectiveness is determined by the pattern of the three variable components mentioned above, that is, the degree of consistency achieved among them.

Integrative contingency theory suggests that differences in organizational environment bring about or require differences in the internal characteristics of organizations. The differences in environments encompass various levels of abstraction: the inter-firm level in an industry, the inter-industry level within a national economy, the inter-sector level (e.g., business *vis-a-vis* non-profit organizations) again within a national economy, and finally the international level. The phase of the research described next focuses on concrete differences at the international level between the U.S. and Japan.

Research Methodology
We have adopted the "middle-range" survey research methodology developed during the last decade (see e.g. Hall, 1977). Although there are limitations inherent in this methodology, it is useful for drawing a comprehensive map of the characteristics of a large number of firms in both countries. The more detailed and intensive research findings of in-depth case studies are reported in the next three chapters.

The variables listed in Figure 2-1 were operationalized and a questionnaire was designed from pilot studies conducted in Japan from 1978 to 1979. The questionnaires were sent to 1000 representative firms in each country. The English version of the questionnaire was sent to the Chief Executive Officer of each of *Fortune*'s top 1000 industrial firms in March, 1980 and 227 were returned. The Japanese version was sent to 1031 industrial companies listed on the Tokyo Stock Exchange, eliciting 291

responses.   The questionnaires in Japanese and English are attached in
Appendices A and B respectively.

2.2 U.S. and Japanese Firms Compared

To check for representativeness, data from the returned questionnaires was
tabulated according to a series of indicators.   Checking the means,
medians, and the ranges of the variables showed that the number of
companies responding seemed to mirror rather closely the population
figures for the different industries in the two countries (Sakakibara et
al. 1980).   The size and industry distribution of the responses are given
in Appendix 2A at the end of this chapter.   We feel reasonably safe in
treating these data as representative of the two countries' business
organizations.[1]

In this section, U.S. and Japanese firms are compared in terms of
environment faced, organizational context, and internal characteristics.

(1) Environment

Product market, input market and inter-organizational relationships with
other organizations are the major components of the business
environment.   Product markets are here compared in terms of their
diversity, heterogeneity, variability, competitiveness and offered
opportunity while input markets are examined in terms of the mobility of
labor.   We compare interorganizational relationships according to the
strengths of constraints imposed by financial institutions, major
customers, suppliers, government, and competitors.   Each dimension is
measured by at least two semantic differential items in the questionnaire.

The results of the comparison are shown in Table 2-1.   The data indicates
that there are significant differences in the diversity, competitiveness,
variability and offered opportunity of the environment.   U.S. firms on the
average face a more diverse market environment in terms of product,
geographical dispersion and promotional strategies, and the markets they
serve are more competitive.   On the other hand, the markets served by

Japanese firms are, on the average, more volatile yet are protected by
higher entry barriers. Finally, the rate of technological change facing
Japanese firms is higher.

Table 2-1   Comparison of Environmental Characteristics[a]

Dimension of the Environment	U.S.	Japan
Markets		
product diversity	4.62	4.20[***]
geographical diversity	5.20	4.26[***]
level of product information	4.86	4.90[*]
diversity of promotional media	4.75	4.43
Competition		
intensity of rivalry	5.66	5.32[**]
inability to influence market conditions	4.00	3.60[***]
average profitability of the principal market	4.21	4.26[***]
entry barriers to the principal market	4.77	5.22
Rate of environmental change		
in technology	4.10	4.46[*]
in demand	3.82	4.09[*]
Constraints imposed by inter-organizational relationships		
with banks and major stockholders	2.81	3.03[***]
with major distributors and customers	2.98	3.75[***]
with major suppliers and subcontractors	2.46	3.71[***]
with government	4.36	3.16[***]
with competitors	2.04	2.64
Mobility of labor market		
for managers	3.46	1.78[***]
for technological experts	3.45	1.97[***]

Notes: a.   The higher the mean score, the more typical is the
               characteristic.
          *   significant at .05 level by t-test of means
          **   significant at .01 level by t-test of means
          *** significant at .001 level by t-test of means

There is also a significant difference in labor market mobility between the two countries. Japanese firms face a less mobile labor market than U.S. firms. Not new, the finding is consistent with the prevalent view that the Japanese labor market is less mobile because of its life-time employment system (typical at least in large firms).

The strengths and range of constraints imposed by interrelationships with other organizations are also different in Japan and the U.S. U.S. firms face stronger constraints imposed by government and regulatory bodies, while Japanese firms feel the constraints imposed by their relationships with distributors, customers, suppliers and competitors to a greater degree than American firms. This result suggests that Japanese companies create closer interorganizational networks with various kinds of organizations. The networks, although constraining decisions within organizations, may have a number of benefits including risk-sharing and long-term stabilization of business. The strong constraints imposed by the government upon U.S. firms probably stem from the relatively adverse historical relationship between business and government in the U.S. as well as from motives to protect the public and promote competition.

To sum up, Japanese firms face a less diverse, less competitive, more volatile and high opportunity environment, and a less mobile labor market. They are, moreover, constrained by interrelationships with other organizations to a greater extent than U.S. firms.

(2) Context

Corporate Objectives
A firm must set operational objectives, the priorities of which are contingent upon the opportunities provided and constraints imposed by its environment matched against the internal capabilities of the organization. Respondents were asked to select the three most important objectives from nine candidates generally thought to be important corporate objectives, and to rank the three in order of importance. Table 2-2 shows the results of this comparison.

Table 2-2 Importance of Selected Goals[a]

Goals	U.S.	Japan
Return on investment	2.43	1.24 ***
Capital gain for stockholders	1.14	0.02 ***
Increase in market share	0.73	1.43 ***
Improvement of product portfolio	0.50	0.68 **
Efficiency of logistic activities	0.46	0.71
Equity/debt ratio	0.38	0.59
New product ratio	0.21	1.06 ***
Public image of the company	0.05	0.20 **
Quality of working conditions	0.04	0.09 **

Notes: a. Mean score of importance (3 points for the most important
            goal, 2 points for the second, 1 point for the third, and 0
            point for others)
      **   significant at .01 level by t-test of means
      *** significant at .001 level by t-test of means

The table shows the existence of three important differences. The first
is the difference in the relative importance of profitability *vis-a-vis*
growth objectives: Japanese firms, on the average, emphasize growth
objectives such as increase in market share and new product ratio, while
U.S. firms stress profitability (ROI) more. Secondly, a striking
difference exists in the ranking of importance of capital gains to
stockholders (i.e., share prices): this objective ranked second by U.S.
firms, is the least important objective of Japanese firms. The stock
market apparently imposes much stronger constraints on U.S. firms.
Finally, there is a difference in the dispersion of scores. The responses
of U.S. firms concentrate on a few objectives such as ROI and capital
gains, while the responses of Japanese firms include a larger number of
objectives including growth, profitability, and the efficiency of logistic
activities.

These differences in the choice of objectives correspond to the
differences in environment touched on earlier. For instance, the pursuit
of a growth objective is more feasible in the high opportunity environment
surrounding Japanese firms, and the emphasis on profitability is needed in
the more competitive environment faced by U.S. firms.

Production Technology

As stated previously, technology is here viewed as a mediating variable between an organization and its environment.[2] The market environment of an organization determines what types of technology are feasible, and these in turn constrain organizational structure and process.

Production technologies are here ranked in terms of five levels of routineness, a scale developed by Woodward (1965). The categories range from *continuous process* (the most routine) to *custom technology* (the most non-routine). As large firms usually utilize more than one technology, each respondent was asked to indicate the approximate percentage of output contributed by each of these five technologies to total production. Table 2-3 shows the average percentages of output derived from the five categories of production technology and the average scores of non-routineness. From Table 2-3 we see that Japanese firms, on the average, have less routine technology than U.S. firms.

Table 2-3 Comparison of Production Technology

Type of production technology	(Score of non-routineness)	U.S. (Mean percentage of total output from each technology)	Japan
Custom technology	(5 points)	12.5	20.2[**]
Small batch, job shop technology	(4)	14.8	17.7[***]
Large batch technology	(3)	35.4	24.5[***]
Mass production technology	(2)	19.3	22.6
Continuous process technology	(1)	17.9	15.0
Average scores of non-routineness		2.86	3.05[*]

Notes: [*]   significant at .05 level by t-test of means
        [**] significant at .01 level by t-test of means
        [***] significant at .001 level by t-test of means

A less routine technology is more flexible and is more suited to coping with a variable environment. Therefore, a consistent relationship between differences in the routineness of technology and in environmental variablility between U.S. and Japanese firms has been found.

Strategy

Broadly speaking, an organization's strategy is defined as "the basic characteristics of the match the organization achieves with its environment" (Hofer and Schendel, 1978, p.4). It is useful to differentiate between three major levels of organizational strategy: (1) corporate strategy which is concerned primarily with the determination of the domain in which an organization chooses to do business; (2) business strategy which focuses on how to compete in a particular industry segment; and (3) functional area strategy which focuses on how to use resources in a particular functional area. The differences in strategy between the U.S. and Japanese firms are analyzed at each of these three levels.

As most of the characteristics are qualitative in nature, the operationalizing methodology developed by Hall (1961) and Hage and Aiken (1967a) was employed in this study. We provided multiple sentences describing the typical characteristics of each dimension of strategy, and asked the respondent to assess the correctness of each sentence as a description of the respondent's company on a five-point scale. The scales are shown in the footnote of Table 2-4.

Several notable differences concerning strategies are indicated in the table. First, it shows that U.S. firms, on average, are oriented toward a wider scope of activities, especially in terms of orientation toward internationalization of production operation.

Second, it was found that U.S. firms are more flexible in their strategic deployment of resources and that they emphasize short-term resource utilization, while Japanese firms emphasize long-term resource accumulation and are slow to follow a withdrawal strategy. This contrast in resource deployment is the most significant difference between Japan and the U.S. along the seven dimensions. This finding corresponds to the differences in environment and objectives cited earlier: it is quite reasonable for the U.S. firms, which give a higher priority to profitability and face a lower opportunity environment, to emphasize mobility and short-term capitalization of resources.

Table 2-4 Characteristics of Corporate Strateg}

Dimension and Indicators of Corporate Strategy	U.S.	Japan
Relatedness of product/market		
The diversification targets are restricted to those product lines which have close commonality with the existing technological base.	3.89	3.84
The diversification targets are restricted to those product lines in which existing strengths in marketing can be applied.	3.49	3.51
Orientation toward internationalization		
Your company has been actively developing foreign markets.	3.87	3.77
Your company has been actively investing in foreign production subsidiaries.	3.21	2.77
Strategic mobility of resource deployment		
Your company does not hesitate to divest from questionable businesses.	3.92	3.29***
Your company has actively acquired new businesses.	3.59	2.32***
Your company concentrates resources in a few strategic market segments.	3.36	3.13*
Long-term resource accumulation		
The recruitment of managerial personnel and technological experts is based upon long-range personnel planning rather than immediate needs.	3.15	3.54***
Your company emphasizes accumulating a diverse base of know-how more than making better use of existing know-how.	2.54	3.19***
Competitive orientation		
Your company competes head-on with competitors.	4.50	3.41***
Your company selects the market segments in which it has advantages and pursues coexistence with competitors.	3.26	3.29
Your company exploits the advantage of being a "follower" and tries to reduce risks in the development of new products and/or markets.	2.43	2.36
Your company is always an innovator which actively takes risks in the development of new product and/or market.	3.31	3.19

Table 2-4 (continued) Characteristics of Corporate Strategy

Dimension and Indicators of Corporate Strategy	U.S.	Japan
Your company consistently seeks high market share and tries to take advantage of cost efficiencies in every market.	4.02	3.81*
Your company aims to produce high quality products with high value added and to rely on non-price marketing strategies.	3.62	3.55
Strategy formulation Strategy formulation in your company is based upon systematic research data and sophisticated analytical methods.	3.34	3.43
The intuitive judgment of experienced executives plays a major role in formulating strategy.	4.04	3.32***
Information is sought extensively even on markets unrelated to present businesses.	2.54	3.17***
Voluntary recommendations made by lower-level managers are frequently followed by senior executives.		
Social responsibility The pursuit of stockholder benefits is thought to be the most important social responsibility of your company.	3.23	3.13
The fulfillment of various social responsibilities is clearly built into the corporate strategy of your company.	3.75	3.90

Notes: a. The higher the score, the more typical is the characteristic (5; definitely true, 4; somewhat true, 3; cannot say one way or the other, 2; somewhat incorrect, 1; definitely incorrect). The followng statements were given reverse scores: No's 2, 3, 4, 8, 16, 22.
       *   significant at .05 level by t-test of means
     ** significant at .01 level by t-test of means
   *** significant at .001 level by t-test of means

Third, U.S. firms emphasize head-on competition and cost-efficiency by accumulating experience in a way suggested by "experience curve theory." This fact implies that strategies are better formulated and stated more clearly in U.S. companies than in the Japanese companies.

Fourth, Japanese firms' mode of strategy formulation differs from the U.S. mode in that the latter emphasize the judgment of experience executives in formulating strategies and the former seek more diverse and redundant information. This difference suggests that the strategy formulation process in Japanese firms involves interaction of various people rather than being based solely upon executive's judgment and, therefore, contains more slack and redundancy.

Table 2-5 shows the average product portfolios of U.S. and Japanese firms according to a scheme developed by the Boston Consulting Group. Our results show that, compared with the Japanese portfolios, the proportion of stars and cash cows is higher and that of dogs and question marks lower in U.S. portfolios. This finding reflects the finding on resource deployment. The U.S. firms, which emphasize short-term and mobile

Table 2-5 Comparison of Product Portfolios

		Competitive Position	
		Strong (First or second in market share)	Weak (Third or lower in market share)
Growth rate of market	Higher	STARS[**] U.S. 30.7% Japan 23.6%	QUESTION MARKS U.S. 18.2% Japan 19.5%
	10%		
	Lower	CASH COWS U.S. 36.2% Japan 34.1%	DOGS[**] U.S. 14.9% Japan 22.9%

Notes: Mean percentages of total sales form each category of products
    ** significant at .01 level by t-test of means

Chapter 2

deployment of resources, have a better product/market portfolio, while
Japanese firms, which seek resource development using a longer
perspective, are slow to follow a withdrawal strategy, and have more dogs
and question marks.

The competitive strategies in the principal businesses of U.S. and
Japanese firms are compared in Table 2-6. It shows that Japanese firms
focus on production strategies, while their U.S. counterparts emphasize
product strategies. The typical Japanese company builds up its
competitive strength by improving production efficiency and product
quality, while the typical U.S. company seeks product differentiation.

Table 2-6   Key Success Factors in the Principal Business[a]

Key Success Factor	U.S. mean(rank)	Japan mean(rank)
Product strategy (product planning, market research for new products, R&D, etc.)	3.65 (1)	3.66 (2)
Promotional strategy (sales management and personal selling, advertising, and other marketing communication strategies)	2.79 (4)	2.77 (4)
Distribution strategy (choice of distribution channel, distribution and inventory program, etc.)	2.71 (5)	1.78 (5)
Pricing strategy (price policy, pricing decision, etc.)	3.27 (3)	2.98 (3)
Production strategy (economy of scale, cost reduction, flexibility of prodution system, etc.)	3.46 (2)	3.80 (1)

Notes: a.   Scores: 5-the most important to 1-the least important
             strategic factor.

Table 2-7 shows that there is no statistically significant difference in
the ratio of R&D expenditures to total sales or in the new product ratio
of the two countries. The lower section of Table 2-7 compares the
relative importance of four kinds of R&D activities. It indicates that
U.S. firms emphasize research to improve their existing products while
Japanese firms emphasize basic research and the development of new
products. This finding contradicts the prevalent view that the U.S.

creates new technologies and Japan improves upon them. However, it is also to be expected that the kinds of R&D activities emphasized by Japanese firms have a longer gestation period than the activities emphasized by U.S. firms.[3] As noted before, Japanese firms have longer perspectives toward resource deployment than U.S. firms, and this allows them to focus more on basic R&D than would otherwise be possible.

Table 2-7   Comparison of R&D Strategy

Criteria of R&D Strategy	U.S.	Japan
Mean percentage of sales accounted for by new products introduced since 1973	23.8 %	19.7 %
Mean percentage of R&D expenditures to total sales	2.81%	2.61%
Relative importance of R&D activities (mean percentage allocation)		
Basic research on new technologies	8.4 %	15.9 %[***]
Research on improving and updating existing products	35.6 %	26.6 %[***]
Development of new products	29.9 %	33.9 %[*]
Development of new production methods and processes	26.1 %	23.6 %

Notes: *   significant at .05 level by t-test of means
       *** significant at .001 level by t-test of means

To sum up, the comparison of contexts indicates that U.S. firms emphasize profitability and stockholders' gain as corporate objectives, utilize more routine technology, are oriented toward a wider scope of activities, emphasize short-term mobile deployment of resources, and have product-oriented competitive strategies. Japanese firms emphasize growth objectives, seek a larger number of objectives, utilize less routine technology, and emphasize longer term accumulation of resources and use a more production-oriented competitive strategy. These differences are largely consistent with the differences in environment that the firms face. It will next be shown that they also correspond to differences in organizational structure and process.

(3) Intra-organizational characteristics

Organizational Structure
From a sociological point of view, an organization's structure can be
described by dimensions measuring the pattern of division of labor and
vertical and horizontal distributions of power and influence within the
organization (Hage and Aiken, 1967a; Hall, 1977; Pugh et al., 1968). The
following four dimensions were used here: (a) degree of formalization, (b)
degree of standardization, (c) degree of centralization, and (d) inter-
departmental distribution of influence.

Figure 2-2 Hierarchical Distribution of Influence upon
Strategic Decision Making within Organizations
(mean scores)

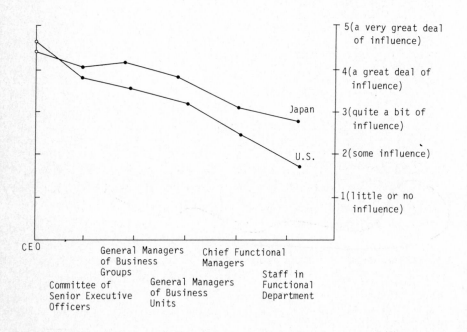

The results as displayed in Table 2-8 indicate that U.S. firms have a more
formalized and standardized structure than Japanese firms. Figure 2-2,

Table 2-8 Comparison of Organizational Structure

Dimension and Indicators	U.S.	Japan
Formalization[a]	3.21	2.99**
The authority and responsibility of every executive or manager are clearly and concretely defined in your company.	3.79	3.50**
The job descriptions for executives and managers are general and, therefore, applied very flexibly (A reversed score is given in calculating the formalization score).	3.36	3.53
Standardization (The average of the percentages of companies employing the following systems.)	70.5	49.3***
Formalized job descriptions	88.4 %	85.2 %
Standard cost accounting system	92.0	73.8
Flexible budgetary control system	63.1	51.7
Performance evaluation system	85.8	65.2
Monthly operation reporting system	97.3	87.9
Management by objectives (MBO)	68.0	55.0
Objective promotion criteria	35.1	54.8
Internal training program for managers	68.9	75.5
Objective formula for wage/salary determination	70.2	62.6
Fixed assets investment analysis system	68.9	42.8
Sales forecasting system	90.2	47.2
Sales review and analysis system	80.0	41.0
Sales force performance appraisal system	68.4	26.9
Competition analysis system	49.8	11.0
Planning system for PR and advertisement	34.7	27.6
Short-range planning system	86.7	87.2
Middle-range planning system	72.4	80.0
Strategic planning system	78.7	34.8
Cash-flow planning system	86.2	93.8
Capital budgeting system	94.2	33.1
Financial investment analysis system	64.4	24.5
Planning-programming -budgeting system (PPBS)	30.7	3.4
Contingency planning system	42.7	5.9
Management information system (MIS)	75.6	21.0
Standardization of lateral relationships (The average of the percentages of companies employing the following structural forms).	47.4	18.1***
Strategic business unit system	50.2	12.8
Project management system	53.8	34.5
Product or brand manager system	55.1	11.7
Matrix organization	30.7	13.4

Notes: a. The higher the score, the more typical is the characteristic (See the note of Table 2-4).
        ** significant at .01 level by t-test of means
        *** significant at .001 level by t-test of means

using the control graph developed by Tannenbaum (1968), shows the distributions of strategic decision-making influence among hierarchical levels in U.S. and Japanese firms. The steeper curve for U.S. firms indicates that the authority is more centralized at a higher hierarchical level in U.S. firms.

Table 2-9 compares inter-departmental distributions of influence. The most striking difference lies in the relative position of the finance and control department. In U.S. firms, this department occupies the second most powerful position, while it is placed fifth in Japan. The greater influence of the finance and control department in U.S. firms obviously coincides with their emphasis on profitability, stockholders' gain, and short-term efficiency of resource deployment. These findings are consistent with the basic premise of "strategic contingency theory" that the power of a department is proportional to its importance in dealing with environmental contingencies threatening the attainment of organizational objectives (Hickson et al., 1971).

Table 2-9 Distribution of Influence between Departments (mean scores)[a]

Department	U.S. (Score of influence)	Japan (Score of influence)
Sales and marketing	3.78	4.08[***]
Research and development	2.71	3.29[***]
Production	3.20	3.66[***]
Finance and control	3.61	3.27[**]
Personnel, labor relations	2.34	2.72[***]
Corporate planning staff	2.76	3.34[***]
Purchasing, procurement	1.93	2.73[***]

Notes: a.   Scores (1, little or no influence; 2, some influence;
3, quite a bit of influence; 4, a great deal of influence;
5, a very great deal of influence)
**   significant at .01 level by t-test of means
*** significant at .001 level by t-test of means

The relative position of the production department is higher in Japan: it occupies the second most powerful position in Japan but the third in the U.S. The high position of the production department in Japanese companies is consistent with their strategic emphasis on production.

The various characteristics of the management control system in multi-divisional organizations are next compared. These results are summarized in Table 2-10.

The first striking finding is the extremely high proportion of divisionalized firms in the U.S. This is consistent with Rumelt's finding (1974) which indicates that the divisional form is the rule among large U.S. firms. It suggests that the divisionalized organization may be well-suited to the socio-cultural setting of the U.S. The next notable difference is that U.S. firms are perceived to have a more sophisticated performance appraisal system and maintain clearer and stronger ties between divisional performance and the financial remuneration of division managers. Third, it is shown that operating decision-making authority is delegated more to division managers in U.S. firms, and their divisions are more self-contained in terms of the functions performed by each division. It is interesting to note that Japanese firms centralize their personnel and finance functions. The centralization of these functions may enable them to develop longer-term policies for resource deployment from a corporate-wide point of view. Fourth, U.S. firms rely more on a vertical network for the control of divisions while Japanese firms rely heavily on a horizontal or lateral coordination network.

It is quite reasonable for U.S. firms, which emphasize profitability and short-term efficiency of resource deployment, to adopt the divisional form, create more self-contained divisions, and use a more sophisticated performance appraisal system with a clearer linkage between divisional performance and financial remuneration. It is hypothesized that the multi-divisional form is more suited to pursue profitability (Williamson, 1975).

Table 2-10   Comparison of Divisional Control Systems[a]

Dimension of Divisional Control System	U.S.	Japan
Percentage of Firms Adopting Divisional Form[a]	94.4 %	59.8 %
(Divisional Function)		
production	96.7 %	85.5 %
sales	94.8	91.5
marketing planning	89.6	82.6
personnel	84.4	35.5
control	82.0	40.1
finance	38.4	12.2
basic research	19.9	28.5
applied research and development	62.1	75.6
purchasing	77.3	52.4
Use of Integrative Devices[b]		
Group executives who are responsible for several business units and report to the chief executive officer	91.7 %	55.1 %
General staff which supports the group executives	63.1	47.3
Task forces that are temporarily organized to solve functional problems common to several business units	40.3	28.9
Teams which are permanently organized to solve functional problems common to several business units	7.8	25.1
Functional coordinator whose primary task is to facilitate collaboration among several business units on functional problems common to them	25.7	26.9
Control Systems[c]		
Mean number of divisions	2.79	1.86[***]
Sophistication of divisional performance evaluation	2.99	2.12[***]
Decentralization of decisions	2.53	2.39[*]
Relationship of divisional performance to financial remuneration of managers	3.40	2.32[***]

Notes: a.   Percentage of the firms in which the function is performed by divisions.
           b.   Percentage of the firms in which the organizational device is adopted.
           c.   Questions are given in Appendix B. A higher score indicates greater possession of the attitude.
           *   significant at .05 level by t-test of means
           *** significant at .001 level by t-test of means

The organizational structure characterized by a high degree of formalization, standardization and centralization is generally termed "mechanistic," while a structure characterized by a low degree in these three dimensions is referred to as "organic" (Burns and Stalker, 1961). Thus, the typical structures of U.S. and Japanese firms may be characterized as "mechanistic" and "organic," respectively.

The organic structure is said to be superior in terms of its adaptability to environmental change while the mechanistic structure is superior in terms of efficiency (Burns and Stalker, 1961; Lawrence and Lorsch, 1967). Consistent with this proposition, we find a consistency between the differences in organizational structure and in environment and context. It is quite reasonable for U.S. firms, which emphasize profitability and short-term efficient utilization of resources, to create a mechanistic structure, while the Japanese firms, which face a more variable environment and emphasize growth and long-term accumulation of resources, maintain an organic structure.

Organizational Processes
Eight aspects of organizational processes are compared in Table 2-11. The first is leadership behavior. Based upon the Ohio State studies (Fleishman and Harris, 1962), Selznick's (1957), and our own (Sakakibara et al., 1980), four dimensions of leadership behavior are identified: (a) human-oriented leadership behavior, (b) task-oriented leadership behavior, (c) information-oriented leadership behavior, and (d) value-oriented leadership behavior. Notable differences were found on two dimensions. U.S. executives tend to be more task-oriented while Japanese executives are more information-oriented.

Next, four modes of conflict resolution within the organization were compared: forcing, *nemawashi* (broad consultation before decision), compromise, and confrontation. The comparative results indicate that U.S. executives put more emphasis on confrontation as a means to resolve conflict while Japanese executives place more emphasis on *nemawashi* and forcing. Lawrence and Lorsch (1967) conclude that confrontation is the most effective means for resolving conflict. Our findings, however, suggest that this is not true in the Japanese setting.

Table 2-11 Organizational Process and Managerial Behavior

Dimension and Indicators of Management Behavior	U.S.	Japan
(Leadership style)		
Human-oriented behavior		
- The organization of your company is designed with some specific executives and/or managers in mind.	3.08	2.94
- Senior executives strive to promote sense of identification with the company among employees.	4.11	4.19
- Senior executives are constantly conscious of developing capability of their potential successors.	3.70	3.72
Task-oriented behavior		
- Senior executives always encourage competition among managers or among divisions.	3.14	3.02
- Senior executilves actively search for problems within your company and take the leadership in solving them	3.88	3.65^{**}
- Senior executives are strict in applying rewards and punishments.	2.91	3.20^{***}
Information-oriented behavior		
- Senior executives always clarify information requests (i.e., what needs to be known) about each division or department.	3.12	3.74^{***}
- Senior executives always try to develop reliable sources of information aside from formal channels of information already available.	3.69	3.75
- Senior executives actively gather information by by themselves about relevant events in and out of your company and about situations on the line.	3.54	3.86^{***}
Value-oriented behavior		
- The value and belief of the chief executive officer is reflected in every system in your organization.	3.60	3.62
- The basic strategy of your company is inseparable from the unique value and belief of the present C.E.O or the original founder.	3.63	3.48
- The organization's climate is inseparable from the unique value and belief of the chief executive officer.	3.55	3.80^{*}
(Conflict resolution)		
Forcing		
- The conflict among executives and managers are promptly resolved based upon superiors' authority.	3.00	3.42^{***}
Nemawashi (broad consultation before decision)		
- Executives and managers exchange information in advance of a formal meeting so that differences in opinion and judgment are not brought up at the meeting.	2.72	3.72^{***}
Smoothing		
- When there is a difference in opinion and judgment among executives and managers, they always seek to find a temporary compromise rather than to impose a final decision.	2.94	3.06

Table 2-11 (continued) Organizational Process and Managerial Behavior

Dimension and Indicators of Managerial Behavior	U.S.	Japan
Confrontation		
- Executives and managers thoroughly discuss differences in opinion and judgment among themselves even though such discussions are time consuming.	3.50	3.32[*]
(Control)		
Control by sharing of values and information		
- Even the first-line employees have intimate knowledge about the basic policy of your company.	2.97	3.82[***]
- Executives, managers, and employees in your comapany share a considerable amount of common information.	3.71	3.54[*]
Control by self-dicipline		
- Your company's control system is based on employees' self-discipline and commitment to work.	2.99	3.48[***]
- Employees' and managers' actions are strictly controlled by rules and by their superiors.	2.41	3.25[**]
Output control		
- The performance of each manager is evaluated by the end results of his/her efforts rather than by the amount of the effort itself.	3.94	3.45[***]
- The performance of each manager is evaluated over 5 to 10 years term so that his/her potential capabilities can be taken into account.	2.96	3.64[***]
(Decision-making and communication)		
- In your company individual managers' initiative is valued more than the harmony of human relations.	3.08	2.82[***]
- Consensus is heavily emphasized in the decisions and actions of each decision unit.	3.03	3.67[***]
- Senior executives have frequent formal and/or informal meetings with line managers and supervisors.	4.03	3.58[***]
- Executives and managers also have close social relationship outside of work.	2.64	3.55[***]
- Important information is usually exchanged informally among executives and managers.	4.14	3.55[***]
(Identification)		
- Employees and managers have a strong sense of identification with your company.	4.20	4.05[*]
- Employees and managers are proud of being members of your company.	4.25	3.79[***]
- Most executives and managers will not leave this company even if a higher pay or a higher position is offered by another company.	3.18	4.08[***]

Table 2-11 (continued) Organizational Process and Managerial Behavior

Dimension and Indicators of Managerial Behavior	U.S.	Japan
(Change-oriented culture)		
- The organization's climate is to pursue and challenge any change.	2.86	3.26***
(Personnel)		
- Career paths for specialists as well as for managerial personnel are clearly defined.	2.84	2.80
- Retirement ages of workers, managers, and executives are clearly defined.	4.00	4.19*
- Planned job rotation of managers is emphasized as a device for developing their capabilities.	2.51	3.11***
- Most executives and managers have no prior job experience outside this company.	2.46	3.70***
- Most senior executives have been promoted from within.	3.96	3.82

Notes: a. The higher the score, the more typical is the characteristic (5, definitely true, 4, somewhat true, 3, cannot say one way or the other, 2, somewhat incorrect, 1, definitely incorrect). Statements no. 5 and 34 were given reverse scores.
   *   significant at .05 level by t-test of means
   ** significant at .01 level by t-test of means
   *** significant at .001 level by t-test of means

Third, the control process is examined in terms of three dimensions: control by sharing of values and information, control by self-discipline, and output control (control on the basis of appraisal of performance output) vs. behavioral control (control on the basis of surveillance and appraisal of behavior). The results of the comparison, shown in Table 2-11, indicate that the control processes in Japanese firms are characterized more by the sharing of values and information and by self-discipline, while the U.S. control systems depend more on output control. These characteristics correspond to the differences in overall structure and the management control systems mentioned earlier. The organic structure of Japanese firms is supplemented by the self-discipline and sharing of values and information among members while the mechanistic structure of U.S. firms is accompanied by output control. These factors combine to make a theoretically consistent match between organizational structure and process (Hage, 1974).

Fourth, the emphasis on group-oriented consensual decision making is compared. As expected, the findings indicate that Japanese managers make decisions in a more group-oriented manner, while U.S. executives stress individual initiative more.

It has been claimed that the behavior and attitudes of Japanese executives are characterized by unusually intensive informal social interactions and by high identification with their companies (see e.g. Ouchi, 1981). The comparative results of the fifth and sixth aspects of organizational process do not support this contention. U.S. executives at top or middle levels exhibit no fewer informal interactions and identify no less with their companies than do Japanese managers.

Seventh, the organizational climate is compared, in particular, with respect to acceptance of change. Our results indicate that Japanese managers are more change-oriented than U.S. managers. This difference in climate also corresponds to the differences in organic vs. mechanistic structure.

Lastly, a comparison of personnel management processes supports the generally held idea that Japanese firms put heavier emphasis on promotion from within.

Personal Predispositions of Members
The personal predispositions of members are compared in terms of six requirements for senior executives: (a) capability as a generalist, (b) value commitment, (c) interpersonal skills, (d) orientation toward innovation and risk-taking, (e) planning and leadership skills, and (f) record of performance.

The comparative results shown in Table 2-12 show that U.S. firms put heavier emphasis on value commitment, innovation and risk-taking, and record of accomplishment, while Japanese firms place more emphasis on capability as a generalist, and credibility and popularity within the company (interpersonal skills). These differences are consistent with the

differences in organizational structure and process: the senior executives
of U.S. firms play a major role in initiating and implementing innovation
in their mechanistic organizations, while Japanese senior executives play
a major role in promoting cohesiveness within their organic
organizations. The findings suggest that U.S. organizations may be better
suited for implementing major changes, while Japanese organizations may be
better suited for implementing incremental changes.

Table 2-12 Desirable Personal Characteristics of Senior Executives

Dimension and Indicators	Mean score of importance[a] U.S.	Japan
Generalist vs. Specialist	3.86	4.03***
Depth of professional knowledge in a special field (R)	3.39	3.73***
General knowledge of the company and its business	4.26	4.35
Ability to integrate diverse information	3.93	4.00**
Value commitment	4.20	4.05***
Sound and consistent values and beliefs	4.19	3.90
Commitment to and identification with company	4.21	4.21***
Interpersonal skills	3.60	3.91
Ability to promote harmony and collaboration	3.77	3.81
Sense of equity and fairness	4.02	4.09**
Credibility with stockholders and bank	3.35	3.58
Popularity and credibility with subordinates	3.24	4.17***
Innovation and risk-taking	3.94	3.43***
Ability to produce and accept new and creative ideas	4.03	3.72***
Willingness to take risks	3.84	3.13***
Planning and leadership skill	4.00	4.08***
Ability to formulate detailed plans	3.54	3.81*
Ability to organize and lead	4.46	4.35***
Record of Accomplishment	3.27	3.10***
Past record of high performance	3.95	3.72
Experience in other companies	2.55	2.47

Notes: a.   The larger the score, the more important is the factor
              (5, indispensable; 4, important; 3, desirable; 2, not
              important; 1, undesirable).
         (R) A reversed score is given in calculating the average score.
         *   significant at .05 level by t-test of means
         **   significant at .01 level by t-test of means
         *** significant at .001 level by t-test of means

In way of summary, a comparison of the intra-organizational characteristics of both nations' firms shows that the structure and processes of Japanese firms tend to be more organic in nature while those of the U.S. firms tend to be mechanistic. The results also indicate that most of the differences in structure and process are consistently related to the differences in environment, strategy and technology of the respective firms.

2.3 Two Modes of Adaptation and Their Strengths and Weaknesses

The results presented thus far have contrasted the environments, objectives, strategies, organizational structures and processes of Japanese and U.S. firms. The differences were perceived to be logically consistent with the contingency theory of organizations. Hence, it can be concluded that both U.S. and Japanese firms, on the average, create consistent patterns which fit the organization to its environment. The patterns are summarized in Table 2-13.

In most discussions, the environment is assumed to be the causal factor in the organization-environment relationship. However, it is also reasonable to assume a two-way causal relationship since the environment is influenced by the actions taken by many (or several powerful) organizations. Further, we assert that the characteristics of firms in each country are derived (in good part) by a common adaptation mode consistent with and largely a result of the country's cultural and institutional setting. We call the mode exhibited by Japanese firms the J-mode, and that of U.S. firms the A-mode. Using Burns & Stalker's terminology (1961), the J and A-modes have characteristics typical of their organic and mechanistic systems, respectively.

Neither mode of adaptation is, in itself, universally superior or inferior to the other. For instance, although the organic systems of Japanese companies have been found to have a higher rate of change (Hage and Aiken, 1967b), the mechanistic systems of American companies are often more efficient in a stable environment (Lawrence and Lorsch, 1967). It is also probable that the organic system of Japanese firms, although suited to change, may be less likely to produce radical changes because their group-oriented consensual decision making is more conducive to compromise and incremental change. Strategies for change on a revolutionary scale are more likely in mechanistic systems in which the initiative of the chief executive can play a more dominant role. Each mode has its own strengths and weaknesses. In light of those strengths and weaknesses, it is possible to specify the situation in which one mode is likely to be superior to the other.

Table 2-13 U.S. vs. Japanese Modes of Adaptation

	A - Mode Adaptation (U.S. mode)	J - Mode Adaptation (Japanese mode)
Environment	diverse,less volatile,bleak; remote relationships with distributors, customers, supplier and sub-contractors; rivalry with competitors; mobile labor market	homogeneous,volatile,opportunity rich close relationships with distributors, customers, suppliers and sub-contractors; somewhat cooperative ralationship with competitors; immobile labor market
Objectives	profitability and stock-holders' gains	multiple objectives with emphasis on growth
Strategy	mobile resource deployment stressing short-term efficiency; head-on competition stressing cost efficiency; product-oriented competitive strategy	less mobile resource deployment and creation of slack, stressing long-term deolyment of resources; coexistence with competitors stressing "niche" and differentiation; production-oriented competitive strategy
Technology	routine	non-routine
Organizational structure	mechanistic structure (high formalization, standardization and centralization); strong power of finance & control department;	organic structure (low formalization, standardization and centralization); weak power of finance & control department and strong power of production department;

Table 2-13 (continued) U.S. vs. Japanese Modes of Adaptation

	A - Mode Adaptation (U.S. mode)	J- Mode Adaptation (Japanese mode)
	divisionalization as the rule sophisticated performance appraisal and clear linkage between performance and financial remuneration; self-contained divisions with vertical control	selective divisionalization; simple performance appraisal and weak linkage between performance and financial remuneration; less self-contained divisions with horizontal coordination network
Organizational Process	task-oriented leadership; conflict resolution by confrontation; decision making stressing individual initiative; output control	information-oriented leadership conflict resolution by broad consultation before action, and by forcing; group-oriented consensual decision making; behavioral control and control by sharing of values and information; orientation toward change; promotion from within
Personal Predisposition of Members	specialist; value commitment; inclination toward innovation and risk-taking	generalist; interpersonal skills

The J-mode of adaptation, characteristic of the average Japanese firm, will be more successful when the following conditions are met:

(1)   the market environment is variable,

(2)   competition in the environment is multifarious,

(3)   the environment has plenty of opportunities,

(4)   a close inter-organizational network is created,

(5)   the input market is not mobile, and

(6)   adaptability to environmental change is the key factor for success.

These conditions are inferred from the characteristics of those industries in which Japanese firms have achieved higher market shares, for example, electronics and related industries,

On the other hand, the A-mode will be more successful under the following conditions:

(1)   the market environment is less variable but occasionally changes drastically,
(2)   competition is "uni-dimensional,"
(3)   the environment is bleak,
(4)   the inter-organizational network is weak,
(5)   the input market is mobile, and
(6)   operating efficiency is the key factor for success.

These conditions are also those under which the organic mode of adaptation does not work well.

As international competition driven by technological innovations becomes more open and pervasive, environments come to impose conflicting demands on organizations. For instance, in the semiconductor industry, operating efficiency and product innovation are simultaneously key requirements. In such a situation, a symbiotic strategy, i.e., one with some combination of the two adaptation modes, will be needed. In fact, between the two extremes, there lies a continuum of possible combinations of the two modes, an issue pursued in more depth later in the book.

In reality, it is well known that successful electronics companies in the U.S. such as IBM, Hewlett-Packard, etc. created highly organic elements in their organization which resemble those of the Japanese firms depicted here, and that successful companies in Japan such as Hitachi, Matsushita, etc. have some mechanistic elements (see e.g. Ouchi, 1981).

The environmental conditions surrounding both U.S. and Japanese firms are changing, and we believe that learning more about each others' adaptation modes is essential to both Japanese and U.S. business, and that we will mutually benefit from it.

Appendix 2A   The Distribution of U.S. and Japanese Samples

Table 2A-1 Size Distribution

Size		Number of Responses	
FORTUNE's ranking of U.S. Industrials[a]	Annual Sales (million of dollars)	U.S.	Japan[b]
1 - 200	Over 1,422	55 (25.7%)[c]	49 (16.9%)[c]
201 - 400	533 - 1,422	40 (18.7%)	65 (22.4%)
401 - 600	278 - 533	38 (17.8%)	54 (18.6%)
601 - 800	170 - 278	46 (21.5%)	35 (12.1%)
801 - 1,000	110 - 170	35 (16.4%)	35 (12.1%)
	70 - 110	0	21 (7.2%)
	Under 70	0	31 (10.7%)
Unknown[d]		13	1
Total		227 (100.1%)	291 (100%)

Notes: a.   The ranking is based upon *FORTUNE*'s 1979 rankings (May 7, 1979 and June 18, 1979).
   b.   Exchange rate used : 1 dollar = 200 yen.
   c.   Percentages exclude unknown firms.
   d.   "Unknown" consists of those responses in which the name of the company or of respondent was not specified.

Table 2A-2   Industry Distribution

Industry	U.S.	Japan
Mining	4 (1.9%)	1 (0.3%)
Food, beverage	20 (9.3)	21 (7.2)
Textile, apparel	8 (3.7)	17 (11.7)
Paper, fiber and wood products	10 (4.7)	11 (3.8)
Chemicals	18 (8.4)	33 (11.4)
Petroleum refining	13 (6.1)	4 (1.4)
Rubber	8 (3.7)	3 (1.0)
Glass, concrete, abrasives, gypsum	5 (2.3)	15 (5.2)
Metal manufacturing, metal products	27 (12.6)	29 (10.0)
Electronics, appliance	27 (12.6)	54 (18.6)
Transportation equipment, Aerospace	3 (1.4)	11 (3.8)
Measuring, scientific, photographic equipment	11 (5.1)	14 (4.8)
Motor vehicle	12 (5.6)	13 (4.5)
Pharmaceuticals, Soap and Cosmetics	11 (5.1)	15 (5.2)
Industrial, farm and office equipment	15 (11.7)	39 (13.4)
Miscellaneous manufacturing (printing, musical instruments, publishing, etc.)	12 (5.6)	10 (3.4)
Unknown	13	1
Total	227 (99.8%)	291 (99.9%)

Notes

1. The samples of responding enterprises were not chosen on a random basis but there is no reason to believe that large biases exist.

   The size and industrial distribution of responding companies are different between Japan and America. On analysis, the difference in average values not only reflects the country difference, but is also a reflection of differences in size and the industrial distribution of companies in the two countries. Needless to say, comparing average values and analyzing the country difference only, is a problematic comparison method. However, between the first 1,000 enterprises of the traded production enterprises section in the Tokyo Stock Exchange and the first 1,000 enterprises in Fortune, though there exist differences in size and industrial distribution, the Japanese companies are reflective of Japan and the American firms are reflective of the U.S. A comparison of the two groups does possess meaning on a country level.

2. This point has strongly been advocated by people of the "technology school" such as Woodward (1965), Perrow (1967), Thompson (1967).

3. This point is contrary to the common understanding that America possesses a desire to do fundamental research while Japan possesses desires to carry out application and developmental research, but it is in agreement with various statistical values. Of course, the size of business enterprises and ratio of sales to R&D are bigger on the American side, so it cannot be said that the Japanese side is high in absolute terms.

References

Burns, T. and G. M. Stalker, *The Management of Innovation*, London: Tavistock, 1961.

Fleishman, E. A. and E. F. Harris, "Patterns of Leadership Behavior Related to Employee Grievance and Turnover," *Personnel Psychology*, 15, 1962, pp.43-56.

Hage, J., *Communication and Organizational Control: Cybernetics in Health and Welfare Settings*, New York: John Wiley & Sons, 1974.

Hage, J. and M. Aiken, "The Relationship of Centralizaton to Other Structural Properties," *Administrative Science Quarterly*, 14, 1967a, pp.366-376.

Hage, J. and M. Aiken, "Program Change and Organizational Property: A Comparative Analysis," *American Journal of Sociology*, 12, 1967b, pp.72-92.

Hall, R. H., *An Empirical Study of Bureaucratic Dimensions and Their Relation to Organizational Characteristics*, Unpublished Ph.D. Dissertation, Ohio State University, 1961.

Hall, R. H., *Organizations: Structure and Process*, 2nd ed., Englewood Cliffs, N.J.: Prentice-Hall, 1977.

Hickson, D. J., C. R. Hinings, C. A. Lee, R. E. Scheck, and J. M. Pennings, "A Strategic Contingencies Theory of Intraorganizational Power," *Administrative Science Quarterly*, 16, 1971, pp.216-229.

Hofer, C. W. and D. Schendel, *Strategy Formulation: Analytical Concepts*, St. Paul, Minn.: West Publishing, 1978.

Kagono, T., *Keiei soshiki to kankyo tekio* (Organizational Adaptation to the Environment), Written in Japanese, Tokyo: Hakuto Shobo, 1980.

Lawrence, P. R., and J. W. Lorsch, *Organization and Environment: Managing Differentiation and Integration*, Boston: Harvard Business School, Division of Research, 1967.

Lorsch, J. W. and J. J. Morse, *Organizations and Their Members: A Contingency Approach*, New York: Harper & Row, 1974.

Nonaka, I., *Organization and Market : Exploratory Study of Centralization vs. Decentralization*, Ph.D. Dissertation, Graduate School of Business Administration, University of California, Berkeley, 1972.

Nonaka, I., *Soshiki to Shijo* (Organization and Market), Written in Japanese, Tokyo: Chikura Shobo, 1974.

Nonaka, I. and F. M. Nicosia, "Marketing Management, Its Environment, and Information Processing: A Problem of Organizational Design," *Journal of Business Research*, 7-4, 1979, pp.277-300.

Nonaka, I., T. Kagono, Y. Komatsu, A. Okumura and A. Sakashita, *Soshiki gensho no riron to sokutei* (Theory and Measurement of Organizational Phenomena), Written in Japanese, Tokyo: Chikura Shobo, 1978.

Ouchi, W., *Theory Z: How American Business Can Meet the Japanese Challenge*, Reading, Mass.: Addison-Wesley, 1981.

Perrow, C., "A Framework for the Comparative Analysis of Organizations," *American Sociological Review*, 32, 1967, pp.194-208.

Pugh, D. S., D. J. Hickson, C. R. Hinings and C. Turner, "Dimensions of Organizational Structure," *Administrative Science Quarterly*, 14, 1968, pp.91-114.

Rumelt, R. P., *Strategy, Structure, and Economic Performance*, Boston: Harvard Business School, Division of Research, 1974.

Sakakibara, K., I. Nonaka, T. Kagono and A. Okumura, "Organizational
    Adaptive Patterns to Environment: Exploratory Study of Integrative
    Contingency Theory," *Hitotsubashi Journal of Commerce,*15, 1980,
    pp.36-56.

Selznick, P., *Leadership in Administration,* New York: Harper & Row, 1957.

Tannenbaum, A. S., *Control in Organizations,* New York: McGraw-Hill, 1968.

Thompson, J. D., *Organization in Action,* New York: McGrow-Hill, 1967.

Williamson, O. E., *Markets and Hierarchies,* New York : Free Press, 1975.

Woodward, J., *Industrial Organization: Theory and Practice,* London:
    Oxford University Press, 1965.

CHAPTER 3   CORPORATE STRATEGY

In this and the following chapters, we will present an intensive qualitative study of the management styles of a selected number of Japanese and American companies. The aim is to analyze in more depth than was possible in Chapter 2, the management strategies and organizational structures of these firms.

It is vital that the companies selected for intensive comparative study, cover a variety of industries. Sixteen pairs of companies were selected from fifteen industries. The pairs chosen for comparison included those in the capital goods and consumer goods (durable consumer goods and non-durable consumer goods) industries, and scientific technology-oriented and non-scientific technology-oriented industries. The company pairs selected are listed in Table 3-1.[1] For a detailed description of the Japanese firms, refer to Appendix C. In addition to the pairs sampled, the study also included high-performance firms of special interest -- certain companies which we felt possessed a distinctive management style. These were Matsushita Electric Industrial Co., Kyocera Corporation and TDK Coporation from Japan, and Hewlett-Packard (HP) from the United States.

A second choice criterion employed here was to follow the general practice of selecting companies representative of industries in terms of performance and size. Having achieved above average performance or dominance in size is an indication that a company is able to cope effectively with the business environment. Our aim was to eliminate, as much as possible, those firms where a lapse in managerial acumen or some similar idiosyncratic factor had produced atypical behavior. Availability of published data and accessibility to the companies was also considered.

Detailed analyses were made of the paired samples using publicly available materials followed by in-depth personal interviews. In this and the following chapters we will present the findings from this analysis, selecting areas which clearly illustrate U.S.-Japan corporate similarities in management strategy and organizational structure, and their differences.

Table 3-1 Company Matches for Comparison

BUSINESS	U.S.			JAPAN		
	NAME	SALES mill. dollars	Number of Employees	NAME	SALES mill. dollars	Number of Employees
Chemicals	Du Pont	13,652	135,900	Toray	2,307	13,926
Semiconductors	TI	4,075	89,875	NEC	3,882	32,800
	Motorola	3,099	71,500			
Electric & Electronic Equipment	GE	24,959	402,000	Hitachi	8,465	72,277
				Toshiba	6,728	63,823
Computers	IBM	26,213	341,279	Fujitsu	2,528	34,019
Food	General Foods	6,601	53,000	Ajinomoto	1,626	5,639
Automobiles	GM	57,729	746,000	Toyota	15,245	48,757
Toiletries	P&G	10,772	59,000	Kao	1,097	4,125
Apparel	Levi Strauss	2,841	48,000	Renown	894	4,185
Pharmaceuticals	Eli Lilly	2,559	28,100	Takeda	1,873	11,023
Industrial Materials	3M	6,079	86,900	Sumitomo Elec.	1,864	11,277
Machine Tools	Cincinnati Milacron	816	13,780	Amada	422	1,134
Beverages	Seagram	2,047	11,000	Suntory	2,995	4,154
Retailers	Sears, Roebuck	25,195	390,000	Seibu	4,061	19,676
Construction Machinery	Caterpillar	8,597	86,350	Komatsu	2,194	16,711
Steel	U.S. Steel	12,492	92,734	Nippon Steel	12,368	71,669

Notes : 1980 Data
Exchange rate used : 1 dollar = 230 yen.

First, we will compare management strategies. Simply defined, management strategy refers to the matching of a company's resources with the opportunities and risks created by its environment -- the creation of a pattern of interaction between the company and the environment. We distinguish here between corporate strategy (strategy encompassing sometimes diverse business lines) and individual business-level strategy. The primary elements of strategy which are addressed in this chapter are: (1) definition of domain; (2) accumulation of the necessary strategic resources; and (3) development of competitive superiority through the management resources accumulated.[2]

3.1 Summary of Findings on Strategy

The main results of our comparative analysis of strategy in this chapter may be summarized as follows:

1. While U.S. companies tend toward relatively *specific definitions of domain*, Japanese companies tend to express *broad direction* to their employees, in a way which allows employees to use their own vision to interpret that direction in a rather free fashion.

2. U.S. companies *actively develop and organize resources* after relatively elaborate analysis and recognition of environmental opportunities and risks, while Japanese companies place more importance upon *continuous in-house resource accumulation* and *development* with a view toward survival under any type of environmental change.

3. U.S. companies favor a *financial management* approach to resource development, while Japanese companies emphasize *human resource development through education and activation*. The former, in fact, tends to be a short-term approach to business achievement, while the latter is oriented more toward long-term survival.

4. While U.S. managers and companies *assume the burden of risk independently*, Japanese companies will *distribute such risk factors* through *inter- and intra-organizational networks*.

5. U.S. companies establish competitive superiority through approaches of *logical, deductive reasoning*, seeking *superiority in products*, while

Japanese companies establish competitive superiority through *inductive, incremental reasoning,* seeking *superiority in production strategy.*

These differences are elaborated upon, below.

3.2 Approaches to Domain Definition and Development of Resources

3.2.1 Defining the Domain -- Functional vs. Directional Definitions

"Domain," as such, is sometimes called "the distinctive survival territory" of a company. A company's domain is typically defined by examining its *raison d'etre*; that is, the response to the question, "What does our company do and why?" The domain defines the "opportunity span" within which the company should develop its specific resources, and includes what technology the company should possess, what products it should supply and what markets it should serve.[3] While domain is established each time a strategy is defined, a comprehensive definition of domain will, at best, clarify and even add to the value of the company. Most firms choose to clearly state their management philosophies which are prerequisite to domain definition, but the two are not infrequently implicitly combined.

The typical U.S. domain definition is relatively market-oriented, with most definitions lying close to the key factors to success (KFS) in a specific market. Let us examine a few examples.

"IBM Means Service" (IBM): The idea is that IBM sells a whole product function, not just machinery, thereby contributing to customer problem solving. "Better Things for Living through Chemistry" (Du Pont): Research and development, in chemistry, with the focus on marketing.

"Make a little, sell a little, make a little more" and the 11th commandment: "Thou shalt not kill a new product idea" (3M). This is a company which started out with sandpaper and continuously developed responses to more and more complex customer needs. Keyed on the precision application of fine coating and bonding technology, 3M relied on autonomous small teams of internal entrepreneurs that responded to smaller size markets by developing more detailed technologies.

"Develop, Make and Sell" (Texas Instruments): Innovation, productivity and market share are the foundation of business development.

"Quality at a Good Price" (Sears): The goal of offering customers high-quality, added value products at a reasonable price.

"48-Hour Parts Service Anywhere in the World" (Caterpillar): A customer-oriented approach to management with the basic policy of rapid after-sales service. Caterpillar maintains 7,000 service stations around the world, a system guaranteeing parts supply within 48 hours of the order.

"Integrity, compassion and a thirst for excellence" (Eli Lilly): Mr. Eli Lilly's description of family values that in the long run have provided his company's basic strategy for the development of new pharmaceuticals and the ethical sales of these products.

"Single Source Responsibility" (Cincinnati Milacron): The approach of producing all related products and parts in-house, allowing the company to take full responsibility for the finished product.

In contrast, there are relatively few Japanese companies which offer such clear definitions of domain or which have management philosophies that are so consistently followed. Even if a domain is identified, it is usually in the form of an extremely macroscopic vision or long-term objective. A few examples are the following.

NEC terms its domain of operations "C&C" for "Computers & Communications." Some 20 years ago, when transistors started to develop into ICs and later, into large-scale integration (LSIs), NEC perceived that the semiconductor developments would bring about major changes in the field of telecommunications and computers. They thought that the digitalization of communications would increasingly integrate telecommunications and computer technologies, and that the next stage of development would involve efficiency improvement through distributed processing or multipolar decentration (which means that several computers are linked together in a constellation-like structure through communications networks). Henceforth NEC has oriented its business operation towards, and it is striving for the ultimate integration of computers & communications, namely "C&C" (Figure 3-1).

Figure 3-1 Perspective of "C & C"

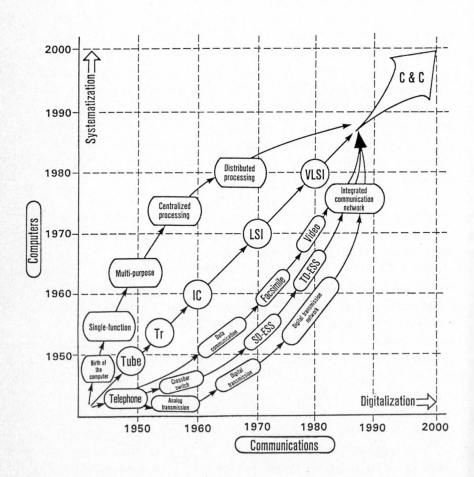

Source : Kobayashi, K., *C & C wa Nippon no chie* (C & C : Japan's Wisdom)
Simul Press, 1980, p. 49.

This rather vague conceptualization is though, more specific than the one used by Sumitomo Electric: "Optopia." This word is meant to evoke a sensitivity among employees toward the future and toward improvements in people's lives along with belief in progress through creative application of scientific knowhow (exemplified in the creation of the word itself). To outsiders such a concept might seem mystifying and obscure, but once the basic ideas have been thoroughly ingested, it provides a shorthand way of bringing into focus the fundamental objectives of the organization.

Suntory, a producer of alcoholic beverages, defines its domain of activity to be the "Lifestyle Culture Industry." Suntory's President Keizo Saji lay down the image of such an industry as, that which transforms the "future needs" (of customers) from the "quantity" level to the "cultural value" level. To become such an enterprise, every employee of the company is encouraged to propose original, creative, suggestions and to try them out in practice. With regards to the alcoholic beverage industry and customers, it means to sell "liquor as a culture." In other words, to become an enterprise which provides "liquor with enjoyment" and "the enjoyment of drinking liquor."

Similarly, the Seibu Distribution Group defines its domain of activity broadly as the "Citizen Industry." The intrinsic difference of the distribution industry from other industries is that it is situated at a closer position to customers. In other words, it is an "interface industry" at the critical boundaries of capital and people. The idea of a "citizen industry" does not follow from the logic of capital flow but from the logic of people. In more concrete terms, it is an industry which should attempt to be in harmony with the logic of the individual varieties of consumers. The Seibu Distribution Group must strive to become a Big Business which understands the individuality and variety of consumers.

Renown, the apparel firm, declares its domain to include the whole realm of "Fashion: Information and Sensation." Information gathering and sensitivity to environmental ques are thought to enable Renown to create and hold leads in home, foods and restaurant chains, as well as its principal business, apparel.

The type of optimism evidenced in the "Optopia" concept is even more conspicuous in Matsushita's: "Producing a supply of materials as inexhaustible as tap water in an effort to create a realm of prosperity." This bears the unmistakable imprint of founder Konosuke Matsushita. Such sentiments might seem self-serving and extreme by western standards, but their ring, especially among Japanese who remember the aftermath of the war, is very cogent. Other companies echo similarly high-blown promises: "Contributing to Global Culture and Industries through Creativity" is the wish of TDK, the tape manufacturer, while Kao proclaims the belief that "A Clean People will Prosper."

These comparisons, which might themselves seem "unacademic" to the reader, indicate that the Japanese company's domain definition is more concerned with expressing the initiative and direction that should be taken by its employees than with the basics of resource deployment. The definitions function to instill a sense of motivation, to heighten employee sensitivity toward the environment, and to stimulate thinking about the meaning of the business. In contrast to the U.S. company's definition stressing market orientation, the Japanese definition is one which leads to activation of the organization as a whole; it expresses a vision from which the corporate "mission" later evolves.

A recurrent Japanese company mission has been to "catch up with and surpass" Western companies. There is little doubt that most of the Japanese companies in this sampling have set their sights on U.S. firms in frantic efforts to grow. A particular case in point is Fujitsu, the only Japanese company specializing entirely in computer manufacturing: its mission to the letter was "catch IBM." Fujitsu president, Takuma Yamamoto commented on this point: "It is said that Fujitsu challenged IBM. Although our true aims are not something that could be expressed with such wishful thinking, saying that we are challenging IBM -- the idea that we are going to beat the industry giant -- is rather effective. It has spirit. It helps boost the morale of our younger people. Frankly speaking, it was the best 'catch phrase' we could have possibly devised."[4]

The more recent "We are GE+IBM" slogan of Hitachi, Ltd. is also this sort of broad but inspiring domain definition.

3.2.2 Active Resource Development vs. Resource Accumulation

(1) Different Approaches to Strategy Formulation

U.S. companies actively develop and organize their resources after carrying out a relatively detailed analysis of environmental opportunities and risks. That is, environmental opportunities are analyzed and in-house resources are *then organized to fit* the situation. Strategic planning in America typically involves concrete features embodying this concept.

GE introduced the "business screen" as a means of rationally distributing resources between business divisions. The unit of resource allocation is the SBU (strategic business unit). The entire company is regarded as a portfolio of numerous SBU's.

In the establishment of a company-wide strategy, a key factor is resource deployment geared to ensure a portfolio balance at present and in the future. A balanced portfolio consists of a suitable distribution of growth businesses which can be expected to rise to a dominant position through capital investment, and businesses which will increase in profitability in step with market maturation and which can be expected to provide a source of in-house income for other investment opportunities. This enables the company to manage resource distribution so as to maintain a balanced cash flow -- the ultimate aim of business screen analysis. This type of concept is predicated upon a strategy of resource development designed specifically to adapt to changing environmental opportunities and risks. Decisions regarding resource development flow essentially from top management. The method is logical and essentially impersonal.

In contrast, Japanese companies, rather than basing resource development upon the careful projections of a thorough analysis of the environment, seek to accumulate an abundance of resources at the in-house level which will allow the company to take advantage of any environmental opportunities and to face any threats when they are encountered. Rather than having the top management or general staff play the leading role in environmental analysis, Japanese top management will generally indicate only the direction to be taken, heavily depending for assessment of opportunities and risks upon middle-level line managers. The idea here is to allow middle-managers and workers to continually make subtle adjustments to long-term plans, and in the process, gradually instill the entire organization with energy and direction.

Behind the resource accumulation and development of **Matsushita Electric Industrial Co., Ltd.** is the philosophy of founder Konosuke Matsushita which he calls "dam management":

> A dam is used to block the flow of a river to store up a water supply, guaranteeing the amount of water needed for daily use regardless of changes in season or weather. The idea of 'dam management' applies the principles of a dam to business, with the aim of maintaining steady, uninterrupted development without major impact from changes in various external factors. There is the equipment dam, capital dam, personnel dam, inventory dam, technology dam, planning and product development dam and so forth. In short, this refers to management allowing margin, elbow room. By placing these types of management dams in key locations, the water accumulated when rivers are flooding can then be discharged in times of drought, avoiding shortages due to changes in the external environment and reacting to these changes in prompt and precise fashion. Such an arrangement will make it possible to carry on stable management at all times.[5]

Matsushita Electric's philosophy and management planning system has, in many ways, a distinctive Japanese character. Like most other Japanese companies, every year on January 10, the company assembles thousands of employees for an "annual policy announcement meeting." The agenda includes reflection upon and evaluation of the previous year, assessments of current and future conditions, forthcoming corporate themes, and the basic attitudes needed to deal with these themes. The slogan for fiscal year 1980, for example, was "React quickly, respond wisely" -- an appeal for the company to respond to market conditions and mobilize its organizational wisdom.

After annual policy has been articulated in broad terms, the members of top management then work together with all division managers to study specific problem areas. They agree upon an "outline for the preparation of management planning." This outline serves as a guide for divisional planning aimed at attaining the goals articulated by the annual policy.

The various divisions take this outline and develop their own long-range, intermediate, and short-range plans. However, long- and intermediate-range plans at Matsushita contain rather loosely worded objectives, with the most specificity in the "business fiscal year plans" (announced on a semiannual basis). These plans contain detailed figures on a wide range of areas --net sales, market share, profits, costs, and others. The divisions submit their fiscal year plans to the head office and after study by top management, the plans become the "basic action plan" of the division. The president's approval of the plans is fairly routine and constitutes a form of mutual agreement by the president and division managers.

At Matsushita, the corporate planning staff is strictly oriented toward providing service, while the divisions themselves have the major responsibility for their own plans. In contrast to the West, the corporate planning staff devotes almost all of its time supplying information to top management, or acting as a "secretariat" in carrying out support activities. One Matsushita executive, in commenting on this planning system, stated: "Our company does not have a long-term plan, but we do have long-term vision."

(2) "Buying" and "Selling" as Strategy

The strategy of U.S. companies involves, as we have seen, thorough analysis of opportunities *followed by* active resource development efforts. In America any business is a potential target for acquisition or divestiture, regardless of its size. U.S. firms, therefore, attempt to ensure their own survival by buying up other companies in growth sectors to augment their own growth, by selling off businesses in deficit or declining sectors, and by taking protective action against take-over bids.

There are several American companies in our sample which have pursued strategies of growth by buying and selling businesses.

The dealings of **Motorola, Inc.** over the last decade or so are a typical example of such activities.[6] Before the 1960's, Motorola was known as a consumer electronics concern. As its name implies, the company started out in the automotive field, building car radios, then, diversified into home audio equipment, television image reception equipment and other business areas. During the same period, it also diversified into communications equipment and semiconductors and, later, into recreation, chemicals, broadcasting and other sectors. In 1974 Motorala sold off its unprofitable "Quasar" television division to Matsushita Electric. As the company pondered what type of business to add to fill the resulting gap, it began to pursue a strategy designed to add coherence to its business portfolio.

It decided to concentrate on data processing-related businesses. Various companies were listed as candidates for acquisition, and the feasibility and economy of various moves was studied. The result was the 1977 purchase of the computer peripheral manufacturer Codex. In three years' time, Codex net sales had increased fourfold, and the purchase is now acknowledged as a major success. In the meantime, Motorola began to think about entering the computer mainframe field and set its sights on a three-pronged business portfolio consisting of semiconductors, communications and information systems. This strategic development eventually led the company to withdraw (in 1980) from the field in which it began -- car radios.

At the present time, the company has established a "new business headquarters" to prepare for advancement into new areas of the electrortics field. Plans call for moves into robotics and CAD/CAM machinery with a net sales target for the early 1990's set at $15 billion.

Ever since 1976 when former U.S. Marine, D.M. Roderick became chairman of **U.S. Steel Corp.**, the company has pursued a path of diversification through a series of acquisitions and asset sales. Such efforts have been particularly intense since 1978, with acquisitions in the plastics and petrochemical fields, construction of plants and equipment, mergers, and the pursuit of other aggressive strategies. The strategy proposed by Roderick for 1980 was "Progress Directed Toward Profit Maximization and Cash Generation."

His boldest move to date was his successful battle with Mobil and Allied to purchase Marathon Oil, America's 17th largest oil company. Describing the future of his company after the mammoth merger, the Chairman said: "I refused to subscribe to the superstition that a company is like a dinosaur in that once it becomes huge in size it will deteriorate and die. Today U.S. Steel is overflowing with vigor and youth."[7]

There are also many U.S. companies which stress internal development of high technology. While suppressing any move toward becoming conglomerates, acquisition is still a vital tool of strategy in these cases as well.

Eli Lilly is an innovative company which invested over $200 million in R&D in 1980. However, it has used acquisition as a method of diversification into medical equipment (in which technological systems differ), cosmetics (where the markets differ) and other fields. An important criterion for acquisition is that the company to be acquired be wholly consistent with Eli Lilly in philosophy and purpose. Thus, in 1977, Eli Lilly bought IVAC Corp., a thermometer maker; in 1978, the implantable pacemaker concern Cardiac Pacemakers, and in 1980, the Physio-Control Corp. It should be noted that Eli Lilly also acquired Elizabeth Arden Inc., a cosmetics firm, back in 1971. In 1980, the share of the company's net sales accounted for by acquired businesses was 17 percent.

The cosmetics field did not really fit the nature of Lilly, and for many years that business seemed to stagnate. A few years ago, the company, in a rare departure from its emphasis on advancement from within, recruited outside experts in a successful attempt to rebuild that particular division. In this diversification effort, not only the takeover of company but also the acquisition of outside managers has proven to be a key source of vitality and growth.

While Takeda Chemical Industries, roughly Eli Lilly's counterpart in Japan, has diversified into foodstuffs, agricultural chemicals, synthetic chemicals, cosmetics and other fields, the approach taken differs markedly from Eli Lilly's in that most of this new business was created through internal development rather than acquisition.

The 3M Company, historically a proponent of in-house development like Eli Lilly, has also used occasional acquisitions as a means for adding momentum to its in-house development. A notable example was 3M's 1972 purchase of Personal Environment Systems Company, a small manufacturer of respirator systems. 3M employed a three-dimensional-forming technology using non-woven polyester as the basis for its development and production of dust mask respirators and established a new division, Occupational Health and Safety Products.

In our target sample, the Seagram Company is a firm which adopted a conglomerate strategy. The alcoholic beverage maker's CEO, Edgar Bronfman, believes that the alcoholic beverage industry is already mature: "It has become more difficult to maintain the growth rates we want without major acquisitions."[8] Bronfman has stated that he is ready to expand into any field other than steel, forestry or nuclear power. This is obviously a company with an extremely aggressive strategy. The contrast with Suntory, Seagram's Japanese counterpart and a company dedicated to the "Lifestyle Culture Industry," could hardly be greater.

(3) The "Under the Table" Concept

In general, most Japanese companies adopt an in-house approach to resource development, experimenting with different business lines, then, selecting the most promising ones to develop fully. This sort of process is sometimes initiated informally at the micro-level, in research institutes or plants.

Sumitomo Electric Industries, Ltd. has used the know-how accumulated in the electric wire and cable field to diversify into a wide range of sectors which include metal products, organic materials, compound semiconductors, cutting tools, data control systems, optical fiber communication systems and so forth. Almost all new recent product and technology developments by the company are the result of in-house efforts, including joint research projects.

The basis for this approach had already been established between 1965-75. Like other Japanese companies up to the early 1960's, Sumitomo

Electric had based its diversification primarily upon borrowed technology. From the late 1960s, however, the company and its employees realized that it would be very risky to rely only on electric wire and cable, the demands for which showed volatile fluctuations. And the company realized the limitation of a strategy of development and growth based solely upon technology from abroad. Hence, Sumitomo opted for a diversification policy keyed on in-house technology. In pursuit of this goal, an R&D policy was adopted which encouraged researchers "to create new things." The seeds for growth in many new directions have since been sown within the company.

The oil crisis of 1974, however, resulted in a change from decentralized to more centralized financial planning. R&D was divided into priority projects and basic research, and investment was concentrated on priority projects involving optic communications, data control systems and fine-quality materials. This type of investment was, of course, possible only because the seeds of growth had been planted in the past.

At the current time, Sumitomo's R&D projects are divided into four stages from basic to near-term applied research, with detailed evaluations conducted at each stage. Sumitomo Electric is one of few Japanese companies with a sophisticated approach to R&D project evaluation. This systematic approach to R&D is a consequence of the fact that the electric wire and cable business -- originally the company's primary field -- is so closely tied to fluctuations in the economy, necessitating a need for strict controls on corporate performance.

A typical example of Japanese corporate research and development is **Toshiba Corporation**'s development of a Japanese-language word processor.[9] The corporation first turned to the task of *kanji* -- Chinese character -- processing back in 1967. The driving force at that time was the desire to create *kanji*-input equipment that anyone could use with ease. Rising to the challenge was Ken-ichi Mori, then, chief researcher at the Toshiba Central Research Center Electronic Equipment Research Laboratory. Although he jumped at the opportunity, the concept of easy *kanji*-input was, itself, difficult to grasp. Much remained to be learned about linguistics, the demand for computer processing capability in

Japanese remained in doubt, and a low priority was assigned to the "unofficial" project (resulting in less than twenty-percent of Mori's time spent on it at work and minimal funding). The project was finally made official in 1976, a prototype produced in 1977, and the commercial potential of a Japanese-Language word-processor demonstrated in 1978. Eleven years had passed since the start of the unofficial project. Today, of course, Toshiba's accomplishment is considered a world-first.

Mori comments on those days:

> The concept of easy *kanji*-input was something hard to grasp. It was like being unable to distinguish between the mountains and the sea. The research center policy was to proceed 'under the table.' In other words, while they encouraged efforts in areas beyond the primary ones of the research center, I was told to hold the time spent on it to under twenty percent of my total time at work. The idea was that I should work alone until my progress was sufficient to develop a tentative time schedule. When I needed to buy books about language or linguistics it came out of my own pocket.

The continuing basic research on computerized automatic *kana* (Japanese phonetic letters) and *kanji* (ideographic letters) conversion was advanced with informal involvement by the research staff; and in the spring of 1976, development prospects were finally established in a formal way. At this stage, the concept was brought above table for the first time. Once a theme is made official, people, material and money are mobilized, but at the same time the researcher must be able to state when the task will be accomplished. This is the reason that the cumbersome under-the-table approach was maintained.

While permission was received to produce an experimental model, approval to commercialize the product faced more difficulty. Division general manager Kimio Tsuzuki harbored doubts about just how many people would purchase word processors for Japanese. He was also concerned about the input method. He thought that the standard "pen-touch" method of having all characters lined up on the keyboard would be easy to get used to, and felt uneasy about *kana* and *kanji* conversion. The division therefore, took tentative steps to develop the pen-touch method, but the main thrust of the plant was covertly in pursuit of "*kana* and *kanji* conversion."

However, worries grew that under these conditions it would be difficult to bring the concept to commercialization, and going on the principle that "seeing is believing," in July 1978, it was decided to invite the divisional manager to take a direct look at the project. The magazine *President* carried a description of that occasion:

> Tsuzuki and the rest of the division managers were ushered into the room where the experimental model was located. A demonstration was conducted by typing in the words 'kana kanji' in kana and having them appear on the screen in kanji. There was obviously a big difference between seeing and hearing because Tsuzuki, who had before said the whole idea was 'risky,' startled everyone present by praising the machine and ordering the designers to commercialize it as soon as possible.

In Japanese companies, middle and lower-level employees are encouraged to suggest concepts for development. The seeds thus sown can and do become the basis for major changes and adaptation. This Japanese approach to development often leads to a "composite technology" -- a synergistic combination of technologies which plays a key role in adaptation (Sakakibara, 1982).

Toray Industries, Inc. has achieved dynamic growth through the "encounter" and "docking" of essential but heterogeneous technologies. For example, *"Ecsaine"*, the suede-like artificial leather , is a joint result of the the development of 0.01-0.09 denier, an ultra-fine textile (itself a world class achievement), and the company's accumulated technological expertise in non-woven fabrics. The key to the development of the carbon fiber *Torayca*, meanwhile, was the synergistic combination of organic compound, polymer design, thread production and baking technologies. As these examples indicate, Toray's technological development has been chiefly characterized by its possession of multiple, heterogeneous in-house technologies, together with the engineering and production prowess necessary to develop these technologies into concrete products.

Similarly, **NEC**'s technological development has been based on the firm's traditional strength in communications technology, and its ability to *integrate* new areas (1) computers, electronic devices (mainly semiconductors), control machinery and other unique technologies, and (2) assembly, testing and quality control technologies, into the mass-

production process. Of tremendous helpfulness to NEC has been its dual
pursuit of communications and computer technologies, with the synthesis of
the two made possible by the semiconductor.

That NEC's composite technological prowess has had a positive impact on
computers and, also, on communications technology, the corporation's
traditional forte, is widely recognized. A good example of the outcome is
NEC's state-of-the-art electronic switchboard, a single system, but one
depending on current technological developments in switching devices,
transmission technology, computers, and so on.[10]

3.2.3 Financial vs. Human Resources

(1) Stress on Cash Flow

Behind the resource development strategies just described is, of course,
the objective of maximizing profits. GE's strategic planning is closely
tied to profits via the management of cash flows, and the diversification
of companies like Motorola and U.S. Steel is motivated by similarly strong
profit motives. Both GE's former chairman, Jones, the man said to have
made the concept of strategic planning an everyday word at GE, and
Roderick, chairman of U.S. Steel, who revolutionized the corporation
through "Strategy for Progress Directed Toward Profit Maximization and
Cash Generation," are men with financial backgrounds.

Accordingly, even after considerable investment, when U.S. companies
decide that a project will not contribute to "corporate growth accompanied
by ample earnings," they tend to abruptly abandon it. There are numerous
examples, such as Du Pont's withdrawal from Corfam, a synthetic leather
said, in the 1960's, to be an epoch-making new product, GE's pullback from
the computer field, General Foods giving up on its chain of non-food
products, and RCA divesting itself of Random House Publishing Company.

Such radical changes are often seen as laudable evidence of willingness to
make the "tough decisions." The 1970 sale of the GE computer division,
for example, is now called a masterpiece of strategic analysis, timing and
financial engineering. GE was the first of the "dwarfs" to withdraw from

the computer business, and the timing was good because GE's competitors were moving toward the next-generation computer. GE was able to negotiate with a large number of potential buyers, and in the end sold the division to Honeywell for an attractive price.[11]

In Japan, withdrawals are extremely difficult because of the fixed nature of human resources. Examples of withdrawals by Japanese companies include the largest spice-maker Ajinomoto from salad dressing, electronics giant Matsushita from computers, and Toshiba from large mainframe computers. But such divestitures are quite rare, and occur only after very protracted periods of decision-making, if then. For example Toray, the textile firm, considered withdrawing from the artificial leather business. After continuous losses for several years, all of Toray's Western competitors had withdrawn. But in a last-ditch effort, Toray embarked on a two-year "probation" period during which time the company's R&D department managed to develop a much improved artificial suede material which was marketed successfully. (More details are cited in the next section.)

(2) The Role of a Healthy Deficit Sector

Japanese corporate resource development is based more on the activation of human resources than on the management of cash flows. Japanese companies are willing to ignore undesirable short-term financial results in favor of long-term human resource development. Transcending specific management styles, the phenomenon is sometimes manifested in keeping "healthy" deficit divisions for the purpose of introducing new information or tension into the organization itself, that is, for the sake of activating the organization and organizational learning.

Suntory's corporate strategy, consists, in short, of continuous new product development. For example, when the sales of the company's first product, a sweet wine called "Akadama," were reaching a peak, Suntory moved into the whisky field; then when whisky was enjoying its best period yet, the company burst into the beer market. Suntory president Keizo Saji offers the following explanation:

> When we started in the beer field the company was truly fired up. I believe that enthusiasm was also a major plus factor -- a

stimulation factor -- for whisky as well. The whisky business
has been comparatively blessed, and we have not had to fight much
of a battle. The period following directly after World War II
was an age of commodity shortages, and whatever we made we
sold. After a while the square-shaped "kakubin" whisky bottle
became a big hit, and we used that product as the locomotive to
move our sales. When the kakubin came to be well known, Suntory
Old became our biggest seller. That resulted in a tranquil mood
which permeated the entire company. That really concerned me,
and I became determined to do something to get everyone fired up
again. I decided that the best way to accomplish that would be
new work. I came to the conclusion that, if the new field were
beer, we could handle the work with our existing technology. The
sales network would be about the same as for whisky and we could
use our marketing in the same way to get the job done. That's
why we decided on beer.[12]

Renown, Inc. expanded and grew by concentrating in the apparel industry,
but it began to diversify in the 1970s. In 1973 Renown Milano, a
restaurant chain, was established, as a joint venture between Renown (40
percent equity) and Lilian, a subsidiary in charge of women's fashion
sales (60 percent equity). In 1976 Renown Foods was created through joint
financing with Ikari Sauce. Renown Foods is a subsidiary producing juice,
soup and instant foods. The establishment of Renown Milano and Renown
Foods differed from that of Durban, Lilian and other previously
established subsidiaries. While the latter two firms were in the apparel
business, the former had no link whatsoever to apparel. They could not
directly utilize Renown's apparel production and sales know-how.

The company's principal field, apparel, continues to enjoy growth; thus,
diversification was not a step taken to counteract stagnation in this
field. While it is clear that the move represents long-term investment,
it was not something implemented according to a long-term profit plan.
Indeed, Renown has a policy of no long-term planning! The view adopted
was to allow growth to develop naturally within each subsidiary and for
diversification to so occur. Although diversification was championed
initially by Renown's former chairman, Onoe, the reasons for it were more
subtle than profit-orientation.

One specific aim dealt with heightening the employee association of
fashion consciousness with the company image, while expanding the concept
of fashion. Of late, the sense of "being fashionable" has expanded beyond

mere clothing to include food, with the hoped-for outcome that a greater sense of the one would have a positive effect on the other. Renown has subsequently established Renown Homes, diversifying into "dwelling fashion."

Renown's president, Hiromichi Inagawa, describes another aim of the company's diversification:

> The most frightening thing that can happen to a company is for every division to be impeccable (because it breeds complacency). In contrast, when there are about three - out of, say, fifteen - major investments for the future that are unprofitable, it puts your mind to rest. When these deficit divisions begin to show profits, then, it will pay to invest in new deficit divisions.[13]

Matsushita's basic structure is built around its divisions -- "in-house subsidiaries" -- each based on a major production item. There are over 40 of these business divisions within the overall Matsushita Group, as well as 14 separate companies listed on domestic stock exchanges and 11 which are unlisted. The Matsushita approach is to successively separate business divisions and to establish them as autonomous subsidiary companies.

Large numbers of business divisions and subsidiaries of this kind exist, each producing quite similar products. In the past, both the Tape Recorder and Radio Divisions developed and marketed stereo cassette players. In a more recent case, the marketing of oven ranges by the Microwave Range Division caused electric oven sales of the Electric Heating Division to abruptly decline. But Matsushita Electric's president, Toshihiko Yamashita, views this type of phenomenon in the following way:

> We thought of having managers take responsibility for each separate group, but to be honest, we don't really have a master plan. In that sense, the business division is far from being the perfect arrangement. But as long as the merits outweigh the demerits, we want to use them and try to compensate for the system's weaknesses in other ways. The system guides the company in a positive direction. At the current time the best performing divisions are those which create friction with others. It is clear that failing to draw territorial lines between business

divisions will cause interference between separate new product
development efforts, but in the interest of progress we tell our
divisions not to fear friction.[14]

The autonomy of the business division or branch company is respected at
Matsushita Electric, because of the entrepreneurial energy arising from
their separate operations.   In-house competition continues to be promoted
even with an overlapping of resources and activities.   In short, a
competitive mechanism has been introduced within the company itself, for
the purpose of increasing in-house tension to help activate human
resources.

Toray had "failed" in its development of the suede-type artificial
leather, "Ecsaine," as mentioned before. The project ended in failure
because the high market demand which was expected never materialized and
Toray's top management had decided to terminate it.   The researchers
requested a two-year moratorium to find an application for the artificial
leather technology accumulated to that point.   Management agreed to this
request, and the research team returned to the fundamentals, launching
detailed studies into the reason behind the special appearance of natural
leather.   Meanwhile, in a separate laboratory, researchers were
enthusiastically pursuing an attempt to create an extremely fine synthetic
fiber.   The artificial leather group hit on the idea of using this new
technology for producing a super fine artificial leather.   The dramatic
melding of the two technologies culminated in the successful development
of "Ecsaine."   Thus, based on the importance of preserving what their
people had learned and of having confidence in them, the initial failure
was turned into a major success.[15]

The type of resource development which stresses human learning tends to be
more long-term in nature than its financial resource oriented
counterpart.   Management continuity is a necessary condition for such
human resource development.   Toray president, Yoshikazu Ito, who addressed
the annual meeting of the *American Chemistry Society* about the development
of *Ecsaine*, told us:

> The meeting hall erupted in surprise. The fact that a team that
> had actually been ordered to disband, was given a two-year
> moratorium, and then produced such outstanding results is

inconceivable in America. In this sense, it seems that Japanese management is more committed to long-term research and development than to short-term financial returns.

Continuity -- of policy, of people, of effort -- is strongly emphasized by the Japanese. Yoshio Maruta, president of the Kao Corporation, stated:

> There was a time when we listened to speeches given or read books written by U.S. management theorists, and believed that we should give their ideas a try sometime, in one form or another. But as it has turned out, I believe now that (uncritical adherence to) those ideas would only have lead us into a slump. A company is not an entity which you are in charge of for only a set period of time; it continues indefinitely. So, even if the flowers do not bloom now, it pays to make the effort to see that they bloom in the next age. Our bodies will waste away, but the company is eternal. It is more important that you make the effort to carry the company on into the next age than to pay out healthy dividends while you are in control. You shouldn't worry about getting applause for your efforts today.[16]

3.2.4 Responding to Changes: Market and Organizational Role Re-definition vs. Network Formation

Distinctive differences exist between U.S. and Japanese companies in the methods they use to reduce environmental risks.

(1) Networks between Competitors

The first difference is in the Japanese formation of networks between competitors. The foremost example is of companies involved in the development of high technology. Although coordinated by the Ministry of International Trade and Industry (MITI), NTT, and other government or quasi-governmental bodies, the networking of competing firms in joint research and through it, the maintenance of networks is a distinctive Japanese touch. Such networks include the *VLSI Technology Research Association*, *Nuclear Power Steel Manufacture Technology Research Association* and others.

In 1975 IBM announced that in the near future, it would be marketing the next-generation mainframe computer -- the so-called FS (future system). This system was intended to contain the VLSI, an epoch-making advance in

high-integration and high-density technology. VLSI development demanded
both massive capital and the exchange of high-level knowledge that had
been accumulating in various parts of the corporation.

At that time, Japanese computer makers were just beginning to gain the
strength to challenge IBM. In 1976 the Japanese government earmarked a
total of 70 billion yen (30 billion consisting of government subsidies) to
be spent over a four-year period to form the *VLSI Technology Research
Association*. A total of five domestic computer makers participated in the
association: Fujitsu, Hitachi, Mitsubishi Electric, NEC and Toshiba.[17]

Hirokichi Yoshiyama, president of Hitachi, was appointed board chairman of
the association, and NEC president, Koji Kobayashi, became its assistant
board chairman. Heading a joint research institute, these two men
coordinated the government spending program. The research staff was
assembled from the member companies and from MITI's Electrotechnical
Laboratory, a part of the Agency of Industrial Science and Technology.
Despite members from such diverse sources, the joint research staff
compiled impressive results in fine processing, process technology and
crystallization, and, thereby, accumulated the technology needed for VLSI
development.

There are also Japanese examples of collaboration between companies
without government leadership. For example, Fujitsu and Toray launched
joint research and development of a computerized Japanese-language laser
printer in June of 1980. This brought together Toray's advanced
electronic photography technology and Fujitsu's computer electronics know-
how to develop the foremost Japanese-language printer in the world. It is
noteworthy that Fujitsu and Toray belong to different corporate groups,
each of them formed around separate financial institutions, as will be
touched on later; and in the field of computerized Japanese-language laser
printers, they are actually business rivals.

A strong impetus to this joint R&D project was the decade-long private
friendship between Rinzo Iwai, manager of Fujitsu's Peripheral Equipment
Department, and Daisuke Miura, head of Toray's New Enterprise Promotion
Department. The existence of strong mutual rivals (IBM Japan and Hitachi)

also provided impetus for this union. Fujitsu president, Takuma Yamamoto, offered the following commentary:

> In this age of globalization, remaining within the borders of conventional corporate groups will cause a company to fall behind in its attempt to create truly top-class world products. Even if people look down at you, a company with rare technology will push on ahead, paying no mind to either criticism or praise. This is our corporate strategy in the effort to win out and survive."[18]

The forming of networks between Japanese companies constitutes an important method for accumulating resources in an environment characterized by difficulty in acquiring businesses and by low between firm mobility of skilled people.

In the United States, there has been unparalleled cooperation between private firms on NASA projects and certainly among universities. However, joint projects between directly competing companies are very rare exceptions. The existence of strong anti-trust regulations surely contributes to such non-cooperation. An over-emphasis on short-term financial successes by individual firms impedes joint effort, as well. "Solutions" will necessarily be suboptimal if the challenges facing an industry are more complex than can be overcome by firms acting individually. We cannot emphasize too strongly that the lesson applies equally well to societies in (after Yamamoto) "this age of globalization."

(2) Networks between Manufacturers and Suppliers

The second difference between U.S. and Japanese companies is that the latter form dense inter-company networks between manufacturers and suppliers. As exemplified by Cincinnati Milacron's "single source responsibility" concept, U.S. companies are more vertically *and* horizontally integrated. In contrast, Japanese companies rely much more heavily on outside suppliers, depending on good relations with companies in their group for mutual assistance. Companies like Toyota and Matsushita are actually more like "production wholesalers" which have their own assembly plants than they are "makers" as such.[19]

Japanese subcontractors use their experience and expertise stemming from specialization to help big companies in the areas of cost, quality, and speed. The frequently lower wages of these subcontractors contribute to lower overall labor costs of the Japanese companies compared to that of U.S. firms with their comprehensive, integrated approaches to production and more uniformly high wages. This is a significant factor contributing to the difference in competitiveness.

In the high technology sectors, U.S. companies are very explicit about their arms-length relationship to venture companies. Only when venture firms have grown and demonstrated substantial profitability, are they acquired as divisions of a business. Examples of such cases include Intersil, a GE semiconductor maker, and Calma, a leading CAD/CAM maker. The U.S. approach to investments in new ventures which have elements of instability and risk is to allow such ventures to be tested in the market before risking capital. This is not common in Japan.

(3) Networks within Channels of Distribution

The third networking difference between U.S. and Japanese companies is that the latter form very close relations with organizations in their channels of distribution. Lasting, human relationships often closely tie manufacturers and distributors, and the market strength of Matsushita, Toyota, Kao and other leading companies in Japan is due, in part, to the size and cohesion of the sales networks that have become part of their corporate networks.

Ajinomoto Co., Inc. is known for the loyalty that it has cultivated and shown over many years. It adopted early a "special license" outlet system and has dedicated itself to the survival and mutual prosperity of its distribution channel members. Market acceptance of its glutamic acid, is always a major theme in the company's strategy, and Ajinomoto has historically worked to develop a network of highly reliable licensed outlets to convince the public of Ajinomoto's value. A nationwide "Ajinomoto Association" was established, and this was combined with a strategy of diversifying and the use of specially licensed outlets classified by product. The Ajinomoto network is now said to consist of approximately 700 major distributors nationwide, 2,000 secondary and tertiary outlets, and over 200,000 retail stores.[20]

While its products pass through the specially licensed outlets, Ajinomoto complements its outlet sales by promotion in volume retailers such as supermarkets and department stores. Ajinomoto's distribution channel policy utilizes the wholesaling function "without turning everything over to them." At the same time, however, wholesalers have also contributed suggestions for Ajinomoto product development on a sustained, long-term basis. Moreover, wholesalers compete in proposing outlets to be licensed, through which they intend to sell newly introduced Ajinomoto products. This has led to even stronger ties and mutual confidence.

Ajinomoto is also moving to improve its production technology and marketing know-how through mergers and other collaborative ties with other firms. These firms include Cereals (corn flakes), Corn Products Company (soup), Ajinomoto General Foods (instant coffee) and The Dannon Company (dairy products). The company's diversification strategy to-date has focused on entering markets that are large or which have great potential for growth. They do not enter undeveloped markets. Effort is concentrated on challenging the dominant product, and over time, Ajinomoto's skills usually enable it to claim second-place. While the success of this approach is based on the accumulation of related technology, it is also the result of forming a strong marketing network.

(4) Networks from Spinoffs

The fourth type of networking characteristic of Japanese companies is their intentional promotion of spinoff enterprises as subsidiaries. As the spinoffs grow, they form an even more extended corporate group. A parent company, Matsushita Electric, arranged for spinoffs by Matsushita-Kotobuki Electronics, Kyushu Matsushita Electric, Matsushita Communication Industrial, Matsushita Seiko, Matsushita Electric Trading and other subsidiaries; each is separately listed on the stock exchange. Toyota Motor Corp. was itself a spinoff of Toyoda Automatic Loom Works, and it later generated spinoff subsidiaries including Toyota Motor Sales (with which it merged in 1982), Aisin Seiki, Nippondenso, Toyota Auto Body,

Aichi Steel Works, Toyoda Machine Works, and Toyoda Tsusho. Hitachi, too, has actively created spinoff subsidiaries.

Even though the parent company is almost always a substantial minority owner of the subsidiary, the companies are to a considerable degree autonomous. While they do retain close links to the parent company, the structure is loosely-coupled, and this eanbles a higher level of adaptability than the more tightly-coupled system of most U.S. subsidiaries. Most U.S. companies, in direct contrast, desire close control over their subsidiaries, with equity ownership of up to 100-percent by the parent company.

There are various reasons for the spinoff of subsidiaries, and the degree of control exercised over subsidiaries varies by group. However, it is quite clear that restrictions on parent company control are imposed by the listing of the subsidiaries on the stock exchange. The following reasons are usually given for the decision to promote such spinoffs in spite of lost control:

(1) Profits may be accumulated for the founders of the spinoff by the selling of stock to outsiders.
(2) Spinning off will require the subsidiary to strengthen its independent ability to adapt to the environment. At times this might even cause conflict between the subsidiary and parent company but this, will in the end, be better for both.
(3) The possibility of advancing into new businesses without changing the parent company's organization reduces the burden on the parent firm.

(5) The Formation of Corporate Groups

A fifth networking characteristic is the formation of Japanese corporate groups based on the former *zaibatsu* (financial conglomerates or cartels). Since this has been covered in much detail elsewhere (see e.g., Imai & Itami, 1981),[21] we will not discuss it here.

Creation of the five types of "soft" extra-organizational structure that we have called networking does, in fact, make for an extended organization of key constituents. This extended organization enables the parent company to, in some instances control, and in other cases to respond more adroitly to the changing demands of its environment. Such networking is typical of Japanese companies. This stands in sharp contrast to the approach of U.S. companies, which draw a sharp distinction between themselves and all other firms through transactions in the market-place and controls exercised through the organizational hierarchy (Williamson, 1975).[22] The evidence of resource distribution by means of the venture capital market and through the company's hierarchical organization in the U.S., suggests that the market principle and the principle of organizational hierarchy in America are treated as separate entities. In Japan, on the other hand, both of these principles tend to be treated as a unified whole.

3.3 Methods of Establishing Competitive Superiority

3.3.1 The Deductive, Logical Approach vs. Inductive, Gradual Adjustment Approach

The heart of business strategy is to tie those resources that comprise the company's core technology to the needs of customers, in a way which enables the company to establish competitive superiority over other firms. Establishing competitive superiority is a complex process because of the often uncertain behavior of competitors, changing needs and preferences of consumers, and advancements in technology. The U.S. approach to establishing competitive superiority is usually a logical, deductive one.

For example, a new product concept is generally derived through logical, deductive means and tested through market research. If the results of the analysis are favorable, a detailed plan integrating the various functions necessary for producing and marketing the product will be made. Actual execution of this plan will follow only after a fairly thorough consideration of feasible alternatives. An instructive illustration is Procter and Gamble's introduction of "Pampers" -- its unique disposable diapers.

(1) The Process of Commercializing "Disposable Diapers" -- Thoroughness
     of Analysis

In the 1950's, a **Procter and Gamble** (P&G) engineer pondered the idea of
producing convenient paper diapers to replace conventional cloth ones.[23]
At that time a type of disposable paper diaper was available, but it was
poor in design and absorption.

The engineer discussed the idea with his colleagues, and convinced the
company to give it a try. Development would cost several million dollars,
so all P&G employees (both male and female) were first asked to consider
the following three principles of product development: (1) Are consumers
actually thinking of a change from conventional diapers?   (2) Does P&G
have the scientific and technological capabilities to develop this new
product?   And (3) if marketed, what are the prospects of attaining ample
profits from the new product?   The idea passed from this initial
examination, to formal consumer research to further determine if consumers
really desired a new type of diaper.   This effort included extensive
telephone interviews, questionnaires, group discussions, household visits
and other measures.

At the same time the consumer research was underway, P&G turned to the
preparations necessary for product development. Scientists and engineers
sought to design a product that would be capable of liberating consumers
from the nuisances of diapers then being used.   Nine months after the
product development team began its work, a diaper pad to be used in
plastic pants was designed. Once the prototype product was completed, the
team conducted another market study -- the pilot test.

Consumers were quite pleased with the idea of a disposable diaper, but ten
cents a diaper was found to be too expensive. The company wondered why it
had overlooked such a simple fact, but once it was grasped, P&G focused on
its next goal: lowering the cost.   This was not an easy problem to
solve. P&G uncovered several feasible cost reduction methods, including
lower-cost raw materials, production and distribution measures. However,
it was decided that these measures alone would fail to significantly
reduce the Pamper's price.   Only one method could lower cost while

maintaining quality. It was upping annual production volume from 400 million to one billion diapers; each diaper could then be sold for six cents.

At this point, P&G ran several other market tests and learned that the number of consumers using Pampers was on the rise. Production was expanded from one experimental line to eight, and the transition from test-marketing to nationwide sales was made. In mid-1970, the production of Pampers reached a level capable of meeting U.S. domestic demand. Nearly two decades had elapsed since the P&G engineer's inception of the idea of disposable paper diapers.

Once a product concept has been formulated on the basis of an idea, verification of its compatibility with customer needs is achieved via market surveys. Forecasts are made of market size and investment profitability, with competitive superiority established through the integration of investment, marketing and production plans. The P&G Pampers project is a good example of following through on the full span of this logical, deductive process. Others who have traveled the same road include Levis (the entry into men's clothing), GE, and General Foods.

(2) Thinking while Running: A New Entry in the Japanese Beer Market

In contrast, the Japanese approach to the process of introducing a product and establishing competitive advantage is much more inductive and less methodical. A typical example is Suntory's entry into the beer market. While the reasons for it have been discussed before, let us elaborate on the background of Suntory's introduction of beer and describe the actual process followed.

The Japanese market was one in which the existing makers (Kirin, Asahi and Sapporo) had developed powerful advantages in production and distribution. New entrants, Takara Beverages, for example, had experienced extreme difficulty in gaining a foothold. Clear brand distinction was needed for successful entry, with this distinction in the early going being focused on taste.

Suntory had attempted an entry into the beer business before World War II, but the effort had ended in failure. President Keizo Saji had, from early on considered a re-entry, and in 1956 he dispatched young engineers to Munich to study the German beer industry. They were followed by four more engineers in 1961, with Suntory's initial strategy being an outgrowth of the observations. It was to target younger age groups with a soft and light, lager-type beer having a European flavor. Suntory first marketed this beer back in April 1963 in the Tokyo area.[24] In May, sales were extended throughout the entire Kanto region. The initial goal was to capture a ten-percent market share in five year's time. The results of the company's entry, however, were less than satisfactory. After gaining a one-percent market share in 1963, the following year witnessed a rise to only 1.2 percent. Since sales of the lager-type beer first marketed were not satisfactory, the next attempt consisted of "bottled draft beer," a typical Japanese example of "if that doesn't work, let's try another solution."

In order to preserve beer for extended periods of time, it is necessary to eliminate various types of microorganisms. Beer which has been pasteurized to eliminate such organisms is known as lager beer, but the distinctive flavor of draft beer is lost in the process. Suntory's "bottled draft" was an attempt to preserve the flavor of draft beer by quickly sterilizing the beer using a special heating process. It was a product retaining the new lager concept, which held close to the flavor of draft beer. A further adjustment to this product concept came with the introduction of "pure draft," which used a micro-filtering method to remove microorganisms. The beginning of this idea may be traced back to Hisakichi Honda, managing director in charge of technology, who learned of an American company which was producing draft beer through a micro-filtering system. The microfilter was a by-product of space exploration, and the Milipore Company of the U.S. was applying the method to draft beer brewing. Using this technology, Suntory introduced its "pure draft" in 1966, and the company's market share jumped in that year to three percent. In the early 1970's, competing makers moved actively to market their own draft beer products, and Suntory carried out a minor adjustment to its marketing strategy, changing the name of its beer from "pure draft" to "Suntory Draft Beer." Various market surveys were carried out, but the surveys were not used to develop a total plan of action. Rather, the approach in the words of one top executive was one of "first give it a try, then regroup if it doesn't go well."

Suntory's product development and marketing strategies stand in stark contrast to that of P&G. Suntory's method of making incremental adjustments to its environmental and competitive conditions as dictated by actual sales is an approach to establishing competitive superiority by "trial and error" -- an inductive, rather than deductive, method. This approach is also characteristic in Japan's apparel and electric home appliance industries.

3.3.2 Elite Guidance vs. Mobilization of "Company-Wide Wisdom"

Another method used by Japanese companies to establish competitive superiority involves the definition of clear but broad strategic objectives by top management, followed by mobilizing the wisdom existing at every level of the company. This approach is used particularly to compete with strong companies from the U.S. and Europe.

Let us examine the case of **Komatsu Ltd.**[25] In 1960 the Japanese government adopted a policy of trade liberalization. This was followed the next year with the announcement of capital deregulation. The construction equipment industry, previously insulated, found itself hit hard. Then, the joint venture of Caterpillar of the United States, the world's largest bulldozer maker, and Mitsubishi Heavy Industries of Japan was announced. At that time, Komatsu was very inferior to Caterpillar both financially and in terms of product reliability. As a result the price of Komatsu stock in 1960-61 plummeted from 300 to 62 yen. There were even rumors that Komatsu would be out of business within three years.

Komatsu reacted outwordly by expressing "absolute opposition to CAT'S Japan entry," while in-house, the company introduced a total quality control (TQC) drive and started a major catchup campaign known as "Countermeasure A." In August 1961 the "Countermeasure A Headquarters" was established, followed by a "Central Quality Committee" the next month. Because the Komatsu bulldozers of that time ranked far below

Caterpillar products in durability, breakdown rate, and other crucial ways, Countermeasure A was focused on closing this gap at the earliest possible time.

The following quality objectives were adopted for Countermeasure A: (1) boost real work hours before the first overhaul from 3,000 to 5,000 hours; (2) achieve a functional rate (ratio of actual operation to down time) of 90 percent; (3) reduce repair costs to 3 times the price; (4) boost vehicle durability from 6,000 to 10,000 hours; and (5) achieve easier machine operation and maintenance. Targeting these goals, Komatsu initiated a survey of Caterpillar's products, then mobilized every level of in-house wisdom toward the development and manufacture of new vehicle types. In September 1962, the "Super," a new type of bulldozer, was released on the market.

In the wake of the 1971 "Nixon Shock," with Total Quality Control measures firmly in place, Komatsu embarked on "Activity B." This new phase sought to boost international competitiveness by placing the focus on market-oriented production and development. Market feedback data was channeled to all Komatsu production plants where it was applied to product improvements and new product development.

Both Countermeasure A and Activity B had their beginnings in plant-level quality control efforts, and were effectively expanded to the company-wide level.

Komatsu's achievement of its company-wide goals was based on feedback from the field to stimulate learning at all levels, thus applying the sum of the company's wisdom to establish competitive superiority. Other companies adopting TQC have used the same methodology.

In contrast, U.S. corporate strategy determination has been "elitist-oriented." In short, planning and strategy staffs, and product managers play a much more prominent role in the drafting of strategy than plant-level initiatives.

The U.S.-style elite-guided, logical, deductive approach achieves major innovation in strategies geared to surpass other companies. In contrast, the Japanese inductive, step-wise gradual adjustment approach seeks to steadily build upon the existing strengths to *evolve* strategy. This difference can be seen in the computer, semiconductor, electrical equipment and other industries. A truly outstanding example, however, is in pharmaceuticals.

Eli Lilly derives major earnings from antibiotics. It is estimated that the Cephalosporin family of antibiotics alone accounted for approximately 20 percent of the company's net sales (between 35 and 40 percent of profits) in 1978.

Antibiotics are a pharmaceutical with effects over a broad range of germs, but they also have a weakness -- the appearance of antibodies. Whenever a family of these medicines is developed, a process of product adjustments and improvement must follow to deal with the emergence of the antibodies. Thus, the Cephalosporin family of antibiotics has in recent years moved from the first to second to its third-generation of products.

The leading products in the Lilly antibiotic line, Keflin and Keflex, are so successful in the market place that they have threatened to involve the company in antitrust problems. These products were in the first-generation Cephalosporin family. Lilly followed with the development of Mandol, Ceclor and other antibiotics but, in the development of the third-generation family, which is effective against gram positive germs, Japanese makers, especially Takeda Chemical Industries, are said to be moving one step ahead. A Lilly supervisor noted: "We make great progress in our development of new product families, but the Japanese makers may very well be more skillful in persistently changing and improving individual product families."

Lilly maintains a cross-licensing agreement witn Shionogi & Company of Japan, and supplies Keflin and Keflex to the Japanese market. However, Shionogi is handling the introduction of the third-generation antibiotic itself. Lilly meanwhile, is working with the Genentech, Inc. to commercialize synthetic insulin made through genetic engineering. This reflects the fact that Lilly remains ahead of its Japanese counterparts in fields requiring advanced technology for major breakthroughs.

3.3.3 Product vs. Production Orientation

What constitutes competitive superiority depends on the peculiarities of individual industries and upon competitive conditions. For this reason, it is difficult to identify general competitive characteristics which distinguish U.S. from Japanese companies. However, Japanese companies do seem to be alike in their common pursuit of superiority in production processes, production technology, and related systems. Relevant industries for comparison include steel, televisions, VTR, automobiles, and semiconductors. The Japanese firms have implemented various types of innovation in production technology, and have achieved competitive superiority on the basis of them. A typical example of this type of development is Toyota's now famous "Kanban System."

(1) Evolving Production Systems

The prototype for **Toyota**'s "Kanban System" dates back to the 1954 adoption of the "supermarket method" in a production plant by it's chief production engineer, Taiichi Ohno. Use of the supermarket method was subsequently expanded to comprehensive assembly and body plants, and became the Toyota Group's principal approach to production control. Originally devised as a ·means for controlling volume at a U.S. aircraft engine plant during World War II, the method is based on the consumer practice of going to a supermarket to purchase what is needed when it is needed. It eliminates inventory stocking in the downstream production processes, with all necessary items brought in during upstream processes. The characteristics of the supermarket system are described in Toyota's corporate history as follows:

1. The conventional procedure was for upstream workers to transport each processed part to the downstream stage when it was completed. This was changed to have workers at the downstream stage go upstream to pick up the parts. Furthermore, a policy was adopted at all plants of carrying just enough parts for five vehicles in each lot.

2. The cargo-carrying vehicles used at each jobsite were eliminated, with forklifts, trailers and other equipment used instead. A set timetable was followed to transport just

enough parts for five vehicles at a loading. Accordingly, the inventory at each production line never exceeded enough for five vehicles, and containers were prepared that were just the right size to allow the forklifts and trailers to carry five units worth of parts.

3. Parts were never allowed to touch the floor, under any circumstances. When an accident or other mishap caused the part stock to disappear or triggered a need to increase its number, the production line conveyor was *stopped immediately to find the source of the problem.*

4. The method of evaluating parts production was revamped. Previously, if 110 units were produced despite a production directive which only called for 100 units daily, it was evaluated as heightened productivity. This was changed and labeled the cause of excess stock in order to drive home the thinking that no employee should have even one piece too many of stock in hand.

5. All parts production went according to a coordinated master-plan. If only enough of a certain part could be produced for 90 finished units when the original plan called for 100, the production of all other parts would be adjusted to turn out only enough for 90 units.

6. Because the part pickups from the upstream stage were conducted in five-unit lots at each jobsite, all parts stocks were held to under five units. Because of this, too, all product lines were specialized; the practice of producing more than one type of part on any one line was eliminated. Various vehicle types were assembled on the same conveyor belt of the chassis line, however.

7. In case of machine breakdown, there was no inventory to act as a buffer, and this dealt a major blow to the production process. This drawback was offset by strengthening the preventative maintenance system in order to eliminate machinery breakdowns. It was an ambitious, but obviously successful undertaking.

The "supermarket system" reduced in-process inventories, thereby reducing cost and increasing material turnover. It also led suppliers' plants and production lines to be synchronized with the Toyota line, extending the results of this technological innovation to those facilities as well.

In 1963, this approach became the basis for adopting the "Kanban System," extending the sphere of application from individual parts processes to rough materials production processes. The Kanban System consists of creating a single kanban (signboard in a square vinyl holder) for each

part. On this board are written the numbers and volumes of other parts
necessary at the downstream production stages. The system ensures that
the necessary items indicated by the kanban are produced in the correct
volume and at the correct time. The kanban links all processes into a
single chain, and holds intermediate stock to a minimum while making
necessary adjustments to the volume of the final assembly process.

Taiichi Ohno compared the Toyota Production System with the traditional
mass-production counterpart typified by Ford's production system:

> The idea of producing the same type of part in bulk -- that
> is, turning out as many parts as possible without changing the
> press die -- still continues to be the common approach at
> production plants today. This is the key to Ford's mass-
> production system. The Toyota system is exactly the
> opposite. The watchword at our production plants is "Make the
> lot as small as possible, and change the press die swiftly and
> surely."
>
> The Ford system requires ready stock throughout the plant in
> order to produce large volumes. The Toyota approach, on the
> other hand, is geared to eliminate the waste associated with
> unnecessary inventory and attempts to control it, in fact, to
> bring such inventory down to zero. To accomplish this goal,
> downstream workers go upstream and pick up the needed parts
> "just in time" for their use. In order to make completely
> sure that the upstream stages produce only the amount picked
> up by the downstream stages, people and equipment must be
> stationed so that all production stages turn out the necessary
> volume. If the downstream stage handles both time and volume
> in scattered fashion, the upstream people and equipment must
> have enough capacity to cope with the variability that
> results. The often unused capacity is clearly wasteful and
> will push up costs.
>
> The true aim of Toyota's production system is the total
> elimination of waste. Strict efforts are made to
> "standardize" production and wipe out variation. The result
> is smaller lots and taking care not to over-produce the same
> item. The Toyota system envisions that in the final market
> each customer will buy a separate, different car, and so care
> must be taken at the production stage in producing each one at
> a time. This is also true at the parts production stage, with
> parts turned out one at a time. In short, this is the idea of
> "one-part basis synchronized production."[26]

In order to customize production, efforts were made to shorten waiting
times. While changing a large press die required between two to three
hours in the decade from 1945-55, by the early 1970's, this had been

reduced to a mere three minutes.

Although efficiency and the elimination of waste are important outcomes of Toyota's production system, there is another important outcome that should not be overlooked.

Toyota's production system is vulnerable to accidents and mishaps. It is overly risky within the traditional paradigm of production control. When an accident occurs at any jobsite, the whole system has to be stopped because Toyota's system is a tightly-coupled one with minimal buffers. The traditional paradigm, assumes that workers on the shopfloor make mistakes at a certain rate, and prescribes stocks at each job-site to provide buffers against such probabilistic errors. Toyota assumes no errors will occur and has virtually no inventory. This is irrational if the cost of lost time from stopping the whole system is greater than that of stocking appropriate inventiories. The traditional argument is logical but not supported by Toyota's experience.

A production system that is recognized to be vulnerable to errors has an important advantage: When the causes of errors are analyzed and measures taken to prevent them in the future are implemented, the system as a whole is improved. Errors may be viewed as probabilistic phenomena from a macro point of view, but each error has its own causes from a micro viewpoint. Toyota's production system enables it to find the causes of errors; the system is thereby improved incrementally. In other words, the production system can learn and evolve. A Toyota executive has said: "The system may incur more costs than traditional ones, but we think of the additional costs as 'tuition for learning.'" QC-circle activities -- "the seeking of 100% quality" -- which will be touched on in the next chapter, are a logical extension of this learning idea.

The heightened efficiency brought about by its production system has given Toyota a major competitive edge. The differences in where competitive superiority is sought will create differences in the methods used to adapt to major changes. A good example concerns the different approaches adopted by GM and Toyota to cope with the first oil crisis. The clear contrast of these approaches deserves a brief mention here.

(2) New Products -- Pulling a Company Out of Danger

The first oil crisis triggered by the October 1973 war in the Middle East, caused the move toward fuel-efficient down-sized cars to become a critical issue at General Motors.[27]

GM had forecast increases in oil prices even before this. The Science Advisory Committee, Public Policy Committee, and Team Management Planning Committee -- groups which included outside directors -- pointed out the need for measures to cope with energy price increases and the small-size imports. By July 1972 the Energy Task Force had been formed. At the beginning of 1973, this task force submitted a report to GM's board of directors forecasting the threat of a gasoline shortage capable of dealing a serious blow to GM's business. GM's management did not take this threat seriously. Although GM president McCall and vice president DeLorean both advocated active efforts to develop small cars, their arguments did not carry enough weight to change the traditional Detroit culture, which espoused the principle that "a big car is a good car." Claiming that GM's management was "completely sealed off from the outside world," DeLorean actually left the automaker. GM, however, had not totally ignored the situation. A project to begin the downsizing of auto bodies was launched in April of 1973. Product planning for this purpose with decentralization of authority among all divisions was initiated company-wide.

In October 1973, the outbreak of the first oil crisis transformed the forecasts of the Energy Task Force into reality. It was vital that emergency action be taken to cope with the oil shortage. The drop in demand triggered by the oil shortage forced GM to shut down 15 assembly plants and lay off 84,000 workers. By the beginning of 1974, the GM market share had plummeted to 37.5 percent, down considerably from the 44.4 percent level maintained before the oil crisis. In December of that year, legislation was enacted demanding that automakers achieve the 20 mile-per-gallon level by 1984.

The decision-making process at GM was accelerated at a January 1974 board of directors meeting for the approval of capital investment items. It was decided to introduce the Chevette, a car slated for design in West Germany and production in Brazil, on the U.S. market on an emergency basis. The tempo of the Chevette development was increased, with work normally requiring three years shortened to the point where the car would enter the market in 1975. Under the GM policy of offering cars in all size and price ranges, reducing the size of a certain model could be expected to decrease the sales of cars in the size categories below it. As a countermeasure, therefore, a plan was drawn up to downsize all cars in the GM line over a three-year period. This plan was announced in January 1974.

Nevertheless, "a big car is a good car" thinking was still strong within GM. In 1974, although the production cost of the company's luxury-class Cadillac Coupe de Ville was only $300 more than that of the small-size Chevy Capri, the difference in sales price was $2,700. The added value of small cars was lower than that of bigger models, and there were still doubts about whether or not consumers really wanted small cars.

U.S. domestic sales in 1974 were 7.2 million units, down 24 percent from the 9.5 million units sold the previous year. However, when the Middle East embargo was lifted in March 1974, the sales of luxury and large models increased. And by the summer, GM and Ford were running up inventories of the small cars they had rushed to produce earlier. This forced more layoffs.

In 1974, Jack Murphy and William Estes rose to the posts of GM chairman and president, respectively. Estes turned his attention to overseas markets, setting out in earnest on development of the "world car." In 1975 the fruit of the downsizing project, the Chevette, was marketed, followed in 1978 by the first world cars, the X-car Chevy Citation. Then, in 1981, after the second oil crisis, GM introduced the J-car which had been jointly designed with Opel of West Germany. The J-car followed the GM strategy of reducing production costs to a minimum through a global division of labor. This was followed by the development of the 1-liter class S-car.

GM coped with the oil crisis by systemizing its product planning and by initiating layoffs. Toyota, meanwhile, turned to heightened operations efficiency.

Toyota surpassed the 2.3-million unit annual production level in 1973.
Then as it was gearing up for three-million units, the first oil crisis
hit.   In a short time, Japanese gasoline prices quadrupled, demand
plummeted, and the cost of materials skyrocketed.[28]

Toyota's response to this crisis was to curb over-production through a
production equipment "seal strategy," while at the same time promoting
line integration.   The latter refers to production of different model
types on the same line.   Specifically, the Corona, Mark II, Carina, and
Celica lines were integrated, as were the Corolla, Sprinter, Publica, and
Starlet lines.   In addition, creative suggestions from Toyota employees
were used to reduce operating costs and strengthen production and
inventory control.   This enabled the automaker to lower its break-even
point to 1.3 million units.

Rationalization of Toyota's production system continued after the first
oil crisis, and yielded major benefits.   The Toyota countermeasure to the
danger was, in short, thorough streamlining of its production system.
The fruits of this effort appear in the following statistics.

    Direct Production Workers
        October   1972   18,000
        February   1975   19,000
        October   1975   19,000
        October   1976   19,000
    Daily Production, Units Produced and Production Index
        1972   9,700   (2 shifts, 4 hours overtime)   100
        1975 (Feb.)   8,500   (1 shift, 0.20 hours overtime)   102
        1975 (Oct.) 10,000   (1 shift, 0.35 hours overtime)   117
        1976   10,700   (1 shift, 0.70 hours overtime)   120

Regardless of GM's focus on large cars and Toyota's tradition of small
sizes, the reactions of these two automakers to the common crisis provide
a clear contrast.   GM sought to handle the situation through a product mix
strategy, while Toyota concentrated its efforts on production technology.

Notes

1. The companies selected in this method must not be average American and Japanese companies. Our objects for comparison must possess above average performance and occupy controlling position's in their respective industries. Accordingly, one must be careful about the difference between these groups of companies compared with those of the last survey. In that survey, we only chose the top 1,000 industrial enterprises from America and Japan. There existed no standards of performance or position in their respective industries.

2. For the definition of the concept of corporate strategy, see Hofer, C.W. and D. Schendel, *Strategy Formulation : Analytical Concepts*, St. Paul: West Publishing Company, 1978.

3. For an analytical definition of domain, see Abell, D. F., *Defining the Business: The Starting Point of Strategic Planning*, Englewood Cliffs, N.J.: Prentice-Hall, 1980.

4. Usui, K., *Fujitsu ga nagare o kaeru* (Fujitsu Changes the Tradition), Written in Japanese, Tokyo: Nippon Recruit Center, 1981, p.172.

5. Matsushita, K., *Jissen keiei tetsugaku* (Practical Management Philosophy), Written in Japanese, Kyoto: PHP Institute, 1978, pp.64-66.

6. The following description is based on *Business Week*, March 29, 1982.

7. Taguchi, T., *"U.S. Steel no kagakujigyo no genjo to tenbo* (The Status Quo and Prospect of the Chemical Business of US Steel)," *Tekkokai (Iron and Steel Industry)*, March 1982.
   "Tekkookoku U.S. Steel no kinyukiki (The Financial Crisis of U.S. Steel, King of Steel Industry)," *Toyo Keizai (The Oriental Economist)*, Nov. 20, 1982.
   Asian Wall Street Journal, February 4-5, 1983.

8. *Business Week*, April 27, 1981, pp.65-68.

9. Interviewed by the authors in September 1982. Also refer to Iwabori, Y., *Toshiba no chosen -- OA-kiki no kakumeiji o unda gijutsu dojo* (The Challenge of Toshiba -- The Technical Environment which Breeds the "Revolutionary Child" of OA Equipment), *Prejidento*, Jan., 1982, pp.214-221.

10. Ikari, M., *Moeru senryakushudan -- C&C-jidai o kirihiraku Nippondenki* (The Strategic Group with High Fighting Spirit -- NEC Pioneers the C&C Age), Written in Japanese, Tokyo: Nippon Recruit Center, 1979, p.170.

11. Fruhan, W. E. Jr., *Financial Strategy*, Homewood: Irwin, 1979, pp.148-179.

12. *Asahi Journal*, June 2, 1978, PP.82-83.

13. Urabe, M., *Tanoshisa no keiei o tsuranuku Renown* (Renown Managing through Joy), Tokyo: Asahi Sonorama, 1980, pp.171-172.

14. Majima, H., *Matsushita Denki no jigyobusei* (Divisional System of Matsushita Electric), Tokyo: Nihon Jitsugyo Shuppansha, 1978, p.156.

15. Ito, M., *Keiei senryaku to kenkyukaihatsu* (Management Strategy and R&D), *Will*, Nov., 1982, p.124.

16. "*Keiei ni okeru Nippon no kokoro* (Japanese Mind in Management)," *Bungei Shunju*, August 1982.

17. Sakakibara, K., *From Imitation to Innovation: The Very Large Scale Integrated (VLSI) Semiconductor Project in Japan*, Working Paper, Sloan School of Management, MIT, Oct. 1983

18. Asahi Shimbun, July 6, 1981.

19. Nakamura, S., *Nippon sangyo guzen no hanei* (The Accidental Prosperity of Japanese Enterprises), Written in Japanese, Tokyo: Toyokeizai Shimposha, 1982.

20. Hasegawa, T., *Ajinomoto no keieisenryaku* (The Management Strategy of Ajinomoto), Tokyo: Hyogensha, 1982.
"Ajinomoto," *NRI Search*, September 25, 1981, pp.25-31.

21. Imai, K., H. Itami and K. Koike, *Naibusoshiki no keizaigaku* (Economics of Internal Organization), Written in Japanese, Tokyo: Toyokeizai Shimposha, 1981.

22. Williamson, O. E., *Markets and Hierarchies*, New York: Free Press, 1975.

23. Following description is based on "P&G Uses Pampers Story to Teach the Consumer about Marketing", *Advertising Age*, April 4, 1977.

24. Ikeda, S., *Suntory no yomikata -- Biiru shinjidai o tsukuru otokotachi* (The Saying of Suntory -- The Men Who Created the New Age of Beer), Written in Japanese, Tokyo: Daiamondosha, 1981.

25. Mito, S., *"TQC no mugensei ni idomu komatsuseisakusho* (Komatsu Challenges the Infinity of TQC)," *Diamond Harvard Business*, July-August 1982, pp.108-117.

26. Ohno, T., *Toyota seisan shisutemu* (Toyota Production System), Written in Japanese, Tokyo: Daiamondosha, 1978, pp.175-176.

27. The following description is based on McCaskey, M. B., *Managing Change and Ambiguity*, Boston: Pitman, 1982.

28. Wakayama, F. and C. Kimoto, *Toyota no himitsu* (The Secret of Toyota), Written in Japanese, Tokyo: Koshobo, 1977.

CHAPTER 4   ORGANIZATIONAL STRUCTURE AND PROCESS:
MAJOR DIFFERENCES IN ACHIEVING INTEGRATION

4.1   Organizing Methods of U.S. versus Japanese Firms

That "structure follows strategy" is a long-held proposition first put
forward by Alfred Chandler in his highly acclaimed analysis of the
histories of General Motors, Du Pont, Sears Roebuck, and Standard Oil of
New Jersey.   Assuming that major structural changes are possible,
Chandler's conclusion was that an organization will devise strategies
which are most appropriate for its environment, its fundamental
objectives, and the strengths of the firm.   It will, then, create that
structure which is best suited for implementing the strategy.   From this
perspective, the act of structuring an organization is essentially a tool
for effectively implementing strategy.   An intensive comparative study of
major Japanese and American firms shows that Chandler's conclusions do not
necessarily apply to Japanese firms and that, indeed, the broader,
integrative contingency theory framework proposed in Chapter 2 is more
appropriate for the analysis of organizations' adaptation to their
environments.

Chandler's study is of divisional decentralization in an earlier era and,
from a world-wide perspective, in a unique culture.   It is perhaps not
suprising that his conclusions may be less appropriate for the
circumstances faced by large organizations today.   It will be shown that
strategies, rather than determining organizational structure, emerge as a
consequence of existing organizational processes and structures in most
Japanese and some U.S. firms.   The realities of Japanese organizations do
not fit Chandler's instrumental view.

Two principal patterns of organization emerge from our comparative
analysis: Bureaucratic Dynamics and Group Dynamics.   Bureaucratic dynamics
refers to organizational characteristics which are structure dominant.
The essence of organizational structure is division of labor and
allocation of decision-making authority.   Relatively greater dependence is
placed in bureaucratic dynamics upon hierarchy for the making and

implementation of decisions.   Decision-making can be characterized as a
process of selecting from among alternatives.   The process serves to
reduce the risk faced by an organization from its environment, but it also
reduces the number of opportunities available to the organization, since
choosing some necessarily precludes the choice of others.   From Max Weber
to Herbert Simon, the essence of organization has been to reduce variety
through the division of labor and hierarchical arrangement of authority.
Problems are divided at the top, then, sub-divided, and lesser parts of
the problem are serially delegated downward through the hierarchy.   Thus,
the most critical role in decision-making is an analytical one played by
an "elite" at the the top of the organization, with successively lesser
roles played by those toward the bottom who, in fact, see and deal with
smaller and smaller parts of the problem.   The most fundamental functions
of variety reduction are those performed, in the bureaucratic dynamics
organization, by the elite (and their staffs) who initiate strategy and
design the basic organizational structure necessary to implement it.

Group dynamics is, on the other hand, process rather than structure
dominant.   Organizations which are group dynamics-oriented depend much
more upon personal interaction processes within and across groups both for
making and implementing decisions.   Variety is reduced, but only after a
phase of purposeful variety amplification, in which many individual
perspectives are brought to bear upon problems that are *shared* not subdivided.   Top management's decision-making role in group dynamics
organizations is relegated to providing very broad direction and incentive
for participating in problem-solving rather than analytically dividing up
the problem into smaller parts.   Although sometimes competing,
participants' roles tend to overlap considerably, and problems are solved
in a progressive, trial-and-error, *incremental* way as alternatives are
considered but not necessarily rejected, and suggestions for solving the
problems are made by many individuals within relatively autonomous groups.

The organizational characteristics just summarized will be discussed in
depth.

4.2 The Strategic-Hierarchical Form of U.S. Firms

The most prominent feature of the strategic-hierarchical organization typical of U.S. firms is the divisional structure. The essence is as follows (Chandler, 1962 and Sloan, 1963)[1] :

1. Strategic decision-making deals with resource acquisition and allocation at the corporate level for long term survival. Operational decision-making deals with the efficient utilization of allocated resources.
2. Operational decision-making is decentralized to the division level. General managers of the divisions are given the authority and capability to make operational -- use of resource -- decisions, usually, in certain division product and/or service areas. Given relative autonomy, the managers are responsible for their divisions' performance as profit centers.
3. The authority to make strategic decisions is concentrated at the corporate level, along with the overall control of the divisions. Division performance is evaluated at the corporate level and the salaries/rewards of division managers are linked with their divisions' performances.
4. Resources are allocated to the divisions on the basis of their return-on-investment (ROI). ROI is central to the evaluation of division performance.

Thus in the divisional system, operational decision-making is delegated downward to the division level (decentralized) while strict control, resource allocation, and other strategic decisions remain centralized at the corporate level. Du Pont and General Motors are the firms which originated the model of divisionalization described. Each company adopted the divisional form in the early 1920's. Their experiences differ, however, in that Du Pont placed greater emphasis upon decentralizing operational decision-making, while GM's emphasis was on centralizing strategic decision-making and increasing corporate control. This discussion of the divisional system as developed in the U.S. is purposely brief since there are several good descriptions of it already available. Of more immediate interest is the Japanese approach.

4.3 The Development of Divisionalization in Japan

The divisionalization innovator in Japan was **Matsushita Electric**. In May,
1933, Matsushita Electric grouped all of its plants into three divisions
and in February, 1934, established a policy of having all of its divisions
responsible for sales as well as production. The employees numbered about
1,800 at that time; hence, the move to divisionalization by Matsushita
Electric was made at a point of smaller scale than at GM or Du Pont.
Konosuke Matsushita made the following comments about the early
divisionalization by his company:

> When the company was small, control by myself was sufficient.
> But as the company grew and many new jobs were created, it became
> impossible for me to know all of the details of every job. It
> was necessary at times to know those details and, then, I had to
> say "Please wait: I'm thinking about another thing." That wasn't
> good. I felt that concerns related to the making of electric
> heaters should be delegated to someone and said to one of my best
> people, "Matsushita has to make electric heaters but I cannot do
> it; so please do it for me." I assigned complete responsibility
> for making heaters to that person, and appointed him to be the
> top manager of that business. That was the beginning of the
> divisional system at Matsushita Electric.
>
> Two purposes are served by divisionalization. First, it makes
> level of performance easier to determine and, secondly, it makes
> management responsibility for that performance more clear.
> Consequently, division performance -- good or bad -- can be
> clearly evaluated. Each division is accountable for generating
> its own profit, and profit earned by one division should not be
> allocated to other divisions. The management of divisions is a
> time of real trial for managers. Fortunately, Matsushita
> Electric adopted this system early, and it has produced our top
> managers.[2]

Note that in this pioneering Japanese case, there was no explicit
consideration of resource allocation to the divisions or of corporate
financial control, *per se*, over the divisions as was the case for the U.S.
firms. Nor was there as careful consideration given to differentiating
the roles of an organization's headquarters and divisions, or
relationships between them. It should also be noted that the development
of general management skill is stressed.

It has been since World War II, especially in the 1950's and 1960's, that
most large Japanese firms have adopted divisional structures. Toshiba

instituted a divisional form in 1950, as did Hitachi in 1952. They were followed by Takeda and Sumitomo Electric in 1960, and by NEC in 1964. The U.S. structure served as an impetus and a model, especially in these more recent cases; however, there came to be important differences from the U.S. system. Hitachi's experience will be instructive.

Hitachi, Ltd. first adopted a divisional form of organization in 1952. Top corporate management was formalized in what has become the *"jomu-kai"* system. In this system, very different from the Western model, the corporate headquarters was divided into management and product divisions, eight in the case of Hitachi (heavy electric machinery, industrial equipment, locomotives and trains, machinery parts, consumer durables, communications equipment, electrical cables/wiring, and steel manufacturing equipment). Positioned within the organization's structure, similarly to corporate staff departments in the United States, each of Hitachi's product divisions contained engineering and sales departments but *not* the plants responsible for the manufacturing. The principal purpose of this corporate-level "divisionalization" was the coordination and integration of the production and sales of the divisions' products. And while the divisions were responsible for the coordination of production and sales, the managers of the producing *plants* were solely responsible for profits and reported directly to the company president.

Of course, it was not logical to have the plant managers responsible for profits when the divisions had authority over matters like sales and the quantity produced. In an attempt to cope with the problems that ensued, the plant managers were removed from direct access to the president in 1962 and placed under divisional control. Thus, Hitachi's divisions became full-fledged line organizations comparable to those in the west. The transition was completed at the end of 1964. If the essence of divisionalization lies in the integration of major functions (e.g., production and sales), Hitachi's "true" divisional system can be said to have started in that year. Then, following GE's precedent, groups of divisions were created in the period from 1967 to 1969.

But the system failed to function as well as expected. And, in 1974, Hitachi reverted to its original "staff divisional form" of the 1950's.

The principal reason for this development was the strength of the traditional view of the organization. That is, the view of it as being centered around plants responsible for profits and reporting directly to the president, with all of the behavioral expectations that are the consequence of this arrangement. In Hitachi executive vice president, Keisuke Arai's words:

> The very vitality of this company has always derived from our management by plant. Our original ("staff-divisional") system had some faults, but the change to line divisions and divisional groups did not produce higher performance. Instead, responsibilities and the focus of our efforts became blurred, and a variety of management problems ensued.
>
> Involving much more than formally defined structure, corporate character -- one formed over many years -- is not something that can be changed easily. So, we decided that it was better to improve our traditional plant-centered system than to throw it away and adopt such a different one.
>
> Since we reverted once again to our plant system with staff coordinating divisions, our company has really been assisted by the energy of people at our plants. We have concluded from our experience that the best organizational system is not one that is somehow ideally best, but one that fits our corporate culture.[3]

Today, Hitachi has 27 plants as profit centers. The sales of particular products are attributed to the plants which produced the goods sold. Each . plant's manufacturing costs, overhead, interest, and costs of assigned internal capital are subtracted from its sales to determine its profit. Each plant manager is responsible for this profit. In the meantime, the staff-divisions at headquarters are responsible for the market share, pricing, and coordination of production with sales for each plant, but from an overall, integrated, company-wide perspective. The budget for each plant is reviewed semi-annually by a budget committee comprised of corporate officers (*jomu-kai*) and the plant managers. Each plant manager presents his management philosophy, problems that his plnat is facing, and explains his budget plan.

The plant manager is assisted within the plant by "design managers" (*sekkei-kacho*) with engineering backgrounds. These middle-management *sekkei-kacho* play an important role not only in designing products but also in forecasting sales, formulating budgets based on the forecasts, and profit planning. It is the end-product of this planning that is submitted to corporate headquarters in the form of an overall plant budget. It is said that Hitachi's plant and top managers have great business acumen because, although having engineering backgrounds, they are grounded very thoroughly in accounting and profit concepts in their years as *sekkei-kacho*.

With the responsibility for profits at the plant level, the volume of plant production is decided at each plant. Each plant exerts self-control, decreasing its output and cutting expenses in the face of declining demand. While this makes for strong "defensive" behavior in reacting to adverse conditions, the locus of responsibility for profit at the plant level has also resulted in conservative planning and missed opportunities for growth. For this reason, the divisions at headquarters (responsible for coordinating production and sales) have been made responsible for monitoring and increasing their plants' market shares. Hence, the important "offensive" aspect of corporate growth is also emphasized.

Divisional systems like Hitachi's offer several contrasts in comparison to Western firms. First, *plants* without a sales department or function are operating successfully as profit centers. In Hitachi's case, this has been a consequence of preserving traditions which developed as the company grew as a maker of heavy electrical machinery. But this form of divisionalization is not unique to Hitachi. As Table 2-10 (in Chapter 2) showed, in 14.5 percent of all Japanese divisionalized firms, the divisions do not have a production function (like Hitachi) and in 8.5 percent they do not have a sales function (contrary to Hitachi). These figures imply that divisions in Japanese firms are often not self-contained and that functional autonomy is emphasized over the integration of functions at the division level. This functional emphasis is more clearly exemplified by the fact that 40.2 percent of Japanese firms have a functional structure (Table 2-10).

The meaning of "functional emphasis," however, differs between the countries. In the U.S. it means that each fuctional manager or department specializes in a function and develops functional expertise, but in Japan it means that each functional manager or department has a holistic view extending beyond an assigned function and that he sometimes invades the functions of other managers and departments. These functional managers and departments as well as divisional general managers work as integrating units, and multiple integrating units usually exist in Japanese companies (Figure 4-1). Tasks of an organization are so divided that the sub-tasks overlap each other. This overlapping, which seems to be "logically inconsistent" to U.S. managers, enables prompt response to environmental changes. An example is Hitachi where one market feedback channel runs to marketing and another runs directly to Hitachi's plants. The feedback loop is, therefore, short and fast but, perhaps more important, results in the possibility of more varied and flexible plant operational responses to changing market conditions. And, as pointed out in preceding chapters, flexibility of operations is a key factor in environmental adaptation. Of course, when divisional units are responsible for coordinating production with sales but the producing plants responsible for profits are attempting to respond directly to changing market conditions, much confusion including conflict is possible; this vital issue is discussed next.

Conflict can be both functional and dysfunctional. At least three conditions must be met for conflict over goals to be functional: First, differences of opinion must be made overt and not remain "hidden" or ignored; second, there must be agreed-upon spokesmen who can articulate those differences; and, third, there must be clear agreement upon and commitment to *superordinate* goals -- those which are more important to the organization as a whole than the immediate goals in conflict. These three requirements are generally met in Japanese companies, allowing conflicts arising from "logically inconsistent" organizational structures to be resolved in a functional manner. Furthermore, as in the Hitachi organization, conflicting issues are sometimes "assigned" to different people and are resolved by confrontation between them. Very unusual in Japan's past experience, Hitachi is said to have a culture which is characterized by enthusiastic "student-like discussion" -- that which emphasizes interpersonal confrontation. As part of this company's culture, the confrontation is constructive and greatly facilitates open discussion and problem-solving.

Figure 4-1 Modes of Integration

U.S. Mode of Integration

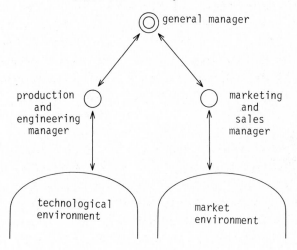

Japanese Mode of Integration

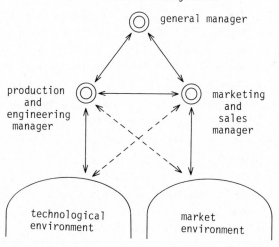

There are always conflicting goals in an organization. It might be said that while U.S. firms seek to balance their goals substantially by the way in which they define standards for the evaluation of performance, Japanese firms like Hitachi translate those goals into specific interpersonal conflicts and depend upon functional conflict resolution for the achievement of overall corporate objectives. Our findings reported in Chapter 2 suggest that conflict is prevalent in both U.S. and Japanese firms. In the U.S., confrontation is the most common resolution method. While emphasis upon confrontation is not commonplace among Japanese firms today, our findings suggest that relative to American firms, a greater variety of means for resolving conflict exists among the Japanese companies.

An organizational design that permits the overlapping of duties also enables information sharing. For instance, as noted before, in Hitachi market information is collected and analyzed independently by the sales department at division headquarters and by the plant. They also exchange sales information frequently, and differences in interpretation trigger further interactions. Assuming that information gathered independently is not so different and that existent differences are adjusted by frequent interactions, the same data base will be held by two (or in some cases several) different departments. This makes it easier for related departments to cooperate. A typical example of a task requiring interdepartmental cooperation is new product development. Sharing the same information enables smoother cooperation of different functional departments in the development of new products. Prompt new product developments or product modifications, which are thought a strength of many Japanese companies, are a result of this overlapping of functions among marketing, production, and R&D departments.

Another contrast between U.S. and Japanese firms evident from the divisionalization issues discussed so far is the way in which major organizational changes are made in the two types of firms. The U.S. example has been one of thorough analysis of alternatives, followed by relatively large, sweeping changes which have been (or are expected to be) long-lasting. In contrast, changes in Japanese firms have been based much more on experimentation, have been relatively frequent, and are more incremental in nature.

Moreover, while ROI is often a key factor in the measurement of division performance in U.S. organizations, Japanese firms are more apt to measure performance in terms of growth in sales or their divisions' return on sales. These standards of performance are oriented more toward the long-term than is ROI. And even more striking, when disparities exist among divisions in their performance along these criteria, the Japanese firm is likely to modify its system of performance appraisal in order to encourage greater harmony between divisions doing well and those doing badly. The following example illustrates this point.

At first primarily a pharmaceutical firm, **Takeda Chemical Industries** adopted a divisional system in June of 1960 with divisions in five areas: (1) manufacturing of pharmaceuticals, (2) sales of medicine and other pharmaceutical products, (3) foods, (4) chemicals, and (5) overseas sales. It added a division for agricultural chemicals in 1966 and, one engaged in cattle breeding in 1971. The pharmaceuticals manufacturing and sales divisions were later combined, and the firm now has six autonomous divisions. As one might suspect, however, there are considerable differences in the return on sales and rates of growth in sales of the different divisions. Takeda's divisions are, therefore, not treated as profit centers. Because of the conflict virtually certain from applying common performance standards to divisions with great differences in potential, Takeda has introduced a unique system of organization-wide profit sharing. The system serves to encourage harmony throughout the company rather than the fractionalization that would ensue from comparing the performance and return on investments of the company's divisions.

Nishimura, a Takeda manager during its transition to the divisional system, describes the circumstances of that time as follows:

> The need for caution in changing Takeda's existing structure was expressed and there were several arguments against adopting the divisional form. One was that sectionalism would occur because people would know and care only about their own division's activities and be unconcerned with the problems and progress of the others or the company as a whole. Another argument was that the division-as-a-profit-center idea was fine if all of the divisions could make strong profits, but that was obviously not

the case. For these and similar reasons, it was argued that it
was too early for Takeda to adopt the divisional system.

The arguments were well-founded. Ninety percent of Takeda's
business was related to the medical field. The rest of the
divisions would be involved with only ten percernt of Takeda's
business, and some would have much less potential than divisions
in the medical field. But, then, I said, "Don't worry about
independence. I know the newer fields are at a disadvantage.
What is necessary is that the more profitable divisions help
those that are less successful. After all, we are all in the
same company."

Another argument was that if certain divisions become strong and
others don't, it becomes difficult to rotate personnel among the
divisions. (After all, who wants to go to a less successful
one?) But the divisional system was inevitable. Different
businesses had to be managed differently. We would have to
address the difficulties with wisdom. Finally, we decided to
adopt Takeda's present divisional system.[4]

The relatively clear distinction between line and staff functions in U.S.
firms is also a point of contrast with Japanese companies. It is said
that Alfred Sloan, in designing GM's divisional system drew from the
existing structures of the Catholic church and traditional military
organizations. Indeed, Weick (1979)[5] has stated that, in many ways, the
dominant metaphor of U.S. business organization is the military metaphor
of conventional strategy and tactics. The "metaphor" of Japanese
organization is different.

While the formal structure of Japanese firms is clearly delineated
according to hierarchical level and function on the organizational chart,
just as for U.S. firms, a careful examination of the processes that
actually occur in Japanese organizations reveals substantial
differences. The reality of Japanese organization is relatively great
flexibility of operations for autonomous units within the "formal
structure." (In terms of a military metaphor, the Japanese firm might be
likened to a constellation of guerilla bands.) The autonomy was seen in
Chapter 2 to contribute to the organization's ability to generate prompt
responses to change. But, in both Western and Japanese firms, mechanisms
must exist for coordinating and integrating the disparate activities
within the organization. We turn to a comparison of such mechanisms in
the next section.

4.4 Integration through Formal Organization versus Processes Facilitating the Sharing of Values and Information

Many devices for organizational integration exist -- from the rules, procedures, hierarchies and plans which are so characteristic of bureaucratic organizations, to more sophisticated "devices" such as liaison people, task forces, special integrating units and matrix organizations. And, U.S. firms are often characterized by explicit, well-defined systems for integrating organization-wide effort. An important such approach is *brand management*, originally developed by **Procter and Gamble.**

The following quote illustrates the essence of the brand management system:

> Brand management is the mainspring and moving force behind all our consumer marketing. The brand management concept assures that each brand will have behind it the kind of single-minded drive it needs to succeed... The brand group is expected to know more about its product and how to increase its consumer acceptance than anyone else in the organization. The brand manager leads the brand group (in) developing the annual marketing plan; developing and executing the advertising copy strategy; planning and selecting media; planning sales promotions; coordinating package design; and analyzing and forecasting business results.[6]

In P&G's case, integration is achieved through its explicit organizational hierarchy, well-defined roles, specific job descriptions, and expertise specific to those roles. That is, integration is achieved by the systematic coordination of specialization throughout the organization. It was shown earlier that roles are far from clearly delineated in most Japanese firms; nor are individual roles and behavior clearly distinguished by job descriptions. Individuals' roles overlap considerably, and individuals (paradoxically, it might seem) operate with substantial autonomy. For these reasons, it is difficult to achieve integration solely through traditional hierarchical means, and a variety of other devices are instituted, the primary functions of which are to facilitate the sharing of values and information ("loose" integration). An example is the contrasting brand management system at Kao Corp.

The brand management system was introduced at **Kao Corporation** in 1968.
While responsible for the promotion of certain brands as in Proctor and
Gamble's case, Kao's managers are often responsible for more than one.
And much more than in the typical U.S. firm, they are encouraged to obtain
and share information from and with *other* brand managers above and beyond
a need-to-know basis. They are also asked to sit in on corporate-wide
Jomu-kai meetings which address performance of and policies for the
different brands. Thus, with "inside" information about each others'
products, the brand managers are able to position their own brands from a
competitive but, also, company-wide perspective. This sharing of
information between brand managers reflects Kao's corporate policy of
emphasizing the sharing of information and knowledge among all
employees. In this regard, Kao's president, Yoshiro Maruta, has stated
the following:

> One of our most important management jobs is to make all of our
> employees willing to cooperate fully, and to make them want to
> continually improve themselves. To achieve this, it is necessary
> for us to provide all kinds of information *equally to everyone*.
> We are doing several concrete things to make this possible.
>
> First, every employee has the right of access to *all* computerized
> information within the company except that information having to
> do with personnel matters. There is the possibility of the
> disclosure of key information to competitors. This problem is
> minimal, however, because it is common for Japanese employees to
> devote their work lives to the same company. Even if there were
> such a problem, we believe that the advantages of widely sharing
> information more than outweigh its cost. Note that this policy
> means that senior employees within the firm should not be privy
> to information which places lower-level employees at a
> disadvantage. All employees have the same information base from
> which to assess opportunities, problems, and the current status
> at both organizational and personal levels.
>
> The second thing which facilitates the sharing of values and
> information is our early morning meetings. Our company has five
> major areas which are related to each other. Those relationships
> are more important than the hierarchy of authority. I do not
> insist upon decision-making authority as president of the
> company. We think that a president is necessary only for
> relationships between the company and those outside it.
> Otherwise, all of us are considered equals within the firm, and
> have equal opportunity for contributing our ideas to it.
>
> Third is our dining room. All of our managers, including me, eat
> lunch with our employees at the same table. This contributes to
> the sharing of information, too.

Fourth, managers' offices and conference rooms are open to everyone, and anyone can come in and talk with us without appointment. People are encouraged to come in and listen even if the discussion going on is not relevant to them.

The fifth thing which contributes to the sharing of values and information (and directly to higher productivity) is our small-group activities. Groups of five to ten people from different areas, such as the packaging line, boiler room, mixing department, and chemical analysis, get together to think of ways to increase the productivity of their jobs. They are able to call upon the expertise of staff specialists when it is necessary. It is not very uncommon for our people to discuss ways to make their own jobs unnecessary.[7]

As shown, there are many devices which contribute to information sharing and, as important, to enriching the interactions of everyday life. As another example, let us look at Suntory which is noted for its "Miyajima plant system."

The principal purpose of **Suntory**'s system is to overcome the barrier between technological and social systems. Operationalizing an idea first learned from Meinan Seisakusho at Nagoya, the plant manager Kishimoto developed the Miyajima plant system in 1968. The system encourages the removal of unnecessary and often artificial distinctions between jobs and the functioning of employees more as generalists than specialists. The consequence at Suntory was more effective performance by fewer people in a simpler organization. A proven success at the Miyajima plant outside Hiroshima, the system was adopted throughout Suntory, although each plant adapted the system to its own circumstances.

Similarly, **Kyocera** is noted for its "kompa" -- regular, informal meetings of Kyocera's employees with their president. Started when the firm was first founded, the kompa is still an important means for president Inamori to share his philosophy and concerns with Kyocera's employees and for winning broad commitment to them. When the company was still small, Inamori visited some section of his firm every night, especially during the Japanese year's-end *Bonen-Kai* season. With Inamori in the middle of a circle, the group would drink and sing and socialize but, also, very fervently discuss the company and their jobs. With everyone's participation encouraged, Kyocera's kompa facilitates mutual understanding and the building of trust throughout the company. Inamori often speaks of "management based on mind"; this quote reflects his philosophy:

> There is no management-versus-worker attitude at Kyocera. We
> are, at the very least, partners who work together. We are, at
> the very best, comrades who get together with love for each other
> and for this company that we created. We work hard for the
> group, and share happiness and hardships as well. Our company
> is, so to speak, a clan. Management based on mind is, first of
> all, trust in each other as partners and showing that trust by
> our actions.[8]

Inamori cannot attend all of the kompa today, since Kyocera has grown so big; nevertheless, the type of meeting described still continues throughout the company, even in Kyocera International at San Diego in the United States (with beer substituted for sake.)   Informal, personal contact between managers and workers in this way contributes to information sharing and greater mutual understanding. It is an important means for achieving integration of organization-wide purpose and effort. This is very different from the hierarchy-dependent "systems methods" for achieving integration which are typical in the United States.

Other traditions contribute to the sharing of values and information in major Japanese firms. They include the hiring and training of all high school and college graduates (all new employees) at the same time. Intensely training and socializing together, they become "alumni of the same company class" with bonds of friendship to each other. Then, when the graduates are assigned to different departments and rotated through different assignments, these bonds create an inter-personal network which facilitates the accumulation and sharing of diverse information even across departments. Such a system is supported by generally good management-union relations.

Good industrial relations are facilitated by company unions in Japan as well as by such often-cited matters as long-term employment, promotion from within, and company bonus systems. But more important than these is the creation and maintenance of trust in matters of every-day work activities. Most Japanese firms experienced labor-management disputes, strikes, and severe conflicts beginning in the period from the late 1940's to the 1950's. More recently, Toshiba experienced a protracted dispute with trade unions from the spring of 1949 until early in 1956. Hitachi's big dispute of 1960 is also well-known. Essential for creating good relationships out of such chaos are a variety of "devices" which fall under the rubric of the human relations movement -- for example, active, continuous problem-solving effort devoted to "every-day concerns," assigning especially good people to the personnel section, addressing issues together before they become major problems (as in the well-known *nemawashi* process), and abolishing differences in dining and bathroom facilities and in dress which directly signal differences in status. All of these acts contribute to the building of the trust which is such an important aspect of Japanese management. These techniques also work for Japanese companies abroad. A timely study by Takamiya (1981)[9] attributed the high productivity of Japanese firms in England to good industrial relations practices built upon persistent attention to the often tiny and subtle considerations of every-day work life.

Even though Japanese firms depend heavily upon such indirect mechanisms for integration in organizations, the formal hierarchy also plays an important role. Especially in organizations which are structured with (for Japanese firms) relatively great emphasis along functional lines, integration depends critically upon key people in the hierarchy, especially the *"kacho"* of middle management. The *kacho* play a key role in both the formulation and implementation of corporate strategy and, therefore, a key role in the integration of corporate-wide effort.[10] They were indeed seen, in Chapter 2, to exert a greater integrating influence in Japanese firms than their middle management counterparts in U.S. firms.

4.5 Individual Learning through Systems vs. Organizational Learning through Groups

Organzational learning is a key to organizational growth and adaptation. Learning in U.S. companies is a highly articulated process integrating all relevant aspects of the organization's system. Highly standardized approaches to training are sought, with intensive training geared to enable new workers to handle their jobs from the very outset.

(1) Manuals Used for Thorough Standardization

In the white-collar sector, as well as for the blue-collar worker, standardization of know-how is attempted to the highest possible degree, with numerous procedures specified in top-quality manuals. Sears, for example, is famous for its meticulously specific manuals.

These high-quality manuals succeed in giving individuals a minimum level of expertise needed in a very efficient fashion. Operations manuals for each of **Sears'** departments list the management organization required for the work to be done, responsibilities and authority of each post, operations management procedures, levels of quality demanded from department managers, educational methods to be used, and other key topics. The manuals are produced by Sears' corporate-level personnel department, in collaboration with all related sectors, and then sent out into the field. They are accompanied by a complete set of other pertinent materials, including a training schedule, training methods, discussion and quiz techniques to check on the results of training, and the forms necessary to run these checks. Because of such great care taken at the preparation stage, it is said that even a total amateur can assume the duties of a store trainer.

Japanese companies, naturally, have also developed official procedures and manuals, but there is a big difference between the U.S. and Japan in what these mannuals actually mean. A Japanese manager of Mitsubishi Electric, U.S.A. offered the following comments on this point:

> The volume of written materials describing work processes in the U.S. and Japan are comparable, but the actual meaning and intentions are totally apart. In America the contents of these descriptions have a direct bearing on contracts and workers' performance within the sphere specified. Work descriptions in Japan, on the other hand, are merely a framework, with everyone crossing boundaries in performing their work. Any overlapping in U.S. manuals would lead to claims of inept management.

As this manager implies, the manuals of U.S. companies are a compilation of know-how which demand strict adherence. In contrast, Japanese companies often do not give specific directions, and if they do they are largely nominal in nature. Here we can see, in part, the concept of the absence of clearly defined duties as a means for increasing the vitality within the organization.

There are both merits and drawbacks to this approach by Japanese companies. Let us examine the problem areas first. Without clear job descriptions and manuals, the burden of Japanese company education is placed on on-the-job training (OJT), and upon the immediate supervisor responsible for that training. The supervisor may be more or less proficient in training, and the new employee's progress can depend, without a formally specified training program, upon his or her chance accumulation of helpful learning experiences. The problem remains whether such experiences are likely to produce genuine expertise. But *even this goal's* merits are subject to differences of interpretation by U.S. and Japanese managers. An employee in the Seibu Distribution Group who received training at Sears commented:

> I believe that there is a fundamental difference in how corporate managers in the U.S. and Japan actually move their firms. At Sears, everyone has a clearly defined role, and the sum of all of the work so defined makes up the total operation. However, the result is that when you ask someone at Sears about the company's management they rarely know much about things outside their particular sphere -- quite a different situation than in Japan. U.S. employees are thoroughly versed in their own duties. Promotion is based on the premise that you master what you are assigned to do, and employees go all out to accumulate job experience and expertise. Establishment of specific job duties makes it easy to organize career programs. Moving through this program in a systematic way will lead to efficient training and top-quality workers. In Japanese organizations I believe there is anxiety about increasing expertise, even if there is considerable knowledge of what goes on within other sectors.

For managerial talent, U.S. companies make active use of the business schools, opting to hire many highly qualified MBA's. This also differs from the Japanese approach with its focus on education at the work site and not recruiting a managerial elite from outside the firm. The latter approach succeeds in producing excellent managers, but may fail to import management theories and concepts needed for the future.

The training programs of Japanese companies forsake individual training in favor of group learning, which utilizes human relationships very

successfully.   The success of the group dynamics approach is derived
largely from the activation resulting from learning activities stimulated
and reinforced by human relationships. This is exemplified by the well-
known QC circle approach.

It is said that small-group activities and the various types of
participative management techniques are a major element of the "Japanese
style of management."   However, such practices are certainly not confined
to Japanese companies.   U.S. firms have used these approaches well, not
just to create better relations for the sake of expedience, but for the
optimal development and utilization of human potential.

Motorola developed its own "Participative Management Program" (PMP) well
over a decade ago.   There are two phases to Motorola's approach -- PMP I
at the plant level and PMP II at the office level. Employees are divided
into small groups, with meetings held on a frequent, even daily, basis.
Group members establish their own standards and base their activities on
them.   Work results are measured and checked daily, weekly, and monthly.
There is also a written suggestion system in operation.   Replies to
suggestions are given within 72 hours, and not through words but concrete
action -- for example, changes in jig tools, improvements in procedures,
policy reconsiderations and so forth.   Of the 45,000 Motorola employees
throughout the United States about one-third participate in PMP.

(2) Detailed Small-Group Activities

The large, very successful companies in both the U.S. and Japan strive to
achieve very good company-employee relations. However, there appear to us,
to be important differences in the attention given to certain
considerations in implenting small-group approaches.   Nippon Steel
Corporation example illustrates such differences.

The small-group activities at **Nippon Steel Corporation**'s Kimitsu Works are
known as JK Activities. The name JK (taken from the Japanese *jishu kanri*
meaning "autonomous management") was adopted to emphasis the autonomous
nature of small-group quality control efforts at the Kimitsu Works. It is
an approach based on integrating individual expression with company growth

and corporate management as shown in Figure 4-2.

In a word, JK Activities strive for autonomous production line control. Introduction of the system and its gaining of acceptance within the organization was no simple matter. Even though autonomous control was strongly emphasized by the head office and by production plant staff, much trial-and-error was necessary within the organization to introduce and keep it functioning throughout the entire Works.

This time line shows that, while JK Activities comprised an autonomous movement, company-wide organization and budgeting efforts had to be conducted to guarantee successful introduction and acceptance. The Kimitsu *JK Secretariat* offered the following two points as important to the development of JK Activities: (1) The introduction of the *JK Union* (a self-management organization consisting of QC circle members) at the same time the activities were launched to assure autonomy of efforts; and (2) the creation of the staff "Management Support Conference" to support JK Activities in a systematic way.

These efforts are symbolic of the JK Activities themselves. That is, while the activities were expressly designed not to create further organization as such, sound cooperation among foremen, department and section managers, and technical staff was vital in gaining acceptance and success of the program. The Kimitsu *JK Secretariat* emphasizes that "the important thing in JK Activities is neither non-interference, nor orders. It is the support of people doing the work." A worker involved in JK Activities agreed: "If the activities themselves were a system of work orders, the whole thing would have become routine overnight." In other words, leadership and control of the Kimitsu JK Activities depended upon a skillful balance between "autonomy" and "systemization." Achievement of this balance was the key to success.

JK Activities operate on the premise that "work manuals are not to be viewed in absolute terms." Open discussion and criticism within the groups are used to "intrude upon and learn from" each other's work areas, with the process aided by competition with other JK groups and cooperation with staff groups. The positive results are immediately standardized and

Figure 4-2 Concept behind JK Activity
(Source: "JK Activity," Nippon Steel Corporation, Kimitsu Works.)

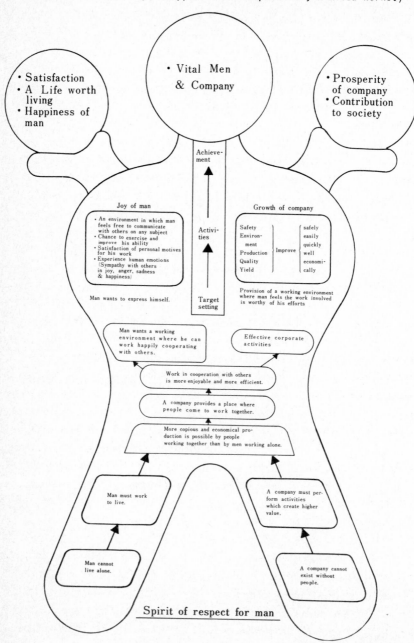

circulated throughout the company. They become a part of the common
working knowledge throughout the organization. Variations in JK
Activities occur, and because they do, it sustains the impetus for
continued in-house learning.[11]

"100% quality," which is the general target of Quality Control Circles in
Japan including JK Circles, may not be rational from a purely economic
point of view, because marginal costs to raise quality from 99% to 100%
may be larger than the benefits obtained by the quality improvement.
"100% quality" or perfection, is however, very important for
organizational learning purposes. By investigating and analyzing the
causes of defects, people and the organization can learn and accumulate
additional know-how. The marginal costs incurred are thought the
"tuition" for organizational learning.

(3) Research and Development Utilizing Group Capabilities

The type of group-oriented learning discussed also shows its strength in
research and development. R&D in America is consigned largely to
individual pursuit, at least in relative terms, whereas in Japan the trend
is for groups to work on given R&D problems. There is little direct
evidence to support this assertion, but several comments appear to
substantiate it. For example, a Hitachi researcher with considerable
experience in the U.S. noted:

> The normal situation in America is for researchers to have their
> own rooms, each pursuing his or her own separate work theme.
> Joint research refers often to, at most, two or three persons,
> and there is, otherwise, little tendency to offer help to
> others. On the contrary, everyone keeps their eyes peeled for a
> chance to push ahead of everyone else with any sort of new
> breakthrough.

In January 1971, **Amada Co., Ltd.** established Amada U.S., a technology
development firm, in Seattle, Washington. The first result to come from
this new firm was a numerically controlled turret punch press used to
drill holes in sheet steel and other substances -- a development which has
grown to become the leading product in the Amada line. This punch press
was developed by a single American engineer. An Amada manager remembered

those days:

> He was an extremely capable engineer, and we were all interested
> in how he would develop his design. He had his own special
> locker and would always shut up all his drawings there before
> going home at night. Everything would stay right there in his
> locker when he went on vacation or was away from work, and nobody
> around him had any knowledge of the design process, the basic
> thinking involved or how far things had come. The final product
> was a big success, yes, but knowing nothing in the interim is not
> the way we like to operate. Suppose he had moved to another
> firm... Amada would have been left empty-handed in the true sense
> of the word.

While there are, no doubt, many exceptions, this type of individual
pursuit is much more typical of the American approach to R&D than is true
in Japan. The Japanese favor a more group-oriented program.

Taiyu Kobayashi made the following comments in an interview when he was
president of **Fujitsu**:

> I believe the strength of Fujitsu lies in our group approach to
> research -- a concept I do not believe exists in the United
> States. From what I have heard, it appears that individual
> abilities are given extremely high evaluation in the U.S.   In
> Japan the trend is to place the stress on evaluation of group
> capabilities rather than the individual. This is particularly
> true at Fujitsu -- we adopted that approach from the very
> beginning. I'm often told by friends in competing firms, "You
> don't seem to have anybody with any talent, but you sure get the
> job done!" Sort of a welcome insult, I suppose. We don't really
> go out in search of great achievement which will scoop everybody
> else.   No, we place more value on cooperative development in
> which everyone has a sense of participation.[12]

The group approach to R&D satisfies the individual's desire to
participate, while lowering the possibility of error due to individual
oversight. But even more important, is that the group structure serves to
stimulate the creative power and volition of its members. Former **NEC**
managing director, Michiyuki Uenohara, offered these interesting words on
this very point:

> Even in America the greatest results are not from researchers
> working totally alone. Statistics will show that results are
> superior when everyone is kept busy. New phenomena will
> generally be overlooked even when experiments are run. These new

phenomena are not the results that one expects to gain -- they usually obstruct the experiment itself -- and efforts are made to reduce such results to the greatest possible degree. It takes a truly penetrating, critical mind to see through to what is really new. When this sensitivity is present, the strange phenomenon triggers the reaction "this might be something I can put to use." New phenomena are seen by many people. But seeing alone just isn't enough -- it is vital to know the meaning of what you are looking at. People who can sense this are the real discoverers, the ones who do the truly original research. When research is pursued in groups, there may be somebody who will see the phenomena. Or, with all the talk of what everyone is having trouble with or how a certain sort of thing would certainly help out, there are many thoughts always hovering in the back of your mind ... That makes a world of difference.

The group-oriented approach of Japanese companies has in many ways evolved from the national and racial characteristics of the Japanese people; the impact of education and general social systems cannot be ignored either. But the group dynamics approach is, just as much, the fruit of conscious management choice for the very reasons cited.

Uenohara elaborates upon the concept as applied to R&D:

We have two projects at NEC -- Basic Technology Project I and Basic Technology II. The former type can be found almost anywhere, but the latter involves special teams designed to force horizontal communication. There are between five and 15 members in a team, which searches out its own problems to kick around. While the general pattern is to keep at it for a year at a time, there is no set time schedule nor are any particular problems presented for study. We do not anticipate "hard" results from this approach. When the researchers gather together, although they talk about the same things, their interpretations differ. Often, they don't get through to one another. We learned that even the same engineers in the same company often do not understand each other. Just to find this out is a major achievement. In the beginning everyone griped about it, and there was plenty of resistance. But I stuck to my guns, and we've been doing it for nearly a decade now. I often liken a research center to a zoo -- if you leave things to fate everyone will build their own cage; but when you tear out the cages, everyone links together. Successful R&D requires cooperation between various types of people, and for that reason I like to peddle the concept of "group creation."

Putting these points together, we find that learning through group dynamics offers the following advantages over individual learning: (1) information sources are more diversified and, with overlapping areas of expertise, the reliability of information is, itself, improved; (2) more ideas on the average (in terms of both volume and diversity) will be created than with individuals learning separately; (3) the breadth of individual learning is increased, with each person learning from everyone else; (4) groups with high cohesiveness will initiate spontaneous learning activities which surpass the demands of the organization itself (for example, carrying a 95 percent quality control target to the 100 percent level). Along with, these advantages, however, there is also the danger that the access to excessive data and the pressure of staying in line (which often comes of a sense of needing to preserve group unity) can choke off different views or conceptual jumps before they have a chance to gain acceptance.

4.6 "Follow Me" vs. Staged Variation

Differences may be identified between U.S. and Japanese companies in their methods of adapting to change in the corporate environment. As the examples we have examined show, U.S. companies tend to react from top management down. These examples included the buying up of Marathon Oil by U.S. Steel; Motorola's withdrawal from car radios (the field in which it started out) in favor of strategic diversification into the three pillars of semiconductors, communication and computers; Du Pont's purchase of Conoco; and GE's withdrawal from the computer business.

In contrast, Japanese companies prefer the bottom-up approach to cumulative change (up from the plant level). Examples include Toyota's Kanban System and QC circles. While in the U.S. model a solid all-inclusive design is present, there can be great difficulties in making fine adjustments during implementation if there are no changes allowed in the basic design. Changes in strategy may, therefore, be implemented in bold and drastic fashion. The typical Japanese model of change incorporates a function for periodic change at the ground level of the company, with adaptation to market shifts carried out in a spirit of experimentation and through fine adjustment. And because the design is usually abstract and all-encompassing, adoption of the individual change model best suited for the current situation faces less organizational resistance from hierarchically sanctioned groups. This mode of change, on the other hand, requires more time for the moving of the entire organization in any sort of bold fashion.

We have described the Japanese company's approach to change as fine adjustment from the bottom up, but this is not to say that top management plays no role whatsoever. Quite to the contrary, Japanese top managers play the critical role of building the incentive and capability to change throughout their organizations. Discussed in earlier chapters, it is this activation of human resources that is the driving force of corporate strategic development and adaptation.

One frequently used means of creating variation in Japanese companies is the staging of movements which stimulate people to contribute their thought. The TQC (Total Quality Control) used at companies like Toyota and Komatsu is one example. Inspiring workers to strive for the goal of winning the coveted Deming Prize for quality control, much of the available human wisdom is elicited. Knowledge is shared, new directions are considered, and innovative efforts are made to create series of small improvements, each contributing to higher quality and serving to reinforce those values which make the organization's culture unique.

Toyota has continued to erect goal after goal geared to mobilize the entire company. "G10" is a comparatively recent example (referring to the goal of capturing 10 percent of the global auto market). Such goals play a key role in motivating all employees to boost corporate performance.

This procedure of organizing movements every several years to strengthen the company is an organizational device adopted by most Japanese firms. QC, TQC and the Deming Prize are all means toward that end, and are certainly not limited to the production plant.

To promote its whisky business, Suntory implemented its "Two Chopstick Strategy," a movement geared to boost whisky sales at Japanese style restaurants where previously the major beverage had been sake. This was followed up by the "Keep Bottle/Whisky and Water Strategies." These strategies were introduced not only as marketing devices, but were also instrumental in starting in-house movements for better productivity as

well. Even more successful as an in-house movement was Suntory's "All of
Us Are Salesmen Strategy," which included everybody from the president on
down.

"Movements" are inspired not just by setting objectives or pursuing
campaigns. Also instrumental has been stirring up a sense of threat to
the firm within the company itself. In the background of Suntory's
strategies was the threat presented by the deregulation of scotch, while
in the case of Toyota, deregulation of imports played a similar role. An
examination of Japanese corporate histories reveals that trade and/or
capital liberalization have served to heighten a sense of crisis within
companies, providing excellent opportunities for in-house movements.
Moreover, there are also high-performance firms, such as Suntory or
Renown, which have intentionally taken on unprofitable market sectors in
order to increase tension within their ranks. President Keizo Saji of
Suntory notes:

> If development is possible without a sense of crisis then all the
> more power to you. But it must be remembered that human beings
> are weak. In that sense, when there is a feeling of crisis --
> that is, when you have a threatened sector in your firm -- it
> imparts a sense of threat to the entire company. That is an
> effective weapon. You could even go so far as to say that the
> company as a whole may become a crisis sector.[13]

There are also distinct characteristics which distinguish the leadership
of highly successful Japanese top managers. They are likely to expend
great effort to create variation, cultivate people, and activate the
organization as a whole.

An approach adopted by Seiji Tsutsumi, chairman of the Seibu Distribution
Group, is to present abstract concepts to employees and, then, demand that
they devise specific methods of operationalizing those concepts. Rather
than preparing answers and indicating specific actions to employees
himself, Tsutsumi presents the general problem and requires his people to
develop their own thinking and concrete plans. There are vivid anecdotes
about how Tsutsumi does this. For example, he refused to approve a plan
submitted by one of his men, and sent it back ten more times for lack of
aggressiveness, sometimes tearing up the plan and showering the employee

with the confetti remains. He finally gave his approval on the 20th submission.

Management and employees have their creativity tested to the extreme. Their strenuous efforts to solve the riddles presented by Tsutsumi prepare them, it is said, to react appropriately to the present age, to correctly read the changes in lifestyles and values, and concomitant changes in the undercurrent of structural demand, and to devise specific countermeasures and investment plans based on that knowledge.

Rejecting subordinates' proposals, or using challenges or shake-ups to overcome complacency and revitalize the organization are common approaches of Japanese top leadership (Okumura, 1982).[14] This type of activity creates a high degree of variation within Japanese firms. As mentioned before, Japanese organizations are relatively weak at curtailing variation by hierarchical means. That is, problems and strategies are not made more concrete at each successively lower level in the hierarchy. The broad challenges, philosophies and directions expressed at the top are echoed at all organizational levels in no more specific form.

Stafford Beer (1981)[15] emphasizes that to reduce variety it is necessary to break problems down into sub-systems' problems, with each subsystem accurately representing the larger system, so that each sub-system can deal independently with its own environment. The contention is that for survival, the overall organizational structure must be designed so that policy, intelligence, control, execution and adjustment functions can be executed in a recursive fashion at each system (including the individual) level within the organization.

The division organization of U.S. companies provides for such recursive processes. There are more self-contained division systems in the U.S. than in Japan; however, in the Japanese organization, levels below the division level are more recursive in nature. Accordingly, when variety is created within the organization, there is very broad effort to reduce it. The consequence of such effort is broad accumulation of knowledge and know-how at the work site. In Japanese organizations this happens most effectively in QC circle activities. QC circles serve as a vehicle for learning in which territory is mutually breached and variation is confronted internally.

4.7 Top Management -- Performance vs. Continuity

We discussed the characteristics of U.S. and Japanese top management leadership in Chapter 2. In this section, we will focus more closely on the stability of Japanese and American top management.

(1) Who Sits on Boards of Directors?

Let us first examine the structure of top management authority. In U.S. companies there is a clear distinction between proposing policy and its execution, with top management confined to thinking of and proposing policy. In this sense, the board of directors is the real locus of policy formulation. Within the board there are usually several sub-committees which handle policy studies and recommendations. Integral to their process is an at least reasonably scientific approach to strategy and policy making, including thoughtful discussions between board members, consideration of increasingly diverse sources of information (in the face of the threat of takeover), and other elements.

In contrast, a Japanese company's board of directors is "simply the place where decisions are ratified." In most cases, actual policy matters are already well-decided by standing committees or behind-the-scenes maneuvering in the divisions involved in the process before submission to the committees. Accordingly, there are hardly any companies which adopt the system of having subcommittees within the board of directors.

Examining the compositions of director boards reveals that the role of external directors in U.S. companies is large, with these persons applying the influence of their respective fields to the policy, choice of top management personnel, and to other key issues. In over 80 percent of U.S. companies, the majority of directors are outside executives (see Table 4-1).

Table 4-1 Comparison of Boards of Directors

	U S A	Japan
Size of the board (number of directors)		
range	7-33 (industrials) 8-27 (non-industrials)	11-43 (industrials) 9-42 (non-industrials)
median	13 (industrials) 15 (non-industrials)	21 (industrials) 22 (non-industrials)
The percentage of companies in which the outside directors are majority	83% (industrials) 88% (non-industrials)	0%
Average age of directors	58 (industrials) 59 (non-industrials)	58
The percentage of companies that have committees of directors	95%	2%
The term of service	1 year	2 years

Source : A survey made by Keizai-doyukai in 1977 and Okumura, A., *Nihon no toppu manejimento* (Japanese Top Management) Tokyo: Daiamondosha, 1982.

Just why do U.S. companies hire so many outside directors? The phenomenon may be due to firm commitment to protecting the interests of shareholders. U.S. corporate managers are constantly operating under the pressures of stock price fluctuations and profitability; it is the role of outside directors to ensure unbiased reactions to such pressures. Moreover, under the restrictions of antitrust legislation, when U.S. firms move actively to purchase other companies, there are many instances when outside legal, industry, or financial expertise is necessary. These are seen to be reasons for the prominent role of outside directors in the United States.

At GM, for instance, a wide variety of people serve as outside directors,

the majority of them serving on "interlocking directorates." In other
words, chairmen of major companies such as P&G or 3M will serve
concurrently as GM directors to help mold GM policy. In addition, many
U.S. company directors have originally been lawyers or management
consultants. Although there are no such persons among the ranks of GM
directors, of equal or greater interest is the inclusion of a female
former Ambassador to Great Britain and a black minister. These directors
appear to be heavily involved in the public policy subcommittee, offering
advice and recommendations on issues which relate to women or minorities.

Outside directors are expected to use their professional expertise to
exert a positive impact upon company policy. At Motorola, this impact
has, at times, been extremely large. A rather dramatic example in a
separate company, was the dismissal of RCA president David Sarnoff. The
RCA executive was visiting Japan at the time, and learned of his dismissal
by the board of directors while locked in negotiations with president (now
chairman) Kazuo Iwata of Toshiba. This example illustrates that boards of
directors exercise powerful personnel authority over the corporate entity,
for the purpose of protecting shareholder interests. Outside directors
also decide management bonuses and salaries. They study company
performance and the efforts made by the top managers to determine the
amounts to be paid. In short, U.S. managers are quite closely controlled
by their boards of directors. Such matters are the prerogative of the
president in Japanese companies, and, in fact, are consigned even· to
people outside of his office.

In contrast to the composition of U.S. boards directors, Japanese boards
are normally made up of internal directors who serve concurrently as
managers of the company. The number of outside directors is small, and
with the nearly total absence of subcommittees within the boards, it
cannot be said that outside executives are actually participating in
policy determination. Most of the outside directors in Japanese companies
participate only as auditors; for example at Toyota, Goro Koyama, former
chairman of the Mitsui Bank, serves as an auditor. Company ties, but
among firms within a given corporate group, are reflected by the presence
of outside directors: Takao Nagata, chairman of Hitachi Zosen
(shipbuilding) serves as an auditor for Hitachi, Ltd., while in the

Sumitomo Group, Masao Kamei chairman of Sumitomo Electric and Chairman Koji Kobayashi of NEC Corporation serve as directors in each other's companies. Nevertheless, the number of such outside directors is extremely small, usually amounting to one or two persons for each 20 to 30 directors.

Over the past two decades or so there have been many attempts to increase the ratio of outside directors. However, the data presented illustrates that the number has not increased. There are several reasons for this. The first is the existence of the lifetime employment and seniority systems in Japan. Under these, employees rise gradually in the corporate hierarchy over a long period of time. The opportunity for promotion to a top management post is vital to motivate and win the sustained loyalty of very promising employees.

The second reason why the number of outside directors has not increased relates to the low mobility of people between companies in Japan. This allows in-house human resource development, with employees accumulating know-how, but much of what is learned is peculiar to the particular company. As a result, relatively little knowledge or skills are gained which are seen to be applicable on the outside. In short, the amount of generalizable knowledge which can be transferred is perceived to be lower in Japan than in the United States, and outside directors are not as likely to be able to guide a firm.

The third reason is that the sense of "the company for the employees" is stronger than that of "the company for the shareholders," making the protection of shareholder interests a secondary concern. The board of directors thus becomes a body more oriented to the interests of the employees than those of the shareholders.

In addition, Japanese companies share stock holdings with other companies in the same group or with similarly affiliated institutions, thus, maintaining stable shareholders. Major banks or life insurance companies will not intervene directly unless a severe emergency demands it.

For these reasons, therefore, the power of Japan's top management is substantial. Toshiba's chairman, Kazuo Iwata, has said:

> Japanese presidents have charisma. They are dictators. They
> decide how high their salaries will be and who will succeed them
> in office. They answer to no one, as long as they stay within
> the bounds of the law. An American president is the chief of a
> team, and has relatively little control over salary or successor.

(2) Top Management Continuity

The basis for the stability of Japanese top management is the
organization's emphasis upon long-term accumulation of in-house resources
and its approach to policy development based on the work site, both of
which were discussed above.

The purpose of long-term in-house resource accumulation is the cultivation
of human potential. The majority of Japanese top managers view the
company as the employees' home and an arena where they improve their
skills, and they strive conscientiously to fulfill their roles as
educators. The philosophy of Matsushita that "you build people before you
build things" was pervasive in our sample.

TDK is a company created through efforts by the founder to industrialize
the Japanese invention of ferrite, and Fukujiro Sono, TDK's chairman, is
well known for his endless enthusiasm for cultivating people. Sono has
stated:

> It hardly need be said that a company must be eternal -- for the
> sake of the shareholders, the employees and the customers
> alike. What can we do to make it so? The answer is to make the
> company itself artistic, cultural in nature, because art and
> culture, indeed, possess elements of the eternal. Art and
> culture in the corporate sense is the ability to perpetually
> create things which are new. This is the word "creativity,"
> which is the corporate philosophy at TDK. But in order to create
> new things you must cultivate people. And when you pass the
> baton on to the next generation, as a manager, the only real
> legacy of any value is human talent.[16]

More specifically, Sono encourages employees to read, actually handing out
reading assignments every month. He passes on a steady stream of books he
has read to his associates, and runs off copies of articles he finds

interesting for circulation.   The chairman makes a special point to be present at all training sessions for newly appointed assistant section managers, giving lectures, reading all employees' impressions, and adding his personal stamp and signature before turning them back in.   Here we see a company president striving to educate his people by close contact on a daily basis.

It is likely that long-term research and development efforts will contribute to a firm's continuity.   Yoshikazu Ito, president of Toray Industries, stated about continuity in research and development:

> Management philosophy is the single most important thing. Former chairman, Shigeki Tashiro, had his own personal philosophy, and was well-versed in U.S. and European chemical firms.   In any case, it takes an extremely long time to change the nature of a company. Holding up over this period requires great patience and constant efforts to maintain a set amount of management resources for such a purpose. This cannot be accomplished through a mere "division of work" -- the only feasible approach is to pass a philosophy on at the top management level.[17]

Continuity in the management of everyday operations in all sectors of the organization can cumulatively lead to major breakthroughs.   Toshiba's chairman, Iwata, was well known during his years as president for stressing the importance of a steady accumulation of commonplace things as one of his "performance recovery" policies.   He has noted, for example:

> When I became president, one of my key policies was the accumulation of commonplace things. This may be likened to the process which eventually developed the "Ultra-C" gymnastics movement. The "flying somersault" which become so popular around the world began with swinging up onto the horizontal bar -- something we learned in junior high school. Repeating the flip movement at the end of the routine, you will turn three full somersaults before landing on the ground. Then when you think that maybe even a few more flips are possible, you work up to four or five somersaults. Superb strategy or technology is the same -- the result of steady and continuous accumulation of effort and endeavor.

A strength of Japanese management is the belief that sustained daily efforts will often blossom into very fruitful outcomes.   But that depends on the continuity of such effort and is inextricably linked to continuity in top management policy.

(3) Top Manager Career Backgrounds

The background of a company's top management is clearly linked to the nature of the company itself and to the strategy being advanced at a particular time.   Let us now examine the career backgrounds of top managers in U.S. and Japanese firms. The previously mentioned "work-site" emphasis in Japan will be seen to have clear implications.

GM is a company that traditionally protects its corporate character, which can perhaps be best referred to as a "strong ROI Culture." The tradition at GM is to have chairmen with a financial background and presidents with a technical background. This is true of the current chairman, Roger B. Smith, and president, F. James McDonald, as well as GM's previous chairman, Thomas A. Murphy, and president, Elliott M. Estes. As at Hitachi, the unspoken rule that men with a plant background can rise to the top seems to be at work -- an accurate reflection of the character of a technology or production-oriented company.

Corporate strategy and top management appear to be congruous at Hitachi and Fujitsu, with Katsushige Mita and Takuma Yamamoto, two men who had been heads of the computer divisions of their respective companies, rising to become president.   Both Hitachi and Fujitsu profess strategies of turning themselves into comprehensive electronics powers and of catching up with world computer giant, IBM. The men most capable of advancing such strategies have been placed in the president's office.   In America, meanwhile, legal expert Irving S. Shapiro became chairman of Du Pont, a company traditionally dominated by "chemists." This was a move calculated to promote both anti-trust legislation countermeasures and the more recent series of corporate acquisition strategies like the buying of Conoco.

An examination of the career backgrounds of top managers reveals several relevant points.   First, the majority of top Japanese managers have technical backgrounds (in R&D or production technology, or they majored in engineering in college). Although our data is not complete for the U.S. side, the study by Brown and Montamedi (1977)[18] is valuable. This study covered a total of 4,000 U.S. managers with salaries of over $100,000 annually, classified by background and covering the period from 1970 through 1976. It shows that there has been a steady increase in managers with financial backgrounds, and they represent the mainstream in U.S. management today. In light of the frequent corporate buying and selling and the extent to which financial efficiency is pursued in the U.S., it is easy to understand why the number of such executives is on the rise. A second trend shown by the study is the large number of managers with a background in management. This development is linked to the fact that the MBA has become a reliable career passport, with those following this route having developed their careers while handling strategy planning, business development or other tasks. A third trend finds very few top managers with backgrounds principally in actual work-site areas of business, marketing or production. This is the most striking difference with Japanese top management, where almost all positions are filled by those with production or marketing backgrounds.

These top managers' career backgrounds are probably an accurate reflection of the problems being faced by U.S. companies today -- problems such as a short-term business orientation, products which do not meet consumer needs, inferior quality and reliability, or falling behind in process development and the increased costs that ensue. It is not illogical to surmise that these problems are, in good part, a result of excessive top management focus on financial affairs, and failing to put good production or sales-related ideas into action. The change of U.S. companies in this direction appears to be a major one, considering that in 1972 most top managers had backgrounds in marketing. In 1970, those from the production sector ranked at the very bottom of the scale. The prevailing opinion in the United States appears to be that production concerns have already been solved. This contrasts sharply with Japanese firms, most of which regard production as the true starting line for thinking about strategy. The "strategic operating policy" mentioned by Wheelwright (1981) zeroes in on this point and, because Japanese companies predicate their strategies upon the need for fine adjustments at the production plant level, the number of top managers from this sector is large.

The criticism and self-examination of U.S. companies in recent years has led to changes in top management ranks, with the emergence of more top managers with engineering or production backgrounds. This is particularly true in the high-tech fields, where the need for R&D, new-product commercialization, and investment in plant and equipment from a long-term perspective has begun to bring those with engineering backgrounds into top management posts. Criticism of those with business school and primarily financial backgrounds, together with the view of the impossibility of adapting to the technological revolution without knowledge of the technology and production involved, has stimulated the beginnings of greater emphasis on the production sector.

In comparison, top Japanese managers have generally been in control of production and/or sales work-sites, and presidents or chairmen with such experience are the rule rather than the exception. They are apt to have thorough knowledge of the work site and the company itself. This factor is important to the formulation of any strategy but is vital for the implementation of strategies which depend critically upon human resource utilization. Japanese companies that are dominated by such top management, possessing excellent organizational skills and adept at nurturing and marshalling human potential, can be said to represent the strength of Japanese industry.

On the other hand, however, Japanese top management may be less likely to take major, radical initiatives. This creates the threat that effective. measures will not be taken in times of very severe crisis or when there is an absence of a reliable model to follow. Furthermore, the minimal control over top management by the board of directors creates a strong possibility that no control will be exercised when it is direly needed; that is, there is literally no means to control top management should it depart from the accepted rules -- a trend clearly evident in most Japanese firms which go bankrupt (even though no such firms were not in our sample). The stable positions of top managers in Japan also creates the possibility of elderly executives remaining too long in their posts for the good of the company; top managers in the U.S. are, on the average, much younger in age. Accordingly, critical themes for Japanese corporate leaders in the future are the development of innovative strategies and the question of how to incorporate self-control mechanisms within the top management structure.

4.8 Firm vs. Loose Values in a Corporate Culture

The majority of the companies in our sample, both Japanese and American, have clear values expressed in their management ideologies. The ideologies vary by company, sometimes centering on corporate domains, as discussed in the chapter on corporate strategy; at other times, they are articulated in the standards of daily behavior prescribed for employees. A comparative analysis of the management ideologies of U.S. and Japanese companies reveals several points of difference.

(1) Management Ideology Stressing Human Relations

The first difference is that the management ideologies of Japanese companies contain many principles prescribing the lifestyles of organization members and their interaction with others. Examples include Suntory's "Give it a try," the "Harmony, Sincerity and Pioneering Spirit" of Hitachi, or Takeda's "Patriotism, Harmony, Study, Modesty and Courtesy." The spirit of harmony advocated by Hitachi and Takeda, as a condition made necessary by frequent member interaction and also emphasized by Kao, Toshiba, and other companies, is of particular interest. Stressing people as the most important resource is common to both U.S. and Japanese companies. However, while U.S. companies treat people as a strategic management resource because of their potential contribution to the business, Japanese companies stress harmony between people for its own inherent importance. That is, U.S. companies appear concerned with the functional contribution of their people; Japanese companies seek development of the person for his or her own sake.

(2) Management Ideology Stressing Ideals

The second difference is the high degree to which corporate ideologies are formalized within U.S. companies. Their management ideologies are put into increasingly concrete form at successively lower levels of the organization. IBM is one of the companies actually pursuing a management ideology close to its corporate ideal.

Most striking at **IBM** is the extent to which its ideologies, for example of "problem solving" or "IBM means service" are thought through to final standards of behavior (see Table 4-2). For example, to solve problems or provide service, it is necessary for each individual to "think" -- doing so is a standard of behavior. The "Zeeland wild duck spirit" is emphasized. Drawn from a story by Kierkegaard, the point is that men, like the "wild ducks of Zeeland," can be debilitated by others' compassionate and good-intentioned but misguided efforts. IBM does not want its employees to hinder others' development -- the demand is for ducks able to fly on their own.

Table 4-2   A Hierarchy of IBM's Management Philosophy

Definition of Domain

"IBM means service" (service: Problem solving aid)

Principles for Operating in the Domain

(1) Respect for the Individual
- Help each employee to develop his potential and make the best use of his abilities.
- Pay and promote on merit.
- Maintain two-way communications between manager and employee, with opportunity for a fair hearing and equitable settlement of disagreements.

(2) Service to the Customer
- Know our customers' needs, and help them anticipate future needs.
- Help customers use our products and services in the best way possible.
- Provide superior equipment maintenance and supporting services.

(3) Excellence Must Be a Way of Life
- Lead in new developments.
- Be aware of advances made by others, better them where we can, or be willing adopt them whenever they fit our needs.
- Produce quality products of the most advanced design and at the lowest possible cost.

In addition, there are four more commonly cited company principles.

Behavioral Norms for Operationalizing the Principles

"Think"
"Zeeland wild duck"
"Business Conduct Guidelines"

Such IBM management ideologies have been translated into concrete standards of behavior in the company's "Management Briefing Letters" and "Business Conduct Guidelines." The Business Conduct Guidelines, for example, give detailed discusssion on fair competition, avoiding ostentation, yet-to-be announced products, delivery according to orders received, discriminatory treatment, orders landed, and on the sales activities of competitors. So, much explicit attention is given to the individual's behavior, and concern for the individual is also strongly reflected by educational programs, an open door policy, the "speak-up program," A&C (appraisal and counseling) program and in several other concrete ways.

At **Texas Instruments,** the key concepts of productivity and market share have been made the bases of a model of productivity improvement. This model illustrates the cornerstone of management strategy at TI -- the requirement of continuously improving productivity. But the model shows that to boost productivity, both the "people effective index" and the vertical "asset effective index" must be raised. The latter expresses how many times greater net sales are than total personnel spending. With improved productivity comes reduced costs, expanded market shares, increased net sales and profits, as well as greater employee-allotted profits.

The IBM and TI examples have been cited to illustrate the very logical way in which corporate ideologies have been made operational in the form of guidelines for corporate activity. They offer a sharp contrast to the way in which ideology is manifested in Japanese firms -- the topic of the following section.

(3) Implanting Management Ideology

In Japanese companies, the degree to which management ideology is formalized is relatively very low. While broad directions for the organization are indicated, much freedom of interpretation is allowed with regard to specifics. For example, although "Citizen Industry," "Lifestyle Culture Industry," "C&C" and other ideological themes all express strategic directions for their organizations, the specifics of how the

organization might fulfill its role within the "Citizen Industry," for
example, are explored (at great length) by each separate work group. The
generality of the ideology's guiding concept allows interpretation and
implementation to be adapted to the conditions facing the firm.

Moreover, rather than instilling management ideology in a top-down,
clearly articulated and formalized way, in Japanese companies the founder
or successor who would restore vitality to the firm uses lectures,
discussions and other interaction with employees to personally spread his
ideology throughout the company. Naozaburo Takao, former vice president
of Hitachi who was responsible for helping to inculcate the ideology of
Hitachi founder Namihei Odaira, utilized any and all opportunities for
lectures or other discourse to communicate "the Hitachi spirit."
Naozaburo offered the following:

> To this day, no one has really attempted a commentary on the
> Hitachi spirit. This spirit is not watered down with awkward
> logic or interpretation. It is communicated simply, almost
> within the context of prophecy, like the riddles of the Rinzai
> Sect of Zen Buddhism. However, this alone now presents
> difficulties in dealing with the large numbers of young employees
> educated in recent years. For example, if the story itself does
> not penetrate to the heart of the person, there must be some sort
> of focus to serve as a clue to the riddle. As the major elements
> of the Hitachi spirit, I suggested "harmony, sincerity, and the
> pioneer spirit." The essence of the Hitachi spirit is something
> which cannot be explained, with any serious attempt to actually
> define it doomed to failure. Harmony, sincerity, and the pioneer
> spirit do not exist like elementary particles within an atomic
> nucleus -- this is a relationship which cannot be broken down
> into separate elements. Other vital elements are also a part of
> the relationship, but words cannot be found to express them in a
> suitable manner. At Hitachi, there are many employees who have
> experienced the Hitachi spirit and who embody this Hitachi
> spirit. They are thinkers with a philosophical, poetic fiber.
> It is my earnest desire that these people strive to express the
> Hitachi spirit in practical, philosophical and poetic
> activities."[19]

"Corporate culture" is the consequence of those processes which are
derived from and take concrete form from a management ideology. It takes
strong men to willing express an ideology, to organize systems consistent
with the ideology, and to carry out the daily activities and rituals which
support it. Corporate culture embodies the values of the organization
which give its members a sense of identity and sets their behavioral

norms. It may also be considered a paradigm which serves to reinforce and justify the organization's values, standards and systems.

It was discovered by McKinsey & Company (Peters and Waterman, 1982)[20] that one characteristic of high-performing U.S. companies is "emphasizing those values that are the key to business."   Such corporate values are enthusiastically pursued up through the CEO to the point of faith. For example, Thomas Watson, the proponent of "IBM means Service," continued lecturing to his staff on how to make customer calls right up to his retirement.   While he was in Dallas, TI's former chairman, Patrick Hagerty, who stressed "innovation" as the company's key concept, made it a practice to stop at the company's R&D center every day on his way home. An expression of the Hitachi spirit is exhaustive discussion without vertical or horizontal discrimination, with all members showing commitment once a direction is agreed upon.   This process has been followed faithfully since the days of Hitachi's founder.   The result of this process is said to be a *samurai*-like company atmosphere, marked by acceptance, expectations of pushing through the just argument, eliminating resentful emotions after discussions are over, making the approval of their peers necessary for the advancement of those who are adept at argument, and other such supporting customs.

President Yoshio Maruta of Kao Corp. argues that for a management philosophy to thoroughly infuse an organization's ranks, all of its members must have access to the same information. To make such access a reality, he encourages the use of computer terminals by all, early morning meetings, interaction between managers and employees while dining, an open-door policy, small-group activities, and other procedures which have been mentioned before.   TDK's chairman, Sono, often strolls through his company's halls, walking into any room at will, and sitting down to discuss company policy with the employees present.

It is in these and many other ways that Japanese and Western top managers, but especially the former, "implant" their ideologies and, in so doing, lay the foundation for the corporate cultures of their firms.

(4) Corporate Culture -- Its Manifestation and Results

A corporation's culture can contribute to (or hinder) adaptation for several reasons. Because it is based upon and reinforces common values which give the organization's members a sense of identity and shared norms of behavior, the corporate culture provides the basis for (1) common decision-making standards to be applied, especially when there are no clear-cut alternatives, (2) resolving conflicts within the organization, and (3) high motivation.

However, corporate cultures may, with an organization's maturity, become constrictive, and even lose their relevance if the values upon which the culture is based become inconsistent with those values that underlie changes in product demand, market structure, societal concerns, etc. That is, a case can be made that corporate cultures, too, must be able to change. Failure to do so will deter organizational adaptation. The following example illustrates a positive contribution to organizational adaptation, hence, growth.

The **3M** management ideology of "People with initiative" and "Make a little, sell a little, make a little more" reflects the company's proven policy of taking a chance on the development of any product with good profit potential. Unlike most large companies, 3M resembles a conglomerate of unrelated research facilities. The origin of 3M's inventive drive dates back to the founding of the company, when the only product manufactured was low profitability sandpaper. For survival, the company had a need to develop new high value-added products. 3M's chairman, Lou Lair, has noted: "When our salesmen visited a client they didn't stop with the office personnel. They went around back into the plants to talk with the workers there. The idea was to find out directly if there was anything necessary which was not being produced by other companies." This concept has since been embodied in one of the company's performance evaluation standards: "25 percent of net sales should come from new products."

The approach, "make a little, sell a little, make a little more," would appear to have little relevance to the usually costly introduction of new products on the consumer goods mass market. 3M does not have a large budget for consumer-directed advertising. The great majority of 3M's consumer goods, in fact, stems from industrial-use products, with the net sales share of consumer-oriented goods being less than 10 percent of total net sales. The company has gotten used to dealing with users possessing professional knowledge of products, and packages often do not have detailed explanations geared for the general consumer. On the negative side, extensive technical nomenclature, a carry-over from industrial business, is also in evidence elsewhere. The company has produced several consumer goods, but often according to Lair, "the package designs varied, making it difficult to tell at a glance that they were even made by the same company." The company's timing has also sometimes been poor. An example being the development of a product to compete with Johnson & Johnson's "BAND-AID" well over a decade after the predecessor was marketed. This was the result of the company's distaste for coming out with imitations and its concerted efforts to develop a version of higher quality. Nevertheless, the result of 3M's approach has been the introduction of over 300 types of new products in just over the past two years.

The management ideology of **Texas Instruments** is "Innovation, Productivity, Share," a theme reflected in the company's spirit of innovation and its low-pricing strategy. More specifically, TI first conducts extensive R&D, then at the product introduction stage, prices the product close to cost in order to market in volume. As the cost gradually comes down with increased production experience, the profit margin widens. This is described by the "experience curve theory."

The approach has yielded amazing results. For example, in 1977 TI marketed a digital watch costing only $19.95, startling its competitors. The success of this new development made possible by technological innovation, however, was plagued by a blind spot in marketing. The company was late in recognizing the shift in consumer demand for liquid crystal digital watches and lost market share. And in the case of calculators, TI overlooked the growing demand for models with alarm clocks, radios, elegant style and other "plus alpha" elements, opening the door for penetration by competitors. Jim Schneider, editor of Merchandising magazine, has summed-up:

TI seems to have neglected the bulk of the calculator market,
which is all fashion. At the last consumer electronics show in
Chicago, Casio Computer, Sharp, and Canon all showed about
fifteen new models with lots of functions. TI showed just two
and they were nothing new.[21]

And because of problems in the digital watch market, TI eventually fell
behind Citizen and Seiko in this field as well.

Alfred Sloan of GM operated under a product strategy of "cars to meet all
budgets, all objectives," and established a divisional organization with a
balance between centralized policy-making and decentralization of
authority in production. Sloan sought the balancing factor for
decentralization in finance:

> It was on th financial side that the last necessary key to
> decentralization with co-ordinated control was found. That key,
> in principle, was the concept that, if we had the means to review
> and judge the effectiveness of operations, we could safely leave
> the prosecution of those operations to the men in charge of
> them. The means as it turned out was a method of financial
> control which converted the broad principle of return on
> investment into one of the important working instruments for
> measuring the operations of the divisions... General Motors is
> not the appropriate organization for purely intuitive executives,
> but it provides a favorable environment for capable and rational
> men.[22]

The successful balance between centralized management and division
autonomy was not limited to Sloan's tenure or his financial orientation;
it was also achieved under managers with superb insight in marketing,
personnel and other fields. In time, however, the post of chairman came
to be dominated by men with financial backgrounds (an exception was James
M. Roach), who placed powerful financial staff not only in the corporate
office but, also, in the individual divisions. The corporation's
orientation became a heavily financial one, making it difficult for its
divisions to pursue a strategy of innovative development in anticipation
of changing market needs. This is said to be one of the reasons why GM
was slow in reacting to the shift in consumer demand for smaller cars.

The same kind of dysfunctional consequence of organizational culture may
be seen in Japanese examples: Hitachi is one. A company which began as a

maker of production materials, Hitachi's profit center was the plant. The individual plants grew conservative in reaction to a strict in-house accounting system. This created delays in product development, and Hitachi is pointed out as a company which has introduced many imitations in the consumer product field. While it is difficult to attribute this outcome solely to matters of corporate culture, it seems plausible that Hitachi failed to make vital matters of system control consistent with its ideology of "harmony, sincerity, and the pioneering spirit."

Several examples can be cited to show how management ideologies are manifested in the corporate strategies of Japanese companies. From Seibu, we find for instance: "The common desire of our group is to respond to the demands of people seeking a peaceful, human lifestyle. We refer to businesses which seek to satisfy this demand the 'Citizen Industry.' This is the fundamental ideology behind our corporate effort." The "Citizen Industry" concept is reflected in the specialized shop strategy of the Seibu Department Store. NEC's "C&C" (Computers and Communications) is also operationalized in its organizational structure, through the corporation's C&C System Research Center, C&C System Headquarters and other facilities which are devoted to "interdisciplinary" computers and communications matters. TDK's "Creativity," an ideology stressing the human element, can be seen in the company's Personnel Education Department, sustained three-year self-management system, frequent adding or dropping of organizations to benefit its employees, and other efforts.

Another example is the "Give it a try" Suntory spirit: "All Suntory executives say the same thing -- that although the company has suffered substantial losses from using this approach, it has helped mold solid executives. They all have experience, and records of 'dishonorable injuries' which have not injured their honor."[23] The Suntory spirit is reflected variously in its personnel systems which are tolerant of such practices. In this case, management ideology is embodied in a more participative, risk-taking mode.

As an American example, among P&G ideologies are "Honesty, integrity, fairness and a respect and concern for others," and "P&G and its employees have an inseparability of interests." Back in 1919, the company staked its future to the fulfillment of this ideology by introducing a new distribution mechanism which did away with wholesalers. The theory was that traditional dependence upon wholesalers made it impossible to control production schedules, and that choosing instead to directly supply retail outlets would result in optimum production and stabilize employment. P&G overcame the fierce resistance of its wholesalers, and in 1923 proclaimed that it had realized America's very first stable employment system. This ranks as a classic example of tenacious and persistent pursuit of management ideology.

These samples demonstrate the importance that companies both in America and Japan attach to management ideology. But there appear to be national differences in how thoroughly the ideologies are articulated, how they are operationalized, and the extent to which they become a part of the corporate culture as a result. The management ideology of Japanese companies tends to focus more on the relationships and behavior of their members, and is less thoroughly articulated but, because of it, is more flexibly interpreted and applied at the work site. A consequence of "Citizen Industry," "Lifestyle Culture Industry" and "C&C," for example, is that members of the organization are able to pursue their own research and draw their own conclusions about the relevance of their work. In Hitachi's management ideology, as well, with its emphasis on behavioral standards, "harmony" may be construed as meaning that everyone should have their say, while "sincerity" can mean product reliability to the production division, honesty with the customer to the marketing division, and budget implementation to the plant manager.

In either the U.S. or Japanese case, a "mature" and inflexible corporate culture may inhibit environmental adaptation. But this might be more so in the more highly articulated and totally-integrated-system U.S. case than in the less well articulated, less specific Japanese case which permits greater freedom of interpretation and more autonomous application at the work site.

In the words of Namihei Odaira, founder of the company, "Hitachi is my thesis, my memorial." In a sense, corporate ideology is that which brings life to one's own values and theories. Surely, the impact of an ideology upon any organization's strategy, structure, and the behavior of its members, depends greatly upon the consistency of the values upon which the ideology is based with those values that are held by the people within the organization. They must "live" that ideology. Also important is the consistency with those values held by the people outside the organization, who are served by it.

4.9 Summary

The major implications of the two basic organizing orientations which were derived from the analysis of U.S. and Japanese firms can be summarized as follows :

1. While U.S. firms tend to design structures to fit their organizational strategies, Japanese firms tend to adopt more flexible structures which, while not designed for particular strategies, permit incremental and more autonomous adaptive behavior.
2. While U.S. firms achieve control through relatively refined, integrated systems that are hierarchy-dependent, Japanese firms depend more upon self-control made possible by the very thorough sharing of values and information which is facilitated by numerous formal and informal mechanisms that serve to integrate purpose and effort.
3. While U.S. firms actively pursue the development of professional knowledge and expertise among an elite of managerial and information specialists, Japanese firms promote learning through formal means throughout the firm, and through informal means that encourage interaction and the sharing of perceptions and information, both within and between groups.
4. While U.S. firms generate change by hierarchical means from the top-down in response to environmental demands and opportunities perceived at the top, Japanese firms rely on considerably greater member participation in the process of enactment -- sensing and defining environmental demands for change -- thus, making for greater variation within the firm, and evoking the motivation among individuals and groups to make the changes required.
5. While even very top management of U.S. firms are evaluated on the

basis of their performance, and their tenure is far from certain, Japanese top management positions are extremely secure. This contributes to organizational stability and makes it possible for the organization to pursue consistent, long-term policies.

6. While U.S. firms appear to base their decisions and policies more upon values that tend to be specific and differentiated according to hierarchical level, Japanese firms foster more general and comprehensively held values and norms. This seems to permit more flexible, autonomous interpretation of how those values and norms are to be operationalized, and more flexible behavior contingent upon the needs for adaptation.

The method of organizing more typical of the Japanese shall be called "group dynamics," while the typical American approach is called "bureaucratic dynamics." Their strengths and weaknesses will be discussed in the next chapter.

Notes

1. Chandler, A. D., Jr., *Strategy and Structure*, Cambridge Mass.: MIT Press 1962.
   Sloan, A. P., Jr., *My Years with General Motors*, New York: Doubleday 1963.

2. *Matsushita Denki Sangyo 50nen no ryakushi* (A Short History of Fifty Years of Matsushita Electric), Written in Japanese, 1978, pp.112-113.

3. *Zaikai* (Financial World), Temporary Edition, Oct. 10, 1981.

4. Haruki, K., *Kenko no mirai o hiraku* (Exploring the Future of Health), Written in Japanese, Tokyo: Nippon Kogyo Shimbunsha, 1971, pp.247-248.

5. Weick, K. *The Social Psychology of Organizing*, *2nd ed.*, Reading, Mass.: Addison Wesley, 1979.

6. Schisgall, O., *Eyes on Tomorrow*, New York: Doubleday, 1981, p.163.

7. Maruta, Y., *Zoku waga jinseikan waga keieikan* (My Management Philosophy, Part II), Written in Japanese, Tokyo: Kao Corp. Public Relations Department, 1981, pp.98-99.

8. Tahara, S., *Ishoku sogyosha no hasso* (Ways of Thinking of Distinctive Entrepreneurs), Written in Japanese, Kyoto: PHP Institute, 1980, pp.46-47.

9. Takamiya, M., *Yoropa ni okeru nihon no takokusekikigyo* (Japanese Multinational Enterprises in Europe) in *Takokusekikigyo to keiei no kokusaihikaku* (International Comparison of Multinational Enterprises and Management), Written in Japanese, ed. by Susumu Takamiya, Tokyo: Dobunkan, 1981.

10. Nonaka, I., *"Katsuryoku no genten -- Nippon no kacho* (Source of Vitality -- Middle Management in Japanese Companies)," *Toyokeizai (The Oriental Economist)*, Feb. 9, 1983, pp.24-31.

11. Nonaka, I. and S. Yonekura, *Innovation through Group Dynamics: JK Activity as Organizational Learning*, Written in Japanese, Discussion Paper, No.107, Institute of Business Research, Hitotsubashi University, Dec. 1982.

12. *Ekonomisuto* (Economist), April 10, 1981, p.2.

13. *Asahi Journal*, June 2, 1978, p.83.

14. Okumura, A., *Nihon no toppu manejimento* (Japanese Top Management), Written in Japanese, Tokyo: Daiamondosha, 1982.

15. Beer, S., *Brain of the Firm, 2nd ed.*, London: John Wiley, 1981.

16. Miyamoto, A., *TDK no koshueki senryaku* (The TDK High Earnings Strategy), Written in Japanese, Tokyo: Sangyo Noritsu University Press, 1983, p.43.

17. *Will*, Nov. 1982, p.122.

18. Brown, W. and K. Montamedi, "Transition at the Top", *California Management Review*, 20-2, 1977, pp.67-73.

19. *Hitachi to sono hitobito* (Hitachi and Its People), Written in Japanese, Privately Printed Edition, pp.226-228.

20. Peters, T. J. and R. H. Waterman, Jr., *In Search of Excellence*, New York: Harper & Row, 1982.

21. Uttal, B., "Texas Instruments Wrestles with the Consumer Market," *Fortune*, Dec. 3, 1979, pp.50-57.

22. Sloan, A. P., Jr., *My Years with General Motors*, New York: Doubleday, 1963, p.140, p.433.

23. Nawa, T., *Santorii* (Suntory), Written in Japanese, Tokyo: Asahi Sonorama, 1980, pp.141-142.

CHAPTER 5 SUMMARY OF QUALITATIVE FINDINGS

A qualitative comparison of American and Japanese major corporations has been presented in the preceding chapters. The qualitative analysis has confirmed and enabled us to understand the differences and similarities between U.S. and Japanese firms which the data of Chapter 2 suggested. The qualitative approach has also allowed us to see the reasons for those differences and similarities in a way which a purely statistical analysis would not have permitted. A summary is presented in this chapter of the major findings so far.

5.1 Differences in Strategy between U.S. and Japanese Companies

Differences in the strategy orientations of U.S. and Japanese companies may be summarized as follows:

a. U.S. companies tend to define relatively specific market domains, while Japanese companies communicate a sense of direction to their employees but one of such breadth that it allows great freedom of interpretation.

b. U.S companies begin active resource development only after considerable analysis of environmental opportunities and risks, while Japanese companies place much greater importance on the continuous accumulation and development of in-house resources which will enable the company to cope favorably with any type of environmental condition.

c. U.S. companies base their resource development decisions primarily upon financial considerations, while Japanese companies stress human resources, learning, accumulated expertise, and activation. The former emphasis tends to be more oriented toward short-term achievement, the latter toward long-term survival.

d. U.S. companies will generally shoulder risks on their own, while Japanese companies will reduce that risk through extensive networks of organizational relationships.

e. U.S. companies strive to establish competitive superiority in a logical, deductive fashion, seeking this superiority through product strategies, while Japanese companies pursue an inductive, incremental

approach, seeking their competitive superiority through production
operations strategies.

These differences are deep and complementary. Companies which conduct
detailed analyses of environmental opportunities and risks and implement
active resource deployment programs, place more emphasis on financial
resources and define their domains more specifically. It is probably
necessary for these companies to be more deductive and logical in
establishing competitive superiority within well-defined business sectors,
and to forecast earnings in those sectors with more precision. The
strategy orientation described in these terms is, on the whole, more
typical of U.S. than Japanese firms. They are said to have a *product
strategy orientation.*

On the other hand, companies which strive to establish competitive
superiority through inductive, incremental means adopt a more inward-
directed than market-specific domain definition, with a large degree of
freedom in making "final" market choices. They, of necessity, emphasize
resource accumulation, keying on experience accumulated through past
operations, and seek to activate learning and contribution at every level
of the company. Such human resource-based development is deemed essential
for long-term survival. The orientation described in these terms is more
typical of Japanese than U.S. firms. They are said to have an *operations
strategy orientation.* The two orientations just described -- product
versus operations -- define the first major dimension of our theoretical
framework of organizational adaptation.

5.2 Key Factors Responsible for U.S. - Japanese Differences

Just what is responsible for this difference in strategy orientation
between the U.S. and Japan? In addition to obvious cultural factors
behind management in the two nations, we believe that the following
considerations deserve close attention.

a. The difference in the pressures for short-term earnings, including
   those imposed by the financial markets and the threat of takeover.

b. The difference in labor market mobility/expectations of "lifetime"
employment.

d. Differences in organizational structure.

Let us take a more detailed look at each of these factors.

5.2.1 Concern with Short-Term Earnings

The emphasis on financial criteria for resource development decisions so
prominent in U.S. product-oriented strategies bears a close relationship
to the pressure for short-term earnings imposed by the financial systems
of that nation.   As seen in Chapter 2, U.S. managers are extremely
sensitive about short-term results that have a bearing on shareholder
profits, whether it be stock price, the profit gained on each share,
dividends or whatever.

An examination of company dividends shows how much importance U.S.
companies attach to the distribution of profits to stockholders.   A
comparison of the earnings per share and dividends declared by Hitachi and
GE, two companies with similar corporate performance, reveals the
following:

(a) GE revises its dividends more frequently than Hitachi.

(b) While GE strives to hold dividend propensity (the percentage of net
profits paid out as dividends) to the 40 to 50 percent level, Hitachi
keeps a constant dividend per share (5 to 7 yen).

(c) From the period 1973 to 1980, both GE and Hitachi's per-share profits
have approximately doubled.   However, while GE has responded by paying
out close to double the dividend per share, Hitachi has only increased
its dividend per share by 6 to 7 yen.

This type of difference is seen among other U.S. and Japanese companies as
well.   Generally speaking, fluctuations in per-share profits are followed
relatively closely by changes in the dividends of U.S. firms.   In
comparison, the rate with which Japanese companies respond to such
fluctuations is lethargic.[1]

Words and actions also reveal the sensitivity of U.S. managers to the evaluations of the stock market. It is common for top management to evaluate the performance of their own company's stock. For example, chairman Wood of Lilly said in regard to recent developments related to Lilly's pharmaceuticals: "I feel that most investors are underestimating (their) latent power" (*Forbes*, February 15, 1982). Our interviews also revealed great top management preoccupation with stock prices. In contrast, the following quote is quite typical of the view of Japanese managers on stock prices:

> I don't really understand if our current stock price is cheap or not, but I do have a feeling that the level around 550 yen is just about right. Last November we conducted a public offering of 25 million shares, and I am happy to say that the price has subsequently risen above the offering price." (Yoshio Maruta, president of Kao Corporation, *Nikkei Sangyo Shimbun* January 19, 1982.)

One of the reasons for the difference in sensitivity between U.S. and Japanese executives is that the former must be cautious about the possibility of a takeover. An example of such an effort, was the attempted takeover of Conoco by a Canadian conglomerate, Seagram. Conoco was the ninth largest oil company in America, with net sales of $18.8 billion. There are only three companies with higher net sales in our sample: GM, GE and IBM, showing that even very large companies can be vulnerable to takeover.

A Motorola executive responded in our interview: "This is a world in which takeovers can occur quite easily, and so there is a need to raise stock prices. This in turn makes it necessary to boost performance above the normal level. Everyone is real jumpy about stock prices, and there is constant monitoring of who is purchasing the stock."

The U.S. stock market is generally said to be sensitive to quarterly reported short-term earnings. Louis Randborg, former chairman of the Bank of America, offered the following comment: "If a company's quarterly earnings are down from the same period of the previous year, there will not be that much impact on stock prices. However, if that slump continues through the next quarter (not one year) the prime shareholders will begin to sell. Naturally, this will cause the stock price to drop."[2]

Accordingly, in order to discourage takeover, steadily raising earnings on a quarterly basis is seen to be essential. The stressful result is a preoccupation with per-share profits, dividends, and other short-term measures of performance. The sensitivity toward stock prices and concomitant emphasis on short-term performance are attributable not only to the threat of takeover. Both are also encouraged by bonus systems, stock option plans, and intra-company control systems.

In Japan, the stock option arrangement has not been broadly adopted, and with a high percentage of stable shareholders and government restrictions on ownership by foreign investors, there is much less threat of a takeover than in the United States. There are, to be sure, cases in Japan like the Amada Company, in which a firm with slumping management has been taken over. Amada's friendly takeover though, was not conducted through stock purchases but through the infusion of new personnel, and new share ownership did not reach a majority. Among the companies in our sample, Suntory's pure takeover of TBS Britannica by purchasing a controlling interest in Britannica shares was a rare exception.

The conditions that force managers to be sensitive to stock prices and the short-term earnings which have a decisive impact upon those prices bring various problems to U.S. companies. Former Bank of America chairman, Randborg, observed: "In America it is said that upper corporate management is constantly placing the focus solely on the pursuit of short-term profits, but this is certainly not limited to them alone. More fundamental is the trend among current-day stock investors to emphasize short-term transactions; company managers are turned into prisoners of this practice. The fact that managers do often prefer to become such prisoners is nothing more than their attempt to protect their own interests. Without a marked increase in the support received from boards of directors, it will be difficult to break free from these shackles and survive."[3] It seems clear that when managers lack a clear long-term philosophy, they tend to establish extremely short-sighted business objectives.

This certainly does not mean that all U.S. companies are short-sighted. To the contrary, most of the U.S. companies investigated here have clearly defined long-term plans and strategies surpassing those of their Japanese counterparts. A problem can occur, however, just from the use of a planning system, if short-term performance evaluation is stressed. When each division must focus on attaining a certain level of earnings within a fixed budget set at the corporate level, it is all too easy to shift funds from projects with long-term paybacks to shorter-term ones. Summed across all divisions, the corporation ends up allocating too little money on long-term strategies, inhibiting long-term adaptation. Japanese corporations tend to lack sophisticated planning systems. Managers do not have to carefully justify all expenditures and as a result are freer to allocate monies to projects with less certain and/or longer-term paybacks.

The buying and selling of control rights on the stock market -- one cause of the pressure to accrue short-term profits -- also has the reverse consequence of facilitating active resource deployment. As we have seen, when it is possible to buy or sell corporate control, there is no shortage of attempts to diversify businesses through the purchase of existing companies rather than bear the burden and risk of in-house development. Motorola's reorganization and the move by U.S. Steel to become a conglomerate are good examples. In Japan's economy, where the buying and selling of corporate control is difficult, whether efficient or not, companies seek development and growth from within.

5.2.2 Labor Market Characteristics

The second cause of the difference in U.S. and Japanese strategy orientation emanates from characteristics of their respective labor markets. The Japanese-style operations oriented strategy, which places such emphasis upon activating human resources, does so because of the obstacles to recruiting outside experts and the custom of single-company, long-term employment within the Japanese labor market. Under these conditions, it is essential to constantly activate a company's employees and to equip them with general skills which will enable them to adapt to changes. In the United States, on the other hand, the ease of procuring managers and engineers with special expertise makes it entirely rational to adopt a strategy of growth through diversification (as in the Lilly's cosmetic case cited earlier), or a strategy of adapting to changes in the environment through lay-offs and re-employment (as in GM's case).

Activity within the labor market stands in direct relation to that in the capital market: strong pressures for change coming from the capital market create the need for increased mobility within the labor market.

In 1980, slumping sales forced GM into deficit, but GM still paid out dividends of $2.95 per share. In that period, however, the number of GM employees was reduced from the 797,000 in December 1979 to 746,000 at the end of 1980. This amounts to an 11 percent drop from GM's peak employment level in 1978. Although these layoffs differed from simple severance because they were accompanied by the right to return on a priority basis, it is easy to understand how such a move would deal a major blow to relations of trust within the company.

Extremely bad conditions in Japan will also lead to personnel reductions, but because of Japan's more lenient capital markets, it is possible to make labor adjustments in a less drastic fashion even in such cases.

In America as well, there are companies -- IBM, Lilly, P&G and HP to name just a few -- which establish non-layoff policies which make it clear that employees will not be released merely because of changing company circumstances. To maintain such a policy, however, it is necessary to keep performance levels high. Considering the pressure from the stock market, it can be said that U.S. managers must endure a considerable handicap in implementing such long-term employment policies.

5.2.3 World-wide Industry Leader or Follower?

The third reason for differences between the U.S. and Japanese strategy orientations is the fact that a great number of Japanese companies played follower to U.S. company leaders.

Generally, those companies which are leaders in their industries have become leaders by their superior use of resources to beget product innovation and establish market loyalties. In contrast, follower companies must search continually for a suitable niche, or else go all-out to raise production efficiency and establish a strategy of superiority in terms of cost advantage or reliability. Followers are given their product concept as such, with the product strategy of the leader naturally shaping the strategies of the followers as well. In the catch-up process, it is more advantageous for followers to concentrate management resources on the improvement of production technology than on product development. This is one reason why Japanese companies have pursued strategies which place emphasis on production operations and their incremental improvement.

The fourth reason for differences in U.S. and Japanese strategy orientations has to do with their methods of organizing. This topic will be covered at length in the latter part of this chapter.

Figure 5-1   Key Factors Responsible for the Differences in Strategy Orientation

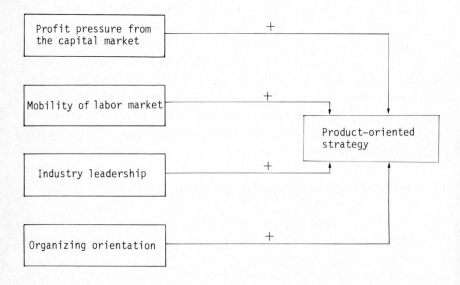

The preceding discussion is summarized in Figure 5-1. This figure depicts

not only the general differences between product (U.S.) and operations (Japanese) strategy orientations, but also helps to explain the differences in orientation between companies within the same nation.

5.3. Strengths and Weaknesses of the Product and Operations Strategy Orientations

The strategy orientations of U.S. and Japanese companies are consequences of their efforts to adapt to the general environmental conditions that they face. Neither approach can be said to be best; each has its own strengths, its own weaknesses.

The Japanese-style operations-oriented strategy seems to possess the following strengths:

a. The ability to adapt to continuing change in an incremental fashion, with minimally disruptive change within the organization, itself.

An operations-oriented strategy which enables such adaptation is most appropriate in an environment in which the demands for change are, themselves, changing in a continuous, not turbulent, way. Postwar Japan, by its own efforts and by borrowing from the West, has been achieving remarkable economic growth. The nation has been faced with the problems of growing and changing demands of a diverse nature. Continuous and detailed adjustments have had to be made to cope with the opportunities and threats wrought by such changes. The adaptation has been incremental, continuous, and successful.

b. The possibility of coordinating complex combinations of diverse and competing elements.

In the operations-oriented strategy, emphasis is placed on both the design of strategy and its implementation to ensure feedback from throughout the organization. With very timely and thorough feedback, a strategy requiring many and diverse responses can be pursued to meet the complex demands of changing organizational environments.

These strengths are ideal for refining existing ideas (as opposed to achieving major breakthroughs). This is why Japanese companies have been so successful at marketing new products during and even after the normal growth stage of the product life cycle for that product form. The successes of Japanese firms in the electric appliances, automobile, semiconductor and other sectors can be traced to this factor.

The weaknesses of the Japanese-style operations-oriented strategy are as follows:

a. Excess slack, inefficient accumulation of resources.

The operations-oriented strategy is geared to the long-term, but it does not create a scenario for long-term growth and, then, acquire and distribute resources to keep pace with that growth. Rather, it seeks to accumulate organizational slack throughout the company in anticipation of unforeseen changes. This, in turn, leads to inefficient resource allocation. Moreover, when such slack does not exist, the company with an operations-oriented strategy finds its ability to adapt to structural changes diminished.

b. Difficulty in adapting to rapid structural change.

Whether such slack is created intentionally or unintentionally, it is necessary that the speed of change be moderate. When structural changes occur rapidly or when there is insufficient organizational slack to adapt to such changes, operations-oriented strategies become less effective, especially in the face of major developments in competing industries. This is the predicament in which Japanese companies in the aluminum and petrochemical fields have found themselves.

c. A strategy of accumulating excess resources is more likely to result in carrying a large number of unprofitable divisions.

The resource development of operations-oriented strategies is progressive and cumulative, with particular consideration given to its impact on human resources. The not infrequent result is slow growth in resource development and profitability.

Other weaknesses of the operations-oriented strategy are:

d. Difficulty in responding to a high level of diversity.

e. Difficulty in making major breakthroughs and changes, because technological systems are so highly linked to existing organizational structures and processes.

The weaknesses described above are evident in product and market portfolios; as found in Chapter 2, Japanese companies tend to own more "question-mark" businesses (those facing high market growth rates but which have a considerable demand for capital) and they have more "dog" businesses (those tending to be unprofitable because of low market growth rates and competitiveness) than their U.S. counterparts. Having more "question marks," when viewed from the corporate level, shows an acutely high level of organizational slack. That is, Japanese companies tend to try to support many new businesses at the same time. Having more "dogs" results from incremental response to environmental changes. Precedence for abrupt redeployment of resources does not exist.

The product-oriented strategy shows an exactly opposite pattern of strengths and weaknesses. The strengths of the product-oriented strategy are as follows:

a. Because resource development is tied more closely to the (often shorter-range) market opportunities for specific product concepts, more efficient resource distribution is possible.
b. Giving less attention to the human consequences, rapid structural changes are made with major redistributions of resources.
c. Major breakthroughs appear more likely because technological systems are less intimately tied to organizational structure and processes.

Its weaknesses are:

a. Less ability of the organization as a whole to adapt to progressive but small changes in customer needs and competitive conditions, because less intense emphasis is given to the *evolution* of the operations and processes of the organization required under such circumstances.

b. Complacency borne of excessively pursuing originality in product concepts or competitive superiority at the expense of inattention to operations and people.

c. Vulnerability to penetration by small-scale niche seekers, when the organization fails to adapt to continuously evolving niches.

Because of these types of weaknesses, while product-oriented companies are more adept at making major breakthroughs, they are less skillful at refining the breakthrough to its absolute best. They will also find it difficult to enter markets such as Japan's, in which competition is carried on in such a complex and multi-faceted way. The operations-oriented firm, on the other hand, may be more adroit in continuously adapting to change but less capable of major breakthroughs.

5.4 Bureaucratic Dynamics versus Group Dynamics: Differences in Organizational Structure and Process

Drawing upon the quantitative description of Chapter 2 and the qualitative analysis of Chapters 3 and 4, two organizing principles have been identified upon which most U.S. and Japanese firms rely as their dominant means of achieving effective organization. The two organizing principles -- Bureaucratic Dyanmics and Group Dynamics -- can be briefly summarized as follows. Firms characterized as Bureaucratic Dynamic rely more heavily upon formal hierarchical authority relationships, clear specialization of functions, and standardized policies, rules, and plans than firms characterized as Group Dynamics. Bureaucratic dynamics tends to be a more descriptive organizing principle of the "average" U.S. firm as presented in Chapters 2 and 4.

In contrast, firms characterized as Group Dynamics rely less upon hierarchy, specialization, and standardized rules but much more upon the extensive exchange of information and sharing of values between individuals and relatively autonomous groups throughout the organization. The sharing and the exchanges are made possible by frequent interactions which largely ignore hierarchical and functional differences. Group dynamics tends to be a more descriptive organizing principle of the "average" Japanese firm described in Chapter 2.

Much is lost in any attempt to reduce complex phenomena to simple "opposites." Nevertheless, the proposed categorization is very useful when trying to gain insight into the strengths and weaknesses of each organizing principle. While not fully demonstrated in a statistical sense, the following strengths and weaknesses are generally supported by the experiences of the firms in this study.

5.4.1 Strengths and Weaknesses

The strengths of the bureaucratic dynamic organization are that:

a. The organization is likely to adapt easily to increases in the information and decision-making load (by means of increasing hierarchical levels or redefining authority relationships).
b. It is, because of accepted rules and routines, able to accumulate and preserve information (e.g., job knowledge, etc.) even when the incumbents are changed.
c. Because the "rules" are systematically integrated (in the form of policies, job descriptions, etc.), behavior is consistent and outcomes predictable.
d. Major changes in structure and processes of the organization can be carried out with relative ease because they tend to be initiated from the top of the hierarchy.
e. Major shifts in strategy and the deployment of strategic resources are facilitated for the same reason.

Bureaucratic dynamics has its limitations, however, viz: as the organizational hierarchy becomes "taller,":

a. Dependence upon hierarchical means for integration necessitates increasingly well-defined positions lower in the hierarchy to ensure predictability of performance (with the negative consequence of

limiting the decision-making opportunities possible for those at lower
levels, hence, diminishing their sense of involvement in their work).
b. Because management is farther removed from day-to-day operations while
   retaining centralized control, the cost of control (e.g. the amount of
   information necessary for it) becomes great, especially when there is
   much environmental change.
c. Information/decision-making burdens at top levels of the hierarchy
   become greater.
d. With relatively great emphasis upon hierarchical management direction,
   the integration of activities laterally often becomes less
   collaborative.
e. The mature bureaucratic dynamic firm is often subject to a number of
   "bureaucratic dysfunctions" such as departmental selfishness, striving
   for sub-optimal goals, mistaking the means as the goals themselves, and
   so on.   The multi-divisional structure mitigates some of these
   difficulties, but divisions, themselves, can be large hierarchical
   structures, and can suffer from the same problems.

The strengths of the group dynamic organization are as follows:

a. Relatively high levels of interaction within and between autonomous
   groups (often with little regard to functional and hierarchical
   differences) contribute to high degrees of involvement and commitment
   to organization-wide as well as group purposes.
b. Because of local control (by group and individuals) which follows from
   broad involvement and commitment, control is less costly.
c. The information/decision-making load borne by top management becomes
   less (much less at the very highest organizational levels).
d. Non-programmed, often "ambiguous" but strategically critical
   information (concerning for example, changing customer needs) is much
   more broadly shared, discussed, and thought about before joint
   decisions are made and acted upon (at best, this yields a smaller
   probability of error in uncertain situations and, at worst, greater
   acceptance of the consequences of error when one is made).
e. Such broad interaction and sharing of information necessarily
   contributes to learning and the accumulation of knowledge of directly
   job-related and broader issues.

f. There is more thorough integration of activities horizontally and vertically, making sub-optimization much less likely.

But group dynamics has its weaknesses, too:

a. The integration of purpose and effort does not automatically follow the announcement of a decision -- meaningful discussion must be facilitated and purposeful direction given.
b. When a great variety of incoming information is not filtered or in other ways reduced by hierarchical means, such reduction must be achieved by other means (this burden is borne primarily by the *"kacho"* of Japanese middle-management with its own attendant costs, some of which are addressed below).
c. Especially since the various parts of the organization are relatively autonomous, there can be misunderstandings, miscommunications, and conflicting decision-making.
d. Because information tends to reside in people's knowledge and expertise more so than in formal rules and policy, group dynamics can be more vulnerable to shifts in key personnel if expertise is not shared broadly enough.
e. The system, based upon the broad sharing of information through interaction, takes much time; changes in behavior, therefore, are slower.
f. Individual members of a group are often subject to strong pressures to conform for the sake of reaching consensus.
g. Finally, the quality of such democratically made decisions is apt to be only as good as the ability and congruence of purpose of those who make them. While the oft-cited "ringi system", of quasi-formal interpersonal networks and overlapping roles is intended to mitigate these problems, it can, indeed, be a part of them. The system is far from perfect.

While the strengths and weaknesses that we have described apply to "pure cases" of bureaucratic and group dynamics, the organizing principles were empirically found to be descriptive of the "average" large American and Japanese firm, respectively. The strengths and weaknesses cited, therefore, should be seriously considered by the managers of both cultures. The implications most central to the purpose of this book are as follows: Firms which rely heavily upon group dynamics as an *organizing principle* are probably better suited to making incremental changes in response to continuously changing environments. In contrast, firms which rely heavily upon bureaucratic dynamics as an organizing principle are probably more capable of making radical changes in response to drastically changing environments. Our data show that these differences typify the average U.S. and average Japanese firm, respectively. Drawing on the analysis in Chapters 3 and 4, we can also demonstrate that the strategies of U.S. and Japanese firms are consistent with their organizing principles and appropriate to the environments which they face.

5.4.2 Factors Determining Structure

Addressing the question of how these differences in organizing might have come about allows us to show the extent to which Chandler's dictum that structure follows strategy applies to Japanese firms.

Based on the findings, arguments can certainly be made for the complementarity of choice of strategy and organizing principle. Bureaucratic dynamics would seem better-suited to a product-oriented strategy geared toward careful analysis of the product environment and major, rapid replacement of resources dictated by changing environmental demands. Conversely, group dynamics seems better-suited to an operations-oriented strategy geared toward incremental, often autonomous, improvements in processes based upon the broad accumulation of knowledge at the operational level. Improvements are most often contributed by those closest to the operations. Such contributions require heightened sensitivity to new information and a commitment to better performance. Both are achieved by the group dynamic organization. Accordingly, bureaucratic dynamics is complementary to a product-oriented strategy and group dynamics is complementary to an operations-oriented strategy. Most often descriptive of U.S. and Japanese firms, respectively, the wisdom of the combinations seems to be demonstrated by the superior performance of our study's firms.

But antecedent to the complementarity of strategy and structure are more basic environmental factors. As was shown in the strategy chapter, pressures for short-term profit arising from the financial markets, mobility within the labor market, and an industry's position within its life cycle had much to do with differences in an organization's strategy orientation, whether product or operations-oriented. These factors almost certainly also have much to do with a firm's dominant organizing principle. For example, firms facing a very mobile labor market (as in the United States) are more apt to preserve routines in the form of rules and formal procedures rather than in the form of unwritten experience on the part of people who may very well leave the firm. Very broad sharing of sensitive information is clearly inappropriate in such cases and, so, there must be a greater dependence upon a formal structure for achieving integration.

Very thorough sharing of information is the basis for integration in group dynamics. But, heavily dependent upon personal interactions, the process of building "consensus" takes much time, and if we take immediate capital-market pressures as a necessary "given," perhaps the faster response of the bureaucratic dynamics model is more appropriate. With less pressure for short-range profitability and facing (or enacting) a more stable environment, slower-paced, incremental change is possible, and the group dynamics organizing model is quite appropriate.

Other factors contributing to the difference in organizing principle applied are size and diversity of the organization. Although size and diversity tend to grow together, in general, as either increases, the information processing load becomes greater for the organization as a whole. The problems of coordination and control become particularly acute at top-management levels for firms leaning more toward bureaucratic dynamics, and near-insurmountable in group-dynamic firms relying heavily for integration on middle-management and lower levels. In the one case, too little information flows upward for accurate decision-making, while in the other, the information redundancy prevents quick response. One implication of our findings is that highly bureaucratic dynamic firms in order to increase the quality of the information flowing internally, must encourage greater group dynamics within relatively autonomous divisions of their organization. And growing, diversified firms that are highly group-dynamic must rely more upon considerations of formal hierarchy, i.e., upon bureaucratic dynamics, to reduce the information load.

5.5 U.S. and Japanese Similarities and Intra-Country Differences

In the last two chapters, we compared the strategies and structures of major U.S. and Japanese firms. In doing so, we focused upon differences between them. Since our cases have been largely well-managed companies, however, it should come as no surprise that there are important similarities as well. They need to be discussed here. There are also important differences, between companies from the same country. These similarities and differences can be explained in terms of the components of our contingency model.

5.5.1 Similarities of Well-Managed Companies

Generally, well-managed companies have a high ability to adapt to changing demands in their environments, to the extent of even changing their domains to those with greater opportunities for growth. Such major changes have been necessary due to technological innovation, changing consumer preferences, increasing international competition, the maturing of industries, and many other reasons. Although the firms discussed here used different means for coping with such changes, most of them have usually adapted very successfully to changes. Some other firms have been less successful in their adaptation. Especially firms in mature industries with very heavy fixed investments have found it difficult to change their core technologies. The steel and auto industries of the United States offer the best such examples, but similar cases exist in Japan as well. Firms facing severe international competition and change in the structure of their industries have responded by diversifying (U.S. Steel) and by forming multinational ventures (GM and Toyota). Nevertheless, the firms that have exhibited the greatest adaptability are those which have, themselves, been versatile, and firms that have had core technologies capable of much future development. In fact, most of the high-performing companies have adapted to changing circumstances by selecting (enacting) environments, shifting their resources, and adapting their core technologies to more promising business fields. Notable examples in the electronics and computer-related field are IBM, Motorola, Hewlett-Packard, NEC, and Fujitsu.

Another similarity shared by the well-managed companies is that, while they were more flexible in their choice of domain than those that were less successful, they also accumulated the managerial, technological, and market know-how that led to distinctive competencies in their new fields. This accomplishment is directly related to their ability to "learn as organizations," what we have called organizational learning.

Organizational learning can occur in many forms, intentional and sometimes unintentional. It is also aided by recruiting personnel with special expertise from outside the firm. Whatever the mode of learning pursued, most of the firms in our cases accumulated knowledge and know-how rapidly and continuously. Examples include 3M, Hewlett-Packard, General Electric, Du Pont, and Eli Lilly in the United States, and Hitachi, NEC, Kyocera, Toray, and Takeda in Japan. These firms built their competitive advantages upon the aggressive accumulation of technological know-how.

Allocating resources for research and development is only one indication of commitment to organizational learning. A major portion of organizational learning occurs at the work site and in field sales. The competitive strengths of firms like Toyota, Matsushita Electric, and Komatsu were achieved, in great part, from the application of knowledge garnered in QC circles at the plant site. The wisdom of their sales forces were key competitive factors for Renown, Suntory, and Levi-Strauss.

The means by which organizations learn are in fact many and diverse. The joint venture in the Japanese market by General Foods and Ajino-moto was a means for General Foods to acquire knowledge about the Japanese market on the one hand and for Ajinomoto to acquire knowledge of more sophisticated marketing techniques on the other. Motorola has accumulated knowledge through frequent acquisitions and divestments. One of Renown's motives for diversifying into the food business was the revitalization stimulated by the added organizational learning required by such a move.

A third similarity of well-managed companies is their higher attention to people and, as a consequence, a greater sense of corporate culture. Knowledge ultimately resides in the people who comprise the organization. The excellent companies, whether American or Japanese, placed high emphasis upon intellectual resources and, because of it (although it was not the only motive for doing so), displayed strong concern for their people. The responses by the executives of IBM, Hewlett-Packard, 3M, Lilly, and Motorola reflected greater attention paid to their people than the average U.S firm. These firms are, consciously or unconsciously, facilitating the sharing and reinforcement of values. This is reflected in distinctive ways of thinking, languages, and behavior patterns which define the corporate culture. HP and 3M's strong orientations toward innovation are examples, as is Hitachi's "Spirit of the *Nobushi*." Matushita and Toyota's cultures are highly operations-oriented. GE's is oriented toward strategic planning. Dominant in Suntory's and Renown's cultures is marketing, and so on. The main theme of an organization's culture directly affects that organization's distinctive competence. On the negative side, overemphasis of a given theme or continued reliance upon a particular thrust when it is no longer appropriate, will be dysfunctional. Even among very successful cases, the dominant cultural orientations which have contributed so much to present or past successes may prove to be impediments to successful strategic choices and future progress.

The fourth similarity among our excellent firms is their ability to proactively shape their environments. The more successful firms in environments of very rapid technological change do not merely react effectively to changing market conditions wrought by the innovations of competitors but are, themselves, instrumental in creating new demand and, in other ways, changing the environment which is relevant for them. This shaping of the firm's environment requires variation within the organization (since it takes variety to reduce variety). 3M, HP, GE, Kyocera, and Toshiba are notable for their experimentation and the subsequent generation of change within their respective industries. Innovations in technology, marketing, and organization of firms like GM, 3M, HP, Kyocera, Toshiba, and (in the past) TI have made them leaders in newly created markets. As such, they have proactively defined the nature of the environments faced by their organizations.

5.5.2 Intra-Country Differences

It is important also to account for differences in the strategies and organization of firms which face the same cultural environment. If we can successfully explain those differences, then, the validity of our contingency model of organizational adaptation and the general strategy and organizing orientation framework which we have applied will be enhanced.

Recall from our earlier discussion that product-versus-operations orientation defines the strategy dimension of our framework, and that bureaucratic-versus-group dynamics defines the organizing dimension of the framework. To briefly summarize the pure types, firms with a product-oriented strategy place relatively great emphasis upon new product innovation as opposed to innovations in production processes. They are capable of redeploying strategic resources quickly in response to changing demands of the environment and, therefore, are able to adapt quickly to major environmental changes. On the other hand, firms with an operations-oriented strategy place greater emphasis upon production. They emphasize the continuous accumulation of knowledge related to production, often by inductive means. As a consequence, they adapt well in an incremental way to continuously (smoothly) changing environments.

Firms with a bureaucratic dynamic organizing orientation tend to rely heavily upon formal hierarchical authority relationships, standardized policies and rules, and detailed planning in order to achieve integration of organizational purpose and activity. Their activities are based upon an analytical orientation. Firms with a group dynamic organizing orientation rely more for such integration upon broad sharing of information and values made possible by very frequent interactions between organizational members across functional boundaries and hierarchical levels. The behavior of group dynamics oriented organizations is more experimental.

The foregoing descriptions are of pure types with combinations of the two

strategy orientations and two organizing orientations possible. The
complexities of real organizations defy their fitting the pure types
perfectly, of course, even for firms within a given country.
Nevertheless, the major differences among the firms studied here can be
depicted in terms of the dimensions of our framework. All of the firms
which have been the subject of our in-depth case studies are classified in
terms of their strategy and organizing orientations in Figure 5-2.

Figure 5-2 Dimensions of Stategies and Organization
            and Interfirm Differences

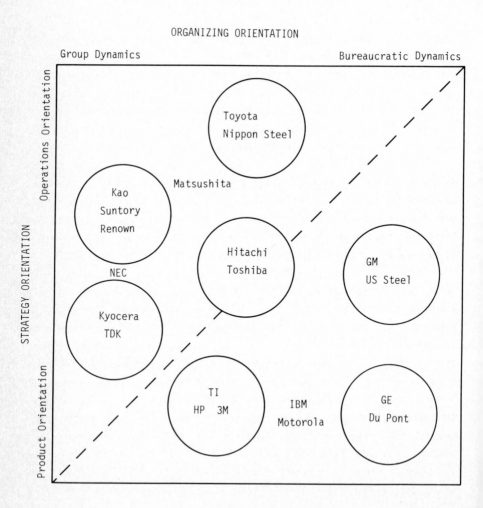

As the figure shows, there are substantial differences between firms which are highly adaptive and innovative such as 3M, HP, or TI and GM or U.S. Steel, in the United States. And the differences are as clear between the Japanese firms like Hitachi or Toshiba with their multi-product lines, and firms like Nippon Steel or Toyota which have highly integrated product lines.

From our earlier, detailed discussion, we know that highly diversified GE and Du Pont rely considerably upon hierarchical authority relationships and that they employ sophisticated systems for strategic planning. In our framework, both firms are strongly bureaucratic dynamic in their organizing orientation. At the same time, their histories reveal the ability to flexibly deploy resources and a product-based strategy; hence, they have a strong product strategy orientation.

In contrast, TI, 3M, and HP, while highly product-oriented along the strategy dimension are, unlike GE and Du Pont, relatively high in group dynamics along the organizing dimension.

GM and U.S. Steel (before its diversification) are strongly bureaucratic dynamic in organizing orientation and lean somewhat more toward operations-oriented than product-oriented strategies. We assign IBM and Motorola a strong product orientation in terms of strategy, and place them between 3M and GM in their organizing orientation.

Among the Japanese companies, Toyota and Nippon Steel place a higher emphasis on strategies concerned with production operations than with products, *per se*; hence, they rate high in the operations strategy orientation. Both firms also depart from the organizing orientation typical for most Japanese companies and can be considered relatively bureaucratic dynamic, although not so greatly as GM or U.S. Steel.

In contrast, Hitachi and Toshiba can both be judged to have a higher product strategy orientation, primarily because highly diversified and facing dynamic industries, they must effectively redeploy strategic resources among their businesses. We note, however, that both in terms of strategy and organizing orientations, Hitachi and Toshiba are about in the middle of our framework. They do not fit neatly into any category.

Consistent with our case discussions earlier, Kao, Renown, and Suntory have very strong group dynamics organizing orientations and strategies that are somewhat more operations than product-oriented.

Kyocera and TDK have a very high group dynamics organizing orientation and a high product strategy orientation.

Although Matsushita Electric had an even higher operations strategy orientation in its earlier years of rapid growth (probably as strong as those of Toyota et al.), Matsushita's strategy is shifting more toward a product-oriented one. It appears "well-balanced" along the group dynamics-bureaucratic dynamics organizing continuum and, so, we see Matsushita in between Hitachi and Toyota.

Finally, with a group dynamics organizing orientation and a somewhat more product than operations strategy orientation, NEC stands between Hitachi or Toshiba and Kyocera or TDK.

While the foregoing classifications represent our best judgment as outsiders (based upon the survey data and interview records reported here, and buttressed by published data about the firms), the classifications are, at best approximate. Nevertheless, they are consistent with and support the following important points:

(1) Highly diversified firms -- GM and Du Pont in the United States and Hitachi and Toshiba in Japan -- tend to be more dependent upon product strategies and bureaucratic organizing dynamics than other firms in their respective countries. Considering the strategy and organizing dimensions jointly, it can be said that these highly diversified firms depend more upon product strategies and bureaucratic dynamics than other firms in each country.
(2) Firms in high technology and innovation areas -- TI, HP, and 3M in the United States and TDK and Kyocera in Japan -- tend to emphasize product-oriented strategies and group dynamics.
(3) Firms in mature industries characterized by few technological break-

throughs -- U.S. Steel before it diversified and Nippon Steel before its implementation of jishu-kanri (JK) activities -- tend to emphasize strategies oriented more toward operations than other firms in their respective countries, and tend to place strong emphasis on bureaucratic dynamics as an organizing principle.

(4) A fourth point reiterating the between-country differences is brought home again by Figure 5-2. The U.S. firms form a cluster in the lower right part of Figure 5-2 while the Japanese firms tend to cluster in the upper-left. Our arguments in Chapters 3-6 addressed this difference. In short, U.S. firms tend, in general, to show greater dependence upon product-oriented strategies and bureaucratic dynamics, while Japanese firms tend to show grater dependence upon operations-oriented strategies and group dynamics.

The foregoing propositions will be tested in the next chapter, in which we will analyze the questionnaire data again.

Notes

1. This is not to say that Japanese companies are taking action contrary to the interests (profit) of the shareholders. For example, for GE investors who purchased stocks at the lowest price in 1974, in return for an initial $65.75 investment the top price in 1980 gave investors a capital gain (gains accompanying stock price increases) of seven dollars and dividend gains of $13.55 -- a total gain of $20.55. For GE the dividend gain percentage was higher than the capital gain -- accounting for 66 percent of the total. Uncompound annual return on investment was 5.2 percent. In the case of Hitachi, meanwhile, for a 127 yen/share purchase, investors reaped a 226 yen capital gain and a 36 yen dividend gain. In short, Hitachi's capital gains were far above the dividend gains -- 86 percent of the total. Uncompound annual return was 34.4 percent. These figures show that investors purchasing Hitachi stock certainly did not find it unprofitable. It should be said, rather, that there is a definite difference between the methods of compensation adopted by U.S. and Japanese companies. American firms tend to pay out short-term dividends, while Japanese firms shift the weight in favor of capital gains.

2. Shiro Ishiyama, *Nichi-bei keieisha no hasso* (Concepts of U.S. and Japanese Managers), Written in Japanese, Kyoto: PHP Institute, 1980, pp.329-30.

3. Shiro Ishiyama, *Ibid*, p.329.

CHAPTER 6   STATISTICAL COMPARISON OF STRATEGY, ORGANIZATION
AND PERFORMANCE:
CONVERGENCE TOWARD A MODEL OF ADAPTATION

The qualitative but in-depth comparisons of large American and Japanese corporations of the preceding two chapters revealed consistent differences in their strategies and organization.   This chapter analyzes the causes and effects of those differences using the questionnaire data from Chapter 2.[1]   The purposes are twofold.   The first aim is to assess the effects of strategy and organization upon corporate performance.   By comparing the high and low performers and analyzing the determinants of performance, the following questions are answered: What are the key factors of success in each country?   To what extent do they differ?   To what extent are they similar?   The second purpose is to further investigate the forces shaping strategies and organizations.   Here the relative strengths of various forces are statistically determined.   Taking corporate performance into account, practical implications of the fit between strategy and structure are drawn and a new theoretical perspective is suggested.

6.1 Measurement: A Multivariate Approach

The qualitative analyses of Chapters 3 and 4 identified two principal dimensions of organizations: their dominant strategic orientation -- whether operations or product oriented, and their dominant organizing principle -- whether dependent more on group or bureaucratic dynamics. These two dimensions will be correlated to other organizational characteristics; new indicators are defined for this purpose.

The first major dimension -- an operations vs. product orientation describes the dominant strategy orientation of the firm.   The operations-oriented strategy focuses upon continuous, incremental improvement of operations, production processes, and existing products, and it places much emphasis on accumulating intra-company capability and "know-how" for future contingencies.   The product-oriented strategy places greater emphasis upon new product development and diversification, relying heavily on the flexible deployment of resources -- e.g., diversification through acquisition and active divestiture of unprofitable businesses.

Table 6-1   Indicators of Strategic Orientation

Dimension and Indicators	Conceptual Definitions	Questionnaire Items
Mobile resource deployment (SRES)	The degree to which a company depends upon corporate-level, active resource allocation	Question 4 (item 6 + 12)*
Emphasis on synergy (SSYN)	The degree to which the relatedness in market and technology is stressed	Question 4 (7 + 14)
ROI emphasis (SROI)	The degree to which return on investment is stressed	Question 13-1 (1)
Product emphasis (SPRO)	The degree to which product strategies are emphasized more than production strategies	Question 5 (1 - 5)
Leadership in innovation (SINN)	The degree to which a company is a leader in product innovations rather than a follower	Question 4 (11 - 2)
Market-share emphasis (SSHA)	The degree to which high market-share is pursued in each product market	Question 13-1 (2) + Question 4 (1)

*   sum of standardized scores

The strategic orientation is described by the six indicators shown in Table 6-1.   The first three indicators primarily measure the characteristics of corporate-level strategic orientation: *mobile resource deployment, emphasis on synergy*, and *ROI emphasis*.   The other three measures are: *product emphasis* (vs. operations emphasis) of business-level competitive strategies, *leadership in innovation*, and *market-share emphasis.* High scores on *mobile resource deployment, product emphasis,* and *leadership in innovation* characterize a product orientation. A high *market-share emphasis* characterizes the operations orientation.

The second principal dimension -- group vs. bureaucratic dynamics -- describes the dominant organizing orientation of the firm. The group dynamics-oriented organization emphasizes an organic mode of management (decentralized, informal, and unsophisticated structures) which relies on shared values and information, frequent interaction, loosely-coupled groups, and actions which are emergent from the bottom, up. The bureaucratic dynamics organization relies on a mechanistic structure (centralized, formalized, and sophisticated structures), hierarchical coordination, and tightly-coupled units, and actions initiated from the top, down.

The dominant organizing mode is measured by the eight indicators shown in Table 6-2. High scores on the first two indicators, *structuring of organization* and *formalization*, characterize bureaucratic dynamics. High scores on the next three indicators, *sharing of values and information, institutionalization of values*, and *human resource emphasis*, characterize group dynamics. *Organizational tension* is an indicator describing some Japanese companies. Two indicators, *total amount of power*, and *relative power of finance and control* indicate the distribution of power within an organization. A high score on *total power* suggests that lower level managers have considerable influence upon strategic decision-making and that the organization's structure is decentralized; a relatively low emphasis upon bureaucratic dynamics as an organizing principle is indicated.

The two principal dimensions -- strategic orientation and organizing principle -- must be correlated to other components of the model: environment, organizational context, abilities required of executives, and corporate performance. The indicators of these constraints are operationally defined by the questionnaire items given in Table 6-3.

Table 6-2   Indicators of the Organizing Orientation

Dimension and Indicators	Conceptual Definitions	Questionnaire Items
Structuring of organization (OSTR)	The degree of sophistication and standardization of management systems	Question 7 (total score) + Question 9 (item 1)*
Formalization (OFOM)	The degree of formalization of organizational rules and procedures	Question 9 (1 - 9)
Sharing of values and information (OSHA)	The degree to which values and information are shared and people identify with the organization	Question 9 (4 + 11 + 20 +10)
Institutionalization of values (OPHI)	The degree to which values and beliefs are embedded in systems and strategies	Question 4 (18) + Question 9 (5 + 23)
Human resource emphasis (OHUM)	The degree to which long-term evaluations, personnel planning and job rotations are employed	Question 9 (2 + 29) + Question 4 (13)
Organizational tension (OTEN)	The degree to which internal competition and strict evaluations are applied	Question 9 (5 + 13 + 18 + 34)
Total power (OPTO)	The total amount of influence that the hierarchical levels have on strategic decisions	Sum of scores of question 10 - 1
Relative power of finance and control (OPFI)	The power of finance and control departments relative to line departments (production, sales and R & D)	Question 10 - 2 (1 + 2 + 3 / 4)

*   sum of standardized scores

Table 6-3   Indicators of Related Variables

Dimension and Indicators	Conceptual Definition	Questionnaire Items
ENVIRONMENT		
Environmental diversity (EDIV)	The diversity of products and markets	Question 1 (1 + 2 + 3)
Environmental variability (EVAR)	The rate of changes in technology and customers' needs	Question 1 (7 + 8)
Dependence on inter-organizational networks (ENET)	The degree to which inter-organizational relationships constrain intra-organizational decisions	Question 1 (10 + 11)
Mobility of skilled employees (EMOB)	The inter-company mobility of managers and engineers	Question 1 (14 + 15)
TECHNOLOGY AND SIZE		
Custom technology (ETJB)	The degree to which a company depends upon custom production technology	Question 3 (1)
Mass production (ETMA)	The degree to which a company depends upon mass production technology	Question 3 (4)
Continuous process (ETPR)	The degree to which a company depends upon continuous process technology	Question 3 (5)
Size (ELNS)	------------------------	log ($ sales)
ABILITIES OF EXECUTIVES		
General management skill (EJGE)	The degree to which general management, planning, leadership and integrative skills are required of senior executives	Question 12 (2 + 6 + 7 + 13)
Interpersonal skill (EJPE)	The degree to which interpersonal skills are required of senior executives	Question 12 (8 + 9 + 10)

Table 6-3 continued (Indicators of Related Variables)

Dimension and Indicators	Conceptual	Questionnaire Items
Entrepreneurial skill (EJEN)	The degree to which risk-taking, value commitments and innovative attitudes are required of senior executives	Question 12 (3 + 4 + 5)

PERFORMANCE

Dimension and Indicators	Conceptual	Questionnaire Items
Strategic position (PSTP)	The degree to which the strategic position of a company is improved	Question 13 - 2 (3 + 7 + 10)
Profitability (PPRO)	The degree to which profitability objectives are attained	Question 13 - 2 (4 + 5 + 12)
Growth (PGRO)	The degree to which growth objectives are attained	Question 13 - 2 (1 + 2)
Human performance (PHUM)	The degree to which the attitudes of employees are improved	Question 13 - 21 (3 + 14 + 16)
Strategic resources (PRES)	The degree to which the strategic (esp. information and knowledge related) resources are accumulated	Question 13 - 2 (8 + 9 + 10)
High-growth businesses (EGRO)	The proportion of sales in growing markets	Stars + question marks (question 2)
High-share businesses (ESHA)	the proportion of sales in the markets where a company has the largest or second largest market share	Stars + cash cows (question 2)

The organization's environment was measured by four indicators: *environmental diversity* and *variability, dependence on inter-organizational networks*, and *mobility of skilled employees*. Organizational context was measured by three indicators of production technologies (percentages of total output produced by custom, mass production, and continuous process technologies) and *organizational size*. The abilities required of executives were measured by three indicators, viz., *general management skill, interpersonal skill,* and *entrepreneurial skill.*

Corporate performance was measured by sixteen items in the questionnaire. Using these items, five separate indicators can be defined: *profitability, growth, improvement of strategic position, human performance,* and *stock of strategic resources.* The sum of responses to the sixteen items was also used as an indicator of *overall performance.*

Measures of the product-market portfolio of each company were also obtained through the questionnaire. The portfolio should be closely related to both strategy and performance. Two indicators described each portfolio's characteristics. One was the proportion of total sales accounted for by *high-growth businesses* (stars plus question marks) and the other was the proportion of total sales accounted for by *high market-share businesses* (cash cows plus stars).

The next two sections investigate some important effects of strategy and organization upon corporate performance.

6.2 Comparison between High and Low Performers

The surveyed companies are divided into two groups, high performers and low performers, using each country's mean overall performance score as the cut-off point.[2] The mean scores of various indicators are compared in Table 6-4. The table also shows the statistical significance of the inter-group differences in mean scores in three ways: inter-country, between high and low performers, and the interaction of the two categories. There are many significant inter-country differences. The following analysis focuses on the relative positions of the high performers and examines their differences and similarities.

Table 6-4 shows that American and Japanese high performers share several features, while having a few intriguing differences.

Table 6-4　Comparison of High and Low Performers

	USA Low	USA High	Japan Low	Japan High	Inter-country	Between performance groups	Inter-action effect
Environmental diversity	14.3	15.0	12.9	13.1	NS	***	NS
Environmental variety	7.4	8.5	8.4	8.9	***	***	NS
Interorganization networks	5.13	5.65	7.58	7.20	***	NS	*
Mobility of skilled employees	6.70	7.13	3.72	3.88	***	NS	NS
High-growth businesses	44.13	53.24	37.87	51.92	NS	***	NS
High-share businesses	60.92	71.16	55.12	62.80	**	***	NS
Custom technology	11.63	11.91	23.23	14.88	**	+	+
Mass production	19.56	20.20	22.90	23.67	NS	NS	NS
Continuous process	14.12	21.58	13.90	14.53	NS	NS	NS
Size	6.45	6.51	5.84	6.08	***	+	NS
Mobile resource deployment	7.31	7.67	5.65	5.57	***	NS	NS
Emphasis on synergy	7.14	7.53	7.40	7.22	NS	NS	+
ROI emphasis	2.40	2.43	1.24	1.13	***	NS	NS
Product emphasis	0.13	0.37	-0.38	0.21	+	*	NS
Leadership in innovation	0.32	1.38	0.62	1.22	NS	***	+
Market-share emphasis	4.28	4.70	4.63	5.33	*	***	NS
Structuring of organization	6.31	7.11	5.57	6.00	***	***	NS
Formalization	0.27	0.64	-0.12	0.57	NS	**	NS
Sharing of values and information	14.03	16.05	14.92	15.53	NS	***	***
Institutionalization of values	10.61	11.09	10.60	11.30	NS	*	NS ⸱
Human resource emphasis	8.22	9.00	9.53	10.02	***	***	NS
Organizational tension	12.36	12.71	12.40	12.75	NS	*	NS
Total power	3.20	3.19	3.69	3.75	***	NS	NS
Power of finance	0.39	0.37	0.31	0.29	***	*	NS
General management skill	15.83	16.60	16.56	16.34	+	NS	*
Interpersonal skill	11.82	12.15	12.20	11.94	NS	NS	+
Entrepreneurial skill	11.68	12.49	10.81	10.68	***	NS	*

$^+$p<0.10　　*p<0.05　　**p<0.01　　***p<0.001

6.2.1 A Higher Product Orientation

Table 6-4 shows that both U.S. and Japanese high performers have significantly higher scores for *leadership in innovation* and *product-emphasis* than their low-performing counterparts, when inter-country differences are controlled for. This indicates that high performers in both countries seek to be leaders in product innovation and to gain a competitive edge by relying on product differentiation. The low performers in both countries, on the other hand, tend to emphasize product innovation less and to place more emphasis on improving their production systems. The entrepreneurial strategy, "Take risks and be innovators" seems to be a good formula for success both in the United States and Japan.

In terms of the model's principal dimension of strategic orientation, the high performers are more "product-oriented" and low performers more "operations-oriented" in both countries. It had been concluded from prior quantitative analysis in Chapter 2 that Japanese companies are, on average, more "operations-oriented" than "product-oriented." The more extensive findings here, however, show that Japanese high performers are more "product-oriented" than both Japanese and American low performers.

6.2.2 A Higher Group Dynamics Orientation

Table 6-4 shows that high performers emphasize the importance of the *sharing of values and information* and the importance of *human resources* more than their low-performing counterparts, regardless of country. This statistically significant finding strongly suggests a relationship between the dominant mode of organizing (in our model) and performance. It is revealing that, while the group dynamics organizing orientation was more typical of Japanese firms *on the whole*, and the bureaucratic orientation was more typical of U.S. firms overall, the high-performing American firms scored even higher in *sharing values and information* and *human resource emphasis* than their Japanese counterparts.

This finding supports Ouchi's assertion (1981) that Z type organizations, which are characterized by long-term employment, slow promotion, and shared values and styles, outperform the A type (more typical of American) organizations. The reasons for their doing so will be discussed later.

Figure 6-1 (A)

Comparison of High and Low-Performing U.S. and Japanese Companies

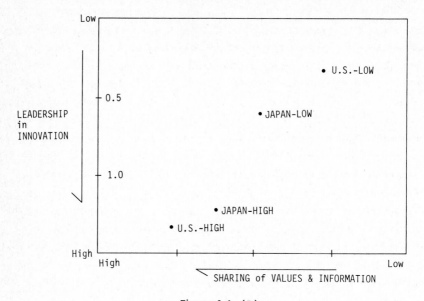

Figure 6-1 (B)

Comparison of High and Low-Performing U.S. and Japanese Companies

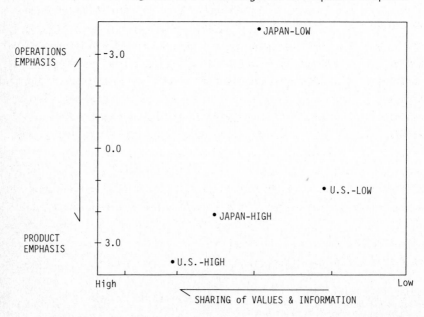

6.2.3   The Combination of Product-Oriented Strategy and Group Dynamics Organizing Orientation

In light of the two findings above, it can be hypothesized that the combination of a product orientation and group dynamics is associated with high performance both in the U.S. and Japan. The hypothesis is confirmed by Figure 6-1, where the mean scores of four groups of companies (the high and low performers in the U.S. and Japan) are plotted. In Figure 6-1 (A), we use *leadership in innovation* as the principal indicator of an "operations vs. product strategy orientation" (on the vertical axis) and *sharing of values and information* as the indicator of "group vs. bureaucratic organizing dynamics" (on the horizontal axis). Figure 6-1 (B) uses *product emphasis* as the principal indicator of strategic orientation.

In each country, the location of high performers is closest to the south-west corner. Among the companies in our sample, Kyocera and TDK in Japan, and Hewlett-Packard and 3M in the U.S. are located in that area (Figure 5-2). Although we are merely reporting our findings here, in-depth analyses of these companies show the logic of this high-performing combination.

The foregoing conclusion must be qualified in several ways. Table 6-4 shows that the high performers also have higher scores in *market-share emphasis* and *structuring of organization* than the low performers in both countries. *This* finding suggests that high performers are also more operations-oriented and bureaucratic dynamics-oriented. Thus the pure combination of group dynamics and product orientation is not sufficient to explain high performance. It is clear that a combination of different strategic and organizing orientations may be optimal. Exactly what conditions make a given combination of strategic and organizing orientations "best" is the topic of much of the rest of this chapter, and is the specific issue of our multi-variate analysis presented later.

6.2.4   Well-Balanced Product-Market Portfolios and a Variable Environment

Another similarity between the high performers of both countries is found

Chapter 6

in their product-market portfolios. Average product-market portfolios of high and low performers in the two countries are shown in Table 6-5.

Table 6-5   Product-Market Portfolios of High and Low Performers

	USA Low	USA High	JAPAN Low	JAPAN High
Stars	23.5 %	36.1 %	18.4 %	31.7 %
Question Marks	20.6	17.2	19.5	20.3
Cash Cows	37.4	35.1	36.7	31.1
Dogs	18.5	11.7	25.4	17.0

The data clearly show that both countries' high performers have more *stars* and fewer *dogs* than the low performers. The product-market portfolio matrix might yet be a valid predictor of corporate performance in spite of criticism of it (Hamermesh, 1979; Kiechel, 1981).

The last similarity observed is in regard to environment. The high performers of both countries face a more variable environment than the low performers. A likely reason may be that variable environments, in which technologies and customers' needs change rapidly, offer greater opportunities for growth and profit than more stable environments. The important implication of this finding, together with the findings concerning product portfolios, is that what business to be in is no less important a decision than what strategy to use in managing it.

6.2.5 Visible vs. "Invisible" Leadership

The most emphatic difference between the U.S. and Japanese high performers lies in the ability required of their executives. As shown in Table 6-4, American high performers require a higher level of ability of senior executives, especially in terms of entrepreneurial skill, than the low performers. The relationship is surprisingly strictly inverse in Japan, where the high performers seem less dependent on able top management, and strong, visible senior executives appear to be more characteristic of low performers. This finding suggests that U.S. senior executives play more prominent decision-making roles and are more directly responsible for corporate performance than Japanese senior executives. Their roles might be more important in American than in Japanese organizations. This requires some explanation.

As suggested in Chapter 4, Japanese executives play indirect and less visible roles as long as their companies perform satisfactorily. When company performance declines, however, their direct intervention becomes necessary and greater ability is required of them. This explains the inverse relationship found. The invisible executive leadership of the Japanese high performers is closely related to the self-organizing and self-adaptive ability of Japanese organizations. As long as the organizations themselves have the ability to adapt to changes and perform well, visible intervention is not required.

6.2.6 Synergy vs. Expanding the Resource Base

Another difference in the relative positions of high performers is found in their *emphasis on synergy* (Table 6-4). American high performers place more emphasis on synergy than do low performers. The relative positions of high and low performers are again reversed in Japan, with low performers showing the greater emphasis. This is consistent with the finding of Chapter 3: high performing Japanese companies accumulate, especially, people-related resources beyond the optimal level for American companies. It is consistent, too, with the diversification of Japanese firms into new areas for the purposes of accumulating people-related resources and to learn from operating in new environments. These actions are closely related to the inter-firm immobility of skilled employees and the difficulty of acquisition in Japan. For long-term adaptability, Japanese companies have to expand their resource bases beyond the short-term optimal level. And high performance enables Japanese firms to maintain the slack necessary for building that base even further.

6.3 Correlation and Regression Analysis: Determinants of Corporate Performance

The combined influences of strategies, orgnizational structures, processes, and executive personality upon corporate performance will be more systematically examined in this section using multi-variate statistical methods. The analytical framework appears in Figure 6-2. The analysis assumes that the performance of a company is directly influenced by its environment, technologies, size, strategy, organization, and executives' personalities.   Per contingency theory, the effects of strategy and organization are also assumed to be contingent upon the environment, technologies, and organizational size.   The interactive effects are shown by two dotted arrows in the figure.   Figure 6-2 shows that strategy and organization are also influenced by other factors. The influence of those factors will be analyzed in the next section.

Figure 6-2   Analytical Framework for the Analysis of
Organizational Adaptation

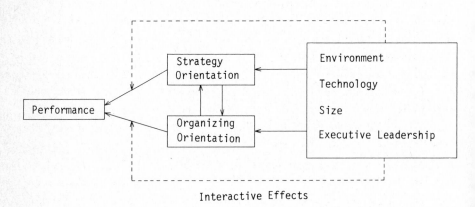

Interactive Effects

6.3.1 Non-Interactive Analysis

Tables 6-6 and 6-7 show how strong the relationships of the various indicators are to performance.   The correlation coefficients shown in

Table 6-6 measure the gross, direct and indirect influences, and the beta coefficients displayed in Table 6-7 measure the net influences upon performance. These tables, however, do not take interactive effects into account.

Table 6-6

Correlations between Performance Indicators and Other Indicators

	Overall performance		
	USA	JAPAN	POOLED SAMPLE[a]
Environmental diversity	.07***	.04	.05***
Environmental variability	.28***	.06	.16***
Interorganizational networks	.11	-.12+	-.03
Mobility of skilled employees	-.01	-.09*	-.05
Custom production	.06	-.15*	-.08
Mass production	-.03	-.02	-.03
Continuous process	.05	.04***	.05**
Organizational size	.03	.22***	.15**
Mobile resource deployment	.13+	-.01	.06
Emphasis on synergy	.13+	-.09	.02
ROI emphasis	.01	-.03	-.01
Product emphasis	.05***	.03**	.04***
Leadership in innovation	.32	.19*	.24*
Market share emphasis	.11***	.15*	.13**
Structuring of organization	.33***	.17**	.25***
Formalization	.15*	.05***	.10*
Sharing of values and information	.46***	.35	.40***
Institutionalization of values	.07***	.24***	.16***
Human resource emphasis	.25***	.17**	.21
Organizational tension	.05	.08*	.07*
Total power	.07	.13*	.12**
Power of finance and control	-.08*	-.15*	-.12**
General management skill	.26*	-.02	.13**
Interpersonal skill	.26*	-.01	.12**
Entrepreneurial skill	.25*	-.03*	.08+
High growth businesses	.18**	.14*	.16**
High market share businesses	.21**	.16*	.16**

a: partial correlation coefficients controlling for country effect
+p<0.10 *p<0.05 **p<0.01 ***p<0.001

Table 6-7 (A) Regression Analysis of Performance

	Total Sample (Beta Coefficient)					
	Overall	Strategic position	Profita-bility	Growth	Human	Strategic resources
Environmental diversity	-.05	-.15	-.01	-.03	-.07	-.07
Environmental variability	.08	.04	.04	.07	.06	.05
Interorganizational networks	.00	.08	-.01	-.05	.01	-.02
Mobility of skilled employees	-.01	.06	.06	.01	-.13	-.03
Custom production	-.08	-.06	-.01	-.05	-.15***	-.11*
Mass production	-.09	-.03	-.05	-.02	-.09	-.10*
Continuous process	.02	-.03*	.03	-.02	-.04**	-.04*
Organizational size	.07	.13*	-.02	-.00	.15**	.10*
Mobile resource deployment	-.04	.04	-.04	-.05	.02	.05
Emphasis on synergy	-.00	.08	-.03	-.02	-.06	.02
ROI emphasis	-.04	-.06**	-.03	.00	-.02	-.03
Product emphasis	.02*	.14**	-.04	-.00	-.03	-.06
Leadership in innovation	.10*	.09*	.06	.06	.02	.01
Market share emphasis	.04*	.08	.14**	.02	-.06	-.01
Structuring of organization	.11*	.00	.09	.10	.03	.05
Formalization	.03***	.03*	.01***	-.04***	.01***	.00***
Sharing of values and information	.29***	.11*	.25***	.20***	.43***	.25***
Institutionalization of values	.07	-.03	.13**	.06	.02	-.06
Human resource emphasis.	-.04	.06	-.02	-.05	-.09	.04
Organizational tension	-.02	-.02	-.05*	.01	-.07	.00
Total power	.02	.08*	-.09*	.01*	.06	.05
Power of finance and control	-.06	-.10*	-.01	-.10*	-.03	-.07
General management skill	-.00	-.07	-.02	-.04	.11*	.07
Interpersonal skill	-.01	-.01	-.01	-.01	.02	-.03
Entrepreneurial skill	-.03***	.06***	-.05***	-.02***	.00	-.05***
Country dummy (Japan = 1)	-.44	-.47	-.32	-.38	-.01	-.44
R^2	.362	.306	.262	.235	.306	.312

*$p<0.05$ **$p<0.01$ ***$p<0.001$

Table 6-7 (B)   Regression Analysis of Performance

	Overall	Strategic position	Profita-bility	Growth	Human	Strategic resources
Environmental diversity	.02*	-.06	.02	.03	-.07	-.04
Environmental variability	.22*	.12*	.13	.05	.17	.10
Interorganizational networks	.07	.17*	.06	.06	-.02	.02
Mobility of skilled employees	-.03	.01	.06	-.04	-.08	-.01
Custom production	.01	-.03	.11	.02	-.08	-.03
Mass production	-.09	-.03	-.09	-.02	-.07	-.10
Continuous process	.12	.03	.16	-.01*	-.01	-.05
Organizational size	-.07	-.06	-.03	-.20*	.00	.03
Mobile resource deployment	.03	.09	.05	-.02	.14	.13
Emphasis on synergy	.04	.16*	-.08	-.01	-.02	.07
ROI emphasis	-.07	-.13	-.01	-.01	.05	-.02
Product emphasis	-.07	.09	-.12	-.02	-.08	-.11
Leadership in innovation	.09	.15	-.01	.11	-.01	-.03
Market share emphasis	-.02*	-.03	.11	-.02*	-.01	-.06
Structuring of organization	.18*	.07	.10	.21*	.03	.05
Formalization	.01***	.03	.01**	-.06*	-.01***	.00**
Sharing of values and information	.35	.10	.34	.23	.43	.26
Institutionalization of values	.04	-.03	.12	-.00	-.04	-.10
Human resource emphasis.	-.01	.09	-.02	.04	.11	-.00
Organizational tension	-.06	-.06	.02	-.04	-.08	-.00
Total power	-.00	.12	-.07	-.03	.08	.04
Power of finance and control	.01	.13	.06	-.08	.07	.02
General management skill	-.01	-.16	.03	.09	.03	.04
Interpersonal skill	.08	.06	.00	.06	.11	.08
Entrepreneurial skill	.00	.00	-.06	-.12	.04	.12
R^2	.343	.303	.262	.212	.312	.206

*$p < 0.05$ **$p < 0.01$ ***$p < 0.001$

Table 6-7 (C)   Regression Analysis of Performance

	Japan					
	Overall	Strategic position	Profita-bility	Growth	Human	Strategic resources
Environmental diversity	-.15*	-.23**	-.05	-.06	-.11	-.15*
Environmental variability	-.01	-.01	-.02	.07	-.01	.04
Interorganizational networks	-.03	.03	-.05	-.11	.04*	-.03
Mobility of skilled employees	-.01	.08	.00	.08	-.13*	-.02
Custom production	-.16*	-.12	-.11	-.09	-.20***	-.17**
Mass production	-.14	-.07	-.04	-.04	-.12	-.15
Continuous process	-.07	-.08	-.11	.02	-.07	-.06
Organizational size	.22**	.30***	.02	.17*	.27***	.21***
Mobile resource deployment	-.14*	-.04	-.10	-.14*	-.12	-.07
Synergy emphasis	-.05	-.02	.04	-.06	-.11	-.04
ROI emphasis	-.01	.01*	-.05	.03	-.04	-.02
Product emphasis	.04	.15*	.02	-.03	.01	-.08
Leadership in innovation	.10	.06	.12	.01	.05	.05
Market share emphasis	.09	.15*	.16*	.00	-.06	.02
Structuring of organization	.08	-.04	.08	.03	.06	.07
Formalization	.05	.03	.05	-.05	.02	-.01
Sharing of values and information	.24**	.10	.15	.10	.35***	.23**
Institutionalization of values	.14*	.03	.17*	.21**	.07	-.04
Human resource emphasis	-.05	.05	-.02	-.11*	-.03	.09
Organizational tension	.05	.03	-.09	.15*	-.04	.04
Total power	.08	.06	-.01	.07	.08	.06
Power of finance and control	-.06	-.02	-.03	-.04	-.07	-.08
General management skill	-.04	-.04	-.07	-.12	.15	.07*
Interpersonal skill	-.10	-.10	-.02	-.08	-.04	-.14*
Entrepreneurial skill	-.04	.07	-.05	.01	-.04	-.13
R^2	.262	.164	.192	.180	.403	.256

*$p<0.05$ **$p<0.01$ ***$p<0.001$

The correlation coefficients confirm the findings in the previous section. *Leadership in innovation* and *sharing of values and information* are positively related to overall performance in the American sample, in the Japanese sample, and the total sample. As expected, the *emphasis on synergy* is negatively related to overall performance in Japan but positively in the U.S., and executives' qualities are, in general, negatively related to performance indicators in Japan, but positively so in the U.S.

The multi-variate analysis shows other important similarities between the two countries. First is the effect of *structuring of organization* upon *overall perfomance*. The effect is positive in all three cases. (.18 in the U.S., .08 in Japan and .11 in the total sample). Thus, bureaucratic dynamics is also an important condition for high performance, although somewhat less so in Japan than in the U.S.

The second similarity is in the effect of *market-share emphasis* upon *profitability*. *Market-share emphasis*, which is an indicator of operations-oriented strategy, is more important to *profitability* than *leadership in innovation*, an indicator of product-oriented strategy, in the three cases (0.11 vs. -0.01 in the U.S., 0.16 vs. 0.12 in Japan and 0.14 vs. 0.06 in the total sample). On the other hand, in the correlation of strategic orientation to *overall performance*, the degree of the product orientation was found to have a greater effect than the degree of operations orientation. These findings are consistent with the notion that a product orientation helps to create or uncover opportunities for growth. An operations orientation, however, helps to exploit existing opportunities. The coexistence of both product and operations orientations, therefore, would seem better than the pursuit of either, by itself.

The most distinctive difference between U.S. and Japanese firms is in the influence of *organizational size*. Size has a significant and positive influence upon overall performance in Japan but has no influence (nonsignificant correlation) or a weak negative influence (beta coefficient) in the United States. In Japan, size has especially strong positive relationships with two specific performance indicators: *human performance* and *stock of strategic resources*. These findings suggest that, large size brings with it advantages in motivating people and in building up strategic resources in Japan. The reasons for this will be discussed in the next section.

The effect of *inter-organizational networks* differs between the countries. It is positively related to performance in the U.S. but negatively so in Japan. As shown in Chapters 2 and 3, the inter-organizational networks are generally stronger in Japan, and a principal outcome was the reduction of risk. The results of our quantitative analysis, however, show that such networks can hinder performance when they are overly developed. There may well be an optimal level of networking somewhere in between the averages typical for the two countries.

6.3.2 Interactive Analysis

In order to take into account the interactive effects upon performance of the variables shown in Figure 6-2, several multiplicative terms were included in the regression analyses.[3] The results of the stepwise, multiple-regressions are as follows:[4]

For the Total Sample

$$PTOL = 57.33 + 0.16 \ OSTR * OSHA - 6.50 \ CNTRY - 2.12 \ OSTR$$
$$\quad\quad\quad (7.73) \quad\quad\quad\quad (9.11) \quad\quad\quad (4.88)$$
$$\quad\quad + 0.33 \ SINN * OSTR - 0.10 \ SINN * SSHA - 6.02 \ OPFI.$$
$$\quad\quad\quad (3.23) \quad\quad\quad\quad (2.38) \quad\quad\quad\quad (2.14)$$
$$R^2 = .359$$

For U.S. Firms only

$$PTOL = 0.55 + 0.04 \ OSTR * OSHA + 0.03 \ EVAR * OSHA - 0.03ETMA$$
$$\quad\quad\quad\quad (1.63) \quad\quad\quad\quad\quad (1.78) \quad\quad\quad\quad\quad (1.80)$$
$$\quad\quad + 0.09 \ SINN * OSTR + 0.55 \ OSHA$$
$$\quad\quad\quad (2.08) \quad\quad\quad\quad (2.00)$$
$$R^2 = .310$$

For Japanese Firms only

PTOL = 34.01 + 0.90 OSHA + 0.34 SINN * OSTR - 0.03 ETJB
      (5.11)   (2.48)   (2.04)
-8.84 OPFI - 1.59 SINN
(2.33)   (1.86)
R^2 = .183

The regression equations show that the *sharing of values and information* (OSHA) and *leadership in innovation* (SINN) do, in fact, contribute to overall performance (PTOL) both countries, but that the effects of these two variables are influenced by other variables. For instance, the effect of *leadership in innovation* is an increasing function of the *structuring of organization* (OSTR) in all three equations. That is, in both countries, *leadership in innovation* (SINN) contributes more to performance in highly structured organizations; this is less so in those less structured. This finding is somewhat inconsistent with existing theories of organization and will be discussed in the next section.

There are also differences between the countries. In the U.S., *structuring of organization* (OSTR) has two multiplicative effects. Its effects are shown by the terms

    0.04 OSHA + 0.09 SINN.

This means that, as *the sharing of values and information* (OSHA) and *leadership in innovation* (SINN) increase, the effects of structuring upon performance become larger. The structuring of organizations, relied on more heavily in American companies than in Japanese firms may, therefore, have even broader implications than surmised. In Japan, *power of the finance and control* (OPFI) actually has a negative effect on performance. Table 6-7 shows that the negative effect is especially strong upon *human performance*. The finance department's power may destroy the sense of unity and willingness of Japanese employees to contribute to their companies.

6.3.3 Discussion of the Findings

The findings in this section show important similarities between the United States and Japan, perhaps assumed but, heretofore, not reported in the literature. Especially noteworthy is the similarity that the *sharing of values and information* and *leadership in innovation* contribute to performance in both countries. The important implication is that the combination of group dynamics and a product orientation -- that combination of strategy orientation and organizing orientation in the south-west corner of Figure 6-1 -- results in higher overall performance than the three other combinations. The characteristics of companies near that south-west corner, e.g., 3M, Hewlett-Packard, Kyocera, and TDK, suggest why this is so. They are examined below.

1. These companies face highly variable environments which afford many opportunities. They actively seek to discover and exploit those opportunities through innovative, entrepreneurial means, capitalizing on the profit premium available early in a product's life-cycle before competitors enter. Such actions are clearly most appropriate and productive in changing environments. To play the innovative and entrepreneurial game in an environment laden with opportunities though incurring some inevitable losses, may be more productive than to employ even the best strategy in a stable and already highly competitive market.

2. The innovative leaps made by these companies help them to keep up with the rapid change and even contribute to it. The continuous, incremental progress of the typical Japanese company does not enable such fast adaptation.

3. The tentative, product-oriented, not infrequently trial-and-error approach of these companies is better suited for discovering latent niches in a changing environment than the analysis-based major market thrusts more typical of American companies. The irony is that rapidly changing environments make environmental forecasts difficult, undermine the basic assumptions of analytical strategy formulation, and make the analytical company more conservative (Peters and Waterman, 1982).

4. The emergent leaps that are occasionally made by the innovative

companies are outside any strategic planning frameworks and create opportunities for self-renewal. These firms are able to unlearn existing "paradigms" and reorganize their resources into new "theories of action" (Pfeffer, 1982).

5. The values of their founders and/or CEO's tend to be widely shared by the people of these companies. Such shared values create a sense of unity and identity (Ouchi, 1980), intrinsically motivate people because of a shared sense of mission, and elicit psychological commitment to an extent that formal rules or orders could not (Selznick, 1957). These organizations are not merely means to achieve individual personal goals but are social institutions to which people dedicate their efforts.

6. These companies build a distinctive corporate culture. It consists of a set of loosely connected beliefs and norms which are less constraining and more flexible than formal rules and policies. They impart to the corporate culture a self-organizing property; they enable the firm to reorganize the order of and relationship between its elements in response to changing situations (Jantsch, 1981). Such firms are better able to adapt to rapidly changing environments.

7. The "high-tech" image of these companies enables them to differentiate their products from others. The image is also helpful in recruiting high-quality, creative engineers and workers who, in turn, produce more innovation. The "high-tech" image is then further enhanced.

The foregoing analysis suggests a new model which differs from the typical Japanese model (the combination of group dynamics and an operations orientation) or the typical American one (a combination of bureaucratic dynamics with a product orientation).

Although the combination of group dynamics and product orientation is "best" among the four pure combinations, this analysis suggests a more complex "optimal solution." For instance, some *market-share emphasis* (a principal element of the operations orientation) is necessary to improve profitability, and the *structuring of organization* (an element of bureaucratic dynamics) was seen to increase overall performance in conjunction with *leadership in innovations*. Their coexistence or symbiosis is desirable for the following reasons:

1. The increasingly complex environments of organizations provide a variety of opportunities, which may be best exploited using different strategies. For example, innovations stemming from a *product orientation* may present new opportunities in the marketplace, but to capitalize upon those opportunities, superiority in production (a strong operations orientation) is also necessary.

2. The respondents in our sample are very large companies in both countries -- they are among *Fortune*'s top one thousand firms in the U.S. and among the companies listed on the Tokyo Stock Exchange in Japan. Companies of this size need some degree of bureaucratic structure, especially to cope with the enormous amounts of information from highly variable environments. Without the structure to sufficiently define company-wide problems and integrate goals and efforts, organizational decision-making can become mired in intergroup processes and conflict.

6.4 Forces Shaping Strategy and Organization

Various studies have proposed factors that significantly affect organizational structure over and above Chandler's strategy influence. They include the environment (Burns and Stalker, 1961; Lawrence and Lorsch, 1969), technology (Woodward, 1965; Perrow, 1967), organizational size (Pugh et al., 1969), leader's personality (Burns and Stalker, 1961; Child, 1972), and socio-cultural factors (Azumi, 1980). It has also been argued that the same factors shape strategy (Porter, 1981). The general analytical framework used here (shown before in Figure 6-2) was constructed on the basis of the studies cited. Three indicators of strategy and two indicators of organization were chosen to evaluate the framework.

Three indicators -- *mobile resource deployment, leadership in innovation* and *product emphasis* -- represent the product orientation toward strategy. *Sharing of values and information* is a measure of the group dynamics organizing orientation, and *structuring of organization* represents bureaucratic dynamics. Table 6-8 shows the correlation between these five indicators and other indicators hypothesized to be determinants of structure, separately for the United States (A) and Japan (B). Table 6-9 shows the results of regression analyses based upon the analytical framework presented.

Table 6-8 (A)

Indicators of Strategy and Organization Correlated with Other Indicators

	U S A				
	SRES	SPRO	SINN	OSTR	OSHA
Environmental diversity	.24***	.29***	.19**	.28***	-.02
Environmental variability	.10	.39***	.40	33***	.13+
Interorganizational networks	-.05	-.01	.03	.15*	-.03
Mobility of skilled employees	.09	.12+	.06	-.01	-.10
Custom production	-.07	.05	.09*	-.02	.07
Mass production	.01	.12+	.15*	.11	.04
Continuous process	-.10	-.45***	-.14	-.09***	.00
Organizational size	-.08	-.05	.07*	.38***	.00
Mobile resource deployment	-	.10	-.17	.30	.09
Emphasis on synergy	-.02	.10*	.08	.09	.16
ROI emphasis	.04	-.17	-.01**	.12**	.12+
Product emphasis	.10*	-	.19	.20***	.08***
Leadership in innovation	.17**	.19**	-	.40*	.31*
Market share emphasis	.19***	.26**	.27***	-.17	.16*
Structuring of organization	.30***	.20	.40	-	.26***
Formalization	.05	.09	.12+***	.34***	.23***
Sharing of values and information	.09	.08	.31	.26	-
Institutionalization of values	.10	.07	-.05***	-.00***	.17***
Human resource emphasis	.06	.10	.23	.39***	.46
Organizational tension	.11	.09	.08*	.22**	.11+
Total power	-.13+	.14+	.19*	.18	.08
Power of finance and control	-.11*	-.03	-.15**	-.04***	-.11***
General management skill	.15	.09	.20*	.29	.32***
Interpersonal skill	.06***	.07	.12+***	.13**	.40***
Entrepreneurial skill	.23***	.11	.30	.21**	.34

+$p<0.10$ *$p<0.05$ **$p<0.01$ ***$p<0.001$

Chapter 6

Table 6-8 (B)

Indicators of Strategy and Organization Correlated with Other Indicators

	Japan				
	SRES	SPRO	SINN	OSTR	OSHA
Environmental diversity	.03*	.21***	.30***	.25***	.17**
Environmental variability	.15*	.27***	.30***	24***	.10
Interorganizational networks	-.05**	-.18**	-.12*	:00	-.10+
Mobility of skilled employees	.15**	.18**	.07	.13*	-.14*
Custom production	-.01	-.02	.10+	.06	-.02
Mass production	-.01	.20***	.07	.05	-.01
Continuous process	.08	-.35***	-.08	-.01	.06***
Organizational size	.09	-.14*	.09	.21***	.29***
Mobile resource deployment	-	-.07	.20***	.27***	.11+
Synergy emphasis	-.07	-.12*	-.13*	-.11+	-.01
ROI emphasis	.10	-.06	.00	.14*	-.04
Product emphasis	-.07	-	.21***	.01*	-.13*
Leadership in innovation	.20***	.21***	-	.17**	.19**
Market share emphasis	.05	.19**	.15*	.09	.17*
Structuring of organization	.27***	.01	.17**	-	.29***
Formalization	.19**	-.07	.05*	.25***	.13*
Sharing of values and information	.11+	-.13*	.19**	.29***	-
Institutionalization of values	.20***	.10+	.23***	.16**	.36***
Human resource emphasis	.11*	-.05	.12*	.37***	.55***
Organizational tension	.12*	.06*	-.01	.24***	.27***
Total power	.09	-.12	.06	.18	.20*
Power of finance and control	-.02	-.10	-.11+	-.02***	-.08**
General management skill	.08	-.04	.06	.24**	.17***
Interpersonal skill	.01	-.03	-.01*	.15**	.21*
Entrepreneurial skill	.11+	-.03	.13*	.18**	.11+

+$p<0.10$ *$p<0.05$ **$p<0.01$ ***$p<0.001$

Table 6-9 (A) Regression Analysis of Strategy and Organizations

	U S A					
	SRES	SPRO	SINN	OSTR	OSHA	OSHA
Environmental diversity	.19*	.12**	.00**	-.03	-.16*	-.11
Environmental variability	-.08	.26**	.26**	.05*	.01	-.01
Interorganizational networks	-.05	-.07	-.10	.12*	-.01	-.04
Mobility of skilled employees	.07	.06	.02	-.08	-.05	-.03
Custom production	-.13	-.08	.11	.01	.06	.07
Mass production	-.04	-.06	.09	-.03	.02	.05
Continuous process	-.04**	-.36***	.02	-.07	.02	.04
Organizational size	-.26**	-.07	-.10	.40***	.02	-.14
Mobile resource deployment				.26***	.03	-.02
Synergy emphasis				.08	.07	.05
ROI emphasis				.05	.08	.08
Product emphasis				.10***	.04**	.03*
Leadership in innovation				.26***	.20**	.16*
Market share emphasis				.03	.08	.02
Structuring of organization	.43***	.09	.30***			.11
Formalization	-.08	-.01	-.08			
Sharing of values and information	-.01	.02	.18*			
Institutionalization of values	.08	.05	-.10			.06
Human resource emphasis	-.00	.01	.03			.38***
Organizational tension	-.02**	-.01	-.02			-.12
Total power	-.22**	.10	.12			-.09
Power of finance and control	-.06	.04	-.08			-.04
General management skill	-.06	-.10	-.08	.21**	.10***	.06
Interpersonal skill	.02*	.05	-.05*	.03	.26***	.18*
Entrepreneurial skill	.20*	.05	.18*	-.06	.11	.10
R²	.279	.332	.357	.448	.289	.401

*p<0.05   **p<0.01   ***p<0.001

Table 6-9 (B) Regression Analysis of Strategy and Organizations

	Japan					
	SRES	SPRO	SINN	OSTR	OSHA	OSHA
Environmental diversity	-.09	.09***	.18*	.11	.09	.05
Environmental variability	.12	.22**	.18**	.09	.01	-.03**
Interorganizational networks	-.07	-.17**	-.11	.00	-.11	-.14
Mobility of skilled employees	.13*	.06	.03	.09	-.10	-.09
Custom production	.02	-.07	-.13	-.08	.02	.03
Mass production	-.03	.07**	-.07	-.05	-.02	-.02
Continuous process	.13	-.22**	-.03	-.06	-.04**	.05**
Organizational size	.06	-.11	-.04	.12**	.20**	.15**
Mobile resource deployment				.19**	.05	-.03
Emphasis on synergy				-.08	.04	.07
ROI emphasis				.11	-.05*	-.03
Product emphasis				-.04	-.17*	-.11
Leadership in innovation				.03	.15*	.09
Market share emphasis				.04	.11	.02
Structuring of organization	.18**	.00	.04			.06
Formalization	.16**	-.02	.08			
Sharing of values and information	-.02	-.13	.10			
Institutionalization of values	.21**	.03	.13			.25***
Human resource emphasis	-.08	-.04	.02			.42***
Organizational tension	.08	.04	-.13			.00
Total power	.05	-.06	.02			.10
Power of finance and control	.05	-.05	-.02			.01
General management skill	-.01	.00	-.01	.15*	.08*	.02
Interpersonal skill	-.07	.08	-.04	.08	.14*	.09
Entrepreneurial skill	.05	-.09	.04	.01	-.03	-.08
R^2	.181	.266	.200	.221	.105	.475

*$p<0.05$ **$p<0.01$ ***$p<0.001$

Table 6-9 (C)   Regression Analysis of Strategy and Organizations

	Total					
	SRES	SRPO	SINN	OSTR	OSHA	OSHA
Environmental diversity	.07	.10***	.07***	.04	-.06	-.05
Environmental variability	.01	.24**	.25***	.08	.03	.01*
Interorganizational networks	-.05	-.14**	-.08	.06	-.07	-.09*
Mobility of skilled employees	.09	.07	.03	.01	-.10	-.08
Custom production	-.03	-.08	-.02	-.03	.05	.06
Mass production	-.04	.02***	.01	-.03	.02	.02
Continuous process	.04	-.30*	-.03	-.08***	-.01*	.04
Organizational size	-.07	-.10*	-.06	.25***	.12*	.02
Mobile resource deployment				.23***	.05	.00
Emphasis on synergy				.01*	.08	.07
ROI emphasis				.09*	.00	.00
Product emphasis				.03	-.08	-.07
Leadership in innovations				.15***	.20***	.14**
Market share emphasis				.03	.10	.04
Structuring of organization	.24***	.05	.18**			.07
Formalization	.06	-.01	.01			
Sharing of values and information	.02	-.06	.17**			
Institutionalization of values	.09	.02	-.01			.14**
Human resource emphasis	-.05	-.01	.01			.42***
Organizational tension	.01	-.00	-.08			-.07
Total power	-.05	-.01	.05			.03
Power of finance and control	-.03	-.03	-.07			-.04
General management skill	-.01	-.03	-.05	.15**	.10***	.04***
Interpersonal skill	-.02	.08	-.04*	-.01	.22***	.16*
Entrepreneurial skill	.09***	-.03	.13*	-.01*	.05	.00*
Country dummy (Japan = 1)	-.28***	-.02	.05	-.12*	-.01	-.16*
R^2	.354	.268	.231	.341	.211	.342

*$p<0.05$ **$p<0.01$ ***$p<0.001$

6.4.1 The Sharing of Values and Information

The sharing of values and information, an important element in the group
dynamics organizing orientation and found to be an important determinant
of performance, is influenced by several factors.

The factors which significantly influence the sharing of values and
information in both countries include *human resource emphasis* and
executives' *interpersonal skill.* The *human resource emphasis* (to include
long-term personnel planning and evaluation, and job rotation) contributes
to the sharing of values and information because job security, longer
term, hence more accurate personnel evaluations, and experiencing many
jobs within a company, all facilitate the building of trust between
organizational members. The building of such trust is more difficult to
implement in the U.S., where the inter-company mobility of people is so
much higher. Once relationships of trust are established, they contribute
greatly to the sharing of values and information in U.S. firms, too. Key
factors are the personnel practices of the firm (Ouchi, 1981; Pascale and
Athos, 1981) and interpersonal skills of senior executives.

A contrasting pattern is found in regard to the influence of company
size. The statistical analysis shows that as the organization becomes
larger, the *sharing of values and information* becomes more difficult in
the U.S., but seems to become easier in Japan. Large size brings the
advantages in Japan, of more motivated and satisfied people and more
strategic resources within an organization, as noted earlier. This is so
because large size has the following consequences in Japan's socio-
cultural and institutional setting:

(1) Because the size of a company is one of the most important
      determinants of the social status of employees and managers, people
      in large companies are more satisfied and identify more closely with
      their firms than those in small firms. This helps in the recruitment
      of competent people.
(2) The large companies usually have clearer and more stringent criteria
      for selecting people; therefore, the employees and managers of large
      organizations are better qualified and more homogeneous than in

smaller companies. Homogeneity helps in the sharing of common values and information.

(3)   Because large companies have more sophisticated personnel management systems, personnel evaluation can be more objective, and job security is also more assured. These factors are of critical importance to the motivation of employees working in an organization for a long period of time.

(4)   Because large companies can provide more diverse career paths, they are for that reason, too, more favored places in which to work.

6.4.2 The Structuring of the Organization

The *structuring of organization* is closely related to the environment's diversity and to organizational size. Relationships between structure and these two indicators are positive as predicted by previous studies (Pugh et al., 1969). As the business of a company becomes more diverse and its size becomes larger, its information processing load becomes commensurately greater. To cope with that load, the organization must define hierarchical reporting relationships, standardize information flow, apply more analytical procedures, and depend more on staff services; that is, the organization must rely more upon structural means for processing information. This logic is common to both countries.

The degree of *structuring of organization* is also positively correlated to *mobile resource deployment* (to include diversification through acquisitions and active divestitures) in both countries. This relationship makes sense because a higher degree of structure makes possible more impersonal, analytical decisions in allocating resources among businesses. It also enables organizations to acquire resources from outside. This finding holds for both countries, even though such resource deployment is less common in Japan.

Structuring of organization has a significant, positive relationship with *leadership in innovation* in the U.S. The relationship is not statistically significant in Japan.

Structuring of organization is positively related to the *mobility of skilled employees* in Japan where such mobility is generally low.   It suggests that a high degree of *structuring of organization* is required when mobility is high.   This, of course, occurs because standardized procedures and rules are necessary to quickly assimilate skilled employees who do not know the organization and their roles in it well. This finding has the broader theoretical implication that the labor and other resource input markets can significantly influence organizational structure. *ROI emphasis*, which reflects pressures from the capital markets also has some relation to the *structuring of organization* in the two countries (Table 6-9).   The important implication of these results is that the usual focus of contingency theory upon product or output markets is too narrow and that differences in the degree of structuring between organizations must be explained, in part, in terms of input market constraints.

6.4.3 Leadership in Innovation

Leadership in innovation, when occurring jointly with *structuring of organization*, was found to be one of the most important conditions for high performance in both countries.   Its statistical relationships with other indicators suggest what is necessary to develop such leadership.

An indicator that has a positive relationship with the innovation leadership position in both countries is *human resource emphasis* (to include long-term personnel planning, evaluation and job rotation). This finding supports the contention that American high performers, especially very innovative ones, rely on long-term employment and share several practices in common with Japanese companies (Ouchi, 1981; Pascale and Athos, 1981).   There are at least three reasons why long-term employment should contribute to greater innovation.

(1) Innovations rely to a considerable extent upon individuals' (or "internal entrepreneurs'") efforts which are often expanded outside of the formal organizational framework even in large organizations (Burgelman, 1983; Kanter, 1983).   Their actions are motivated not so much by their formal responsibilities or extrinsic rewards but by their identification with the organization and its purposes.   This identification is largely the result of long-term personnel planning

and the commitment to individuals demonstrated by the organization.

(2) The evaluation of an innovator's performance should be made only after a long period of time. A short-term, premature evaluation may discourage internal entrepreneurs and their teams.

(3) Innovations entail risks. The success or failure of an innovation often depends upon unforeseeable contingencies. An individual's true contribution can be fairly evaluated only after a number of trials over some period of time.

In the U.S., *leadership in innovation* is also related to the *entrepreneurial skill* of senior executives and to *structuring of organization*. The former relation suggests that entrepreneurial skill is rewarded with promotion in high-performing U.S. firms and can, therefore, contribute even more to the firm's leadership in innovation. Moreover, entrepreneurial executives become role models for future, potential internal entrepreneurs. The relationship between *leadership in innovation* and *structuring of organization* needs some explanation. Earlier studies and our own earlier analysis have argued that innovative organizations are less structured (Burns and Stalker, 1961; Lawrence and Lorsch, 1967). It should be noted that most earlier studies focused upon the group or department level rather than corporate level. The American organizations studied here are among the largest, and the implication of our finding is that such organizations need a formal structure to coordinate their huge numbers of groups and teams, even though each such team may be, for its size, more organic and group dynamics-oriented than in less innovative organizations. Because organizational chaos can result from extremely innovative changes, the issue of structure is all the more important: it is vital for reducing substantial organizational anarchy without diminishing innovation.

In Japan, *the entrepreneurial skill* of senior executives is not strongly correlated to *leadership in innovation* of the firm. Instead, the *institutionalization of values* -- embedding top management's values, beliefs, and strategic visions within the organizational culture -- plays a more important role in innovation by the firm.

6.4.4 Product vs. Operations Orientation

Product emphasis was found to be another feature of high performers in
both countries although the typical Japanese company is less product-
oriented than the typical American firm. This strategic orientation is
correlated significantly to environment, technology, and organizational
size in both countries. The common relationships are as follows:

(1) The more homogeneous the environment, the less emphasis on the
     product mix.
(2) The more variable the environment, the more emphasized the product
     mix is.
(3) The companies employing continuous process technologies are less
     product-oriented.
(4) The larger the company, the less its products are emphasized.

Although there are differences in degree, these patterns are common to
both countries.

6.4.5 Mobile Resource Deployment

Mobile resource deployment is a vital element of the product-oriented
strategies of American firms. As noted before, it is closely related to
structuring of organization in both countries.

Mobile resource development correlates negatively with the *total power* in
the U.S. sample. This means that in order to actively reallocate
resources, the power to make strategic resources decisions needs to be
concentrated at the top and/or the influence of lower-level managers needs
to be circumscribed. The reallocation of resources often causes inter-
departmental conflict; the concentration of power promotes smoother
reallocation even when middle or lower-level managers have conflicting
interests. *Entrepreneurial skill* is also required of top management. It
correlates positively with *mobile resource deployment*.

Mobile resource deployment is positively related to the *mobility of
skilled employees* in Japan. The availability of skilled employees from

outside the firm, which is generally low in Japan but variable among industries, places greater reliance upon resource reallocation from within the company. The *entrepreneurial skill*, that is positively correlated with *mobile resource deployment* in the U.S., does not have a strong influence in Japan. Instead, *institutionalization of values* -- values articulated through the philosophies and visions of Japanese corporate leaders and embedded in corporate cultures -- is more important in influencing (has a higher correlation to) *mobile resource deployment*.

6.4.6 Forces Shaping Strategy and Organization

The preceding analysis of the five indicators representing the two principal dimensions of organizational adaptation uncovers several important factors shaping strategy and organization.

Figure 6-3 Forces Affecting Strategy and Organization

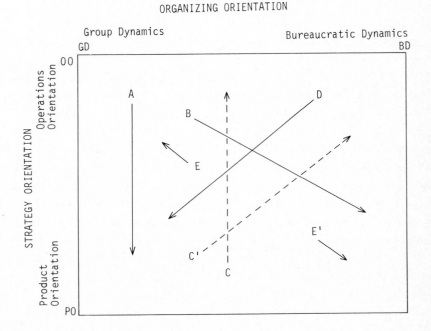

ORGANIZING ORIENTATION

High environmental variability and diversity pull the organizations in both countries in the direction of a product-oriented strategy (arrow A in Figure 6-3). Homogeneity and stability push organizations in the direction of operations-oriented strategy.

The mobility of labor and externally imposed pressure for profits make organizations more product-oriented and bureaucratic dynamics-oriented. This is more true in Japan than in the U.S. The relationship may be generally applicable, however, because American companies that do face clearly more mobile labor markets and competitive capital markets are, on the average, more product-oriented and more bureaucratic dynamics-oriented. This is depicted by arrow B in Figure 6-3.

The effect of organizational size is somewhat complicated. In Japan large size is attended by a stronger operations orientation but appears to be independent of the organizing dimension because it necessitates increased structuring of organization (bureaucratic dynamics) and, at the same time, increased sharing of values and information (group dynamics). The effect of size in Japan is shown by arrow C in the figure. In the U.S. organizational size pushes organizations toward the bureaucratic dynamics and operations orientations (as shown by C').

There are also very instrumental forces acting to shape the organization from within. Long-term personnel evaluation and executive leadership make organizations in both countries more product-oriented (more innovative) and more group dynamics-oriented. This is shown by arrow D. The effect of leadership is clear from our data, although the form of leadership exercised is different in the two countries: Visible enterpreneurial leadership is more prominent in the U.S., while less visible, indirect leadership -- embedding values into visions and organizational cultures -- is more in evidence in Japan.

Taking into account the factors discussed so far, there remain some important inter-country differences. Japanese companies are, on the average, more group dynamics-oriented and operations-oriented (shown by arrow E) and Americans firms are more bureaucratic dynamics and product-oriented (shown by E'). This difference reflects the idiosyncratic socio-cultural forces peculiar to each country, as we have seen.

The analysis of previous sections showed that the combination of a group dynamics and product orientation outperforms the other combinations of organizing and strategy. The forces shown by arrows A and D tend toward a group dynamics and a product orientation; the forces shown by arrows B, C, C', E and E' do not. The "internal force" D is more controllable than the "external force" A. Thus, *executive leadership* and *long-term human resource management* are the keys to creating the good combination.

6.5 Implications and Conclusions

Two principal dimensions of organizational adaptation -- strategy and organizing orientations -- were identified in the qualitative analysis of this study. Using indicators of those dimensions, the effects of strategy and organization upon corporate performance were statistically derived, and the forces shaping organizations were identified. The findings of the preceding analyses appear in Figures 6-4 (A) and (B).

These findings suggest that the combination of group dynamics and product orientation, typified by entrepreneurial, creative companies in variable environments, outperforms other combinations both in the United States and Japan. This combination of strategy and organizing orientation is different from the combination typical of American firms (bureaucratic dynamics and product orientation) or typical of Japanese companies (group dynamics and operations orientation). In order to achieve truly optimum performance, the typical Japanese company must become more product-oriented and the typical U.S. company must rely more on group dynamics (Figure 6-5).

The findings also suggest that a symbiotic combination which includes some elements of bureaucratic dynamics and the operations orientation as well as those of group dynamics and product orientation, can be more appropriate than the pure combination of group dynamics and product orientation. This is especially so in variable environments.

Figure 6-4   (A) Factors Affecting Performance
(Path Diagram, U.S.A.)

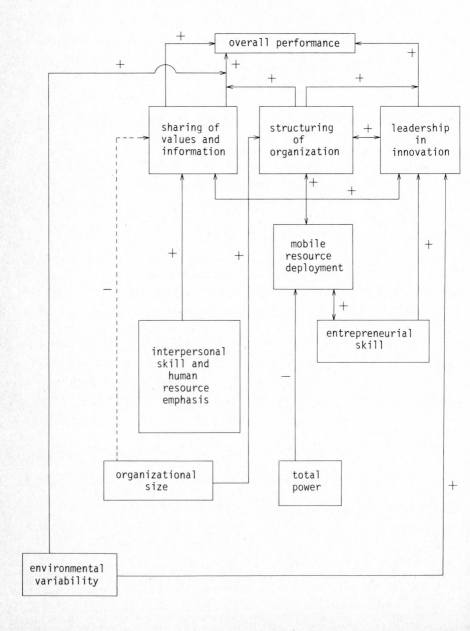

Figure 6-4 (B) Factors Affecting Performance
(Path Diagram, JAPAN)

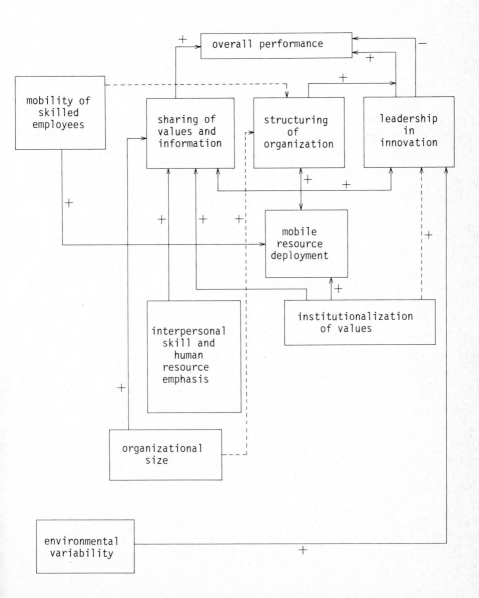

Figure 6-5 Combinations of Strategic and Organizing Orientations

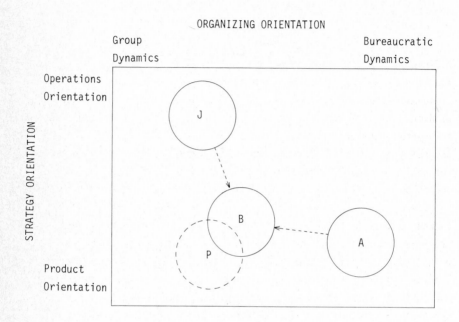

J : typical Japanese combination
A : typical American combination
B : best performing combination
P : pure combination of group dynamics
    and product orientation

As shown by our qualitative studies in Chapters 3, 4, and 5 group
dynamics-oriented organization relies on organic (decentralized, informal,
and unsophisticated) management systems, shared values and information,
and frequent interaction within and between loosely coupled groups.   The
actions generated within the group dynamics-oriented organization are
guided less (and constrained less) by strategic plans, policies, and

sophisticated planning procedures; the emergent actions tend to be more autonomous, empirical, and pragmatic. The more autonomous empiricism contributes to greater intra-organizational variation (Weick, 1969). This variation results, in turn, in the greater probability of discovering hidden market niches and experimenting with new ideas and actions that are necessary for proactively adapting to changing environments.

The underlying rationale of the group dynamics organizing orientation is different from the traditional rational model underlying the bureaucratic dynamics orientation that is exemplified by the average American firm: the rational model prescribes that the executives of organizations must predict environmental change, identify threats and opportunities, formulate strategic plans, and then guide organizational actions accordingly. Ashby's law of requisite variety provides the rationale: rational organizations have to create and maintain an equilibrium between environmental variety (the variety facing them) and organizational variety. To do so is called variety engineering (Beer, 1981). In contrast, however, organizations that rely on group dynamics generate more organizational variety than required to maintain equilibrium with their environments. It is the redundant variety that is accumulated which enables these organizations to actively cope with environmental uncertainty. Its rationale is provided fully by the evolutionary model of organizations, which will be fully developed in the next chapter (Weick, 1979).

The present environments of American and Japanese companies change rapidly and are becoming even more uncertain. The hallmarks of group dynamics have been more evolultionary. For this reason, it is submitted that the group dynamics orientation is indispensable for coping with increasingly turbulent environments.

Although the high-performing and more typical Japanese combinations share the group dynamics orientation, they differ in strategic orientation. The high-performing combination is more product-oriented and innovative, while the typical Japanese combination is more operations-oriented and incremental in its progress. The typical Japanese combination is better suited for making continuous improvements in production processes and existing products than in innovating new products (and attending processes). Many Japanese companies have achieved their strength because of this strategic orientation. It, however, is not as likely to produce those "leaps in creativity" which may be necessary for survival in turbulent environments. In order to cope with the turbulence, Japanese companies must become more product-oriented while maintaining their group dynamics orientation.

To reiterate, the typical American company must increase the importance that it attaches to group dynamics. The keys are emphasis upon human resources and executives' interpersonal skills. This conclusion is wholly consistent with recent arguments stressing the importance of human resources (Ouchi, 1981; Pascale & Athos, 1981) and the role of executives' symbolic behavior in creating organizational cultures (Deal & Kennedy, 1982).

The typical Japanese company must become more product-oriented, especially in regard to demonstrating stronger leadership in product innovation. The key in this case is the institutionalization of values of the founders or top management which will strongly encourage internal entrepreneurs to make those "creative leaps." The task of achieving the highest-performing combination is assuredly difficult, because many forces -- organizational size, production technologies, environmental diversity, and Western and Japanese socio-cultural forces -- pull the organization in divergent directions. It is hoped though, that the framework of our analysis and our findings may be helpful in pointing out the proper directions for companies to take.

Notes

1. The questionnaire was sent to the *Fortune* top 1,000 corporations in the U.S. and to 1,031 industrial corporations listed on the Tokyo Stock Exchange in Japan for the year 1980. 227 companies responded in the U.S. and 291 companies in Japan. For the outline of the questionnaire, see Chapter 2, and Appendix A and B.

2. As the mean score of overall performance differs significantly

between the two countries, a different cut-off point (each country's mean score) was applied to each country. The Japanese mean was 2.81 and U.S. 3.24. The number of high performers is 165 and 93 and that of low performers 107 and 104 in Japan and in the U.S., respectively.

3. The interactive (or contingent) effect of a variable X upon Z (the criterion variable) can be mathematically expressed as follows:

$$Z = a_0 + a_1 X + a_2 XY + a_3 Y,$$

where Y is also a variable affecting Z. The net effect of X upon Z is shown as $(a_1 + a_2 Y)$. This means that the effect of X increases as the value of Y increases if a_2 is positive. This means, in turn, that having a higher score of X is more valuable when the score of Y is high. If a_2 is negative, the reverse is true.
Based upon this formula, the following multiplicative terms are included in the regression list besides the 26 variables used in the prior non-interactive regression analysis:

(EDIV) * (OSTR), (EDIV) * (OSHA), (EVAR) * (OSTR), (EVAR) * (OSHA), (SRES) * (OSTR), (SRES) * (OSHA), (SINN) * (OSTR), (SINN) * (OSHA), (OSTR) * (OSHA), and (SSHA) * (SINN).

4. The figures are partial regression coefficients (not beta coefficients). The figures in parentheses are t-values.

5. *ROI emphasis*, which reflects pressures from the capital (another important input) market, also has some influence upon the *structuring of organization* in the two countries (Table 6-9).

References

Azumi, K., *"Soshikikozo no chikaku - Igirisu, Nippon, Sueden no hikaku* (Perceptions of Organizational Structure: A British, Japanese and Swedish Comparison)," Written in Japanese, *Soshiki Kagaku (Organizational Science)*, 13-4, 1980, pp.26-36.

Beer, S., *Brain of the Firm, 2nd ed.*, London: John Wiley, 1981.

Burgelman, R. A., "A Process Model of Internal Corporate Venturing in Diversified Major Firm," *Administrative Science Quarterly*, 28, 1983, pp.223-244.

Burns, T. and G. M. Stalker, *The Management of Innovation*, London: Tavistock, 1961.

Child, J., "Organization Structure, Environment and Performance : The Role of Strategic Choice," *Sociology* 6-1, 1972, pp.1-22.

Deal, T. and A. W. Kennedy, *Corporate Culture*, Reading, Mass.: Addison-Wesley, 1982.

Hamermesh, R. G., "Administrative Issues Posed by Contemporary Approach to Strategic Planning : The Case of Dexter Corporation," Working Paper, Boston: Harvard Business School, 1979.

Jantsch, E., "Unifying Principles of Evolution" in E. Jantsch (ed.), *Evolutionary Vision*, Boulder, Col.: Westview Press, 1981.

Kagono T., I. Nonaka, K. Sakakibara and A. Okumura, "Mechanistic vs. Organic Management Systems : A Comparative Study of Adaptive Patterns of U.S. and Japanese Firms," *Annuals of the School of Business Administration*, Kobe University, 25, 1981, pp.115-145.

Kagono, T., I. Nonaka, K. Sakakibara and A. Okumura, *Nichi-bei kigyo no keiei hikaku* (Comparative Study of U.S. vs. Japanese Management), Written in Japanese, Tokyo : Nihon Keizai Shimbunsha, 1983.

Kanter, R. M., *The Change Masters*, New York: Simon and Schuster, 1983.

Kiechel, E., "Oh Where, Oh Where Has My Little Dog Gone? Or My Cash Cow? Or My Star? " *Fortune*, Nov. 2, 1981, pp.148-154.

Lawrence, P. R. and J.W. Lorsch, *Organization and Environment*, Boston: Harvard Business School, Division of Research, 1967.

Nonaka, I., T. Kagono and S. Sakamoto, "Evolutionary Strategy and Structure," Working Paper, Tokyo: Institute of Business Research, Hitotsubashi University, 1983.

Ouchi, W. G., *Theory Z*, Reading, Mass.: Addison-Wesley, 1981.

Pascale, R. T. and A. G. Athos, *The Art of Japanese Management,* New York: Simon and Schuster, 1981.

Peters, T. J. and R. H. Waterman, Jr., *In Search of Excellence*, New York: Harper & Row, 1982.

Pfeffer, J., "Management as Symbolic Action: The Creation and Maintenance of an Organizational Paradigm" in L. L. Cummings and B. M. Staw (eds.), *Research in Organizational Behavior, vol.3*, Greenwich, Conn.: JAI Press, 1980.

Porter, M. E., *Competitive Strategy*, New York: Free Press, 1980.

Pugh, D. S., D. J. Hickson, C. R. Hinnings and C. Turner, "The Context of Organization Structure," *Administrative Science Quarterly*, 14, 1969, pp.115-126.

Schumpeter, J. A., *The Theory of Economic Development*, Cambridge, Mass.: Harvard University Press, 1934.

Selznick, P., *Leadership in Administration*, New York: Harper & Row, 1957.

Weick, K. *The Social Psychology of Organizing, 2nd ed.* Reading, Mass.: Addison-Wesley, 1979.

Woodward, J., *Industrial Organization: Theory and Practice*, London: Oxford University Press, 1965.

CHAPTER 7 AN EVOLUTIONARY VIEW OF ORGANIZATIONAL ADAPTATION
SUMMARY AND IMPLICATIONS

Important differences in the strategies of U.S. and Japanese organizations, and in the ways in which they adapt to their environments, have been presented in this study. The reasons for these differences, the strengths and limitations of each, and their impact upon performance have been discussed. The principal findings are summarized here, and four major types of environmental adaptation are proposed on the basis of those findings. Factors are discussed which affect the forming of the different adaptive modes with special attention to the environment. A new theoretical perspective is presented and theoretical and practical implications are drawn out.

7.1 Summary of the Findings

A. Analysis of the survey data indicated very consistent differences between U.S. and Japanese firms in their strategies, organizational structures and processes, the traits of their managers, their organizational goals, and in the environments which they faced. It is submitted that these differences were responsible for the substantially different patterns of organizational adaptation which were observed for Japanese companies relative to American. The differences are summarized in Table 7-1.

B. Our comparative study of the strategies and "responses" to their environments of the two nations' firms disclosed the following differences:

1. While U.S. firms define their domains with relative precision and specificity, Japanese firms define their domains very broadly, indicating only general organizational directions and imparting visions with the barest "forest" outlines of corporate strategy. This, however, performs a sensitizing function -- making everyone aware of goals and issues -- and also requires broad participation in

Table 7-1 U.S. vs. Japanese Modes of Adaptation

	A - Mode Adaptation (U.S. mode)	J - Mode Adaptation (Japanese mode)

Environment	diverse,less volatile,bleak;
	
	remote relationships with
	  distributors, customers,
	  supplier and sub-
	  contractors;
	rivalry with competitors;
	
	mobile labor market
		homogeneous,volatile, opportu-
		  nity rich;
		close relationships with
		  distributors, customers,
		  suppliers and sub-
		  contractors;
		somewhat cooperative relation-
		  ship with competitors;
		immobile labor market

Objectives	profitability and stock-
	  holders' gains
		multiple objectives with
		  emphasis on growth

Strategy	mobile resource deployment
	  stressing short-term
	  efficiency;
	
	head-on competition stress-
	  ing cost efficiency;
	
	product-oriented competitive
	  strategy
		less mobile resource
		deployment
		  creation of slack, stressing
		  long-term development of
		  resources;
		coexistence with competitors
		  stressing "niche" and
		  differentiation;
		production-oriented
		competitive strategy

Technology	routine	non-routine

Organization-
al Structure
	mechanistic structure
	  (high formalization,
	  standardization and
	  centralization);
	strong power of finance &
	  control department;
	
	divisionalization as the rule
	sophisticated performance
	  appraisal and clear linkage
	  between performance and
	  financial remuneration;
	self-contained divisions
	  with vertical control
		organic structure
		  (low formalization,
		  standardization and
		  centralization);
		weak power of finance &
		  control department and
		  strong power of production
		  department;
		selective divisionalization;
		simple performance appraisal
		  and weak linkage between
		  performance and financial
		  remuneration;
		less self-contained
		  divisions with horizontal
		  coordination network

Organization-
al Process
	task-oriented leadership;
	
	conflict resolution by
	  confrontation;
		information-oriented
		  leadership;
		conflict resolution by broad
		  consultation before action,
		  and by forcing;

Table 7-1 (continued) U.S. vs. Japanese Modes of Adaptation

	A - Mode Adaptation (U.S. mode)	J- Mode Adaptation (Japanese mode)
	decision-making stressing individual initiative; output control	group-oriented consensual decision-making; behavioral control and control by sharing of values and information; orientation toward change; promotion from within
Personal Predisposition of Members	specialist; value commitment; inclination toward innovation and risk-taking	generalist; interpersonal skills

order to interpret and make such general direction operational. Perhaps just as important, such equivocality gives organizational members the opportunity to participate very meaningfully.

2. While U.S. firms seek to develop their available physical and financial resources only after relatively thorough analysis of the environment, the opportunities it provides, and the risks entailed, they then deploy those resources as efficiently as possible (explicitly accounting for risks of understocking, etc.); Japanese firms emphasize the accumulation -- the overstocking -- of not only physical and financial but, also, people-related resources within the organization in a variety of ways. The rationale is that by over-stocking, the organization will be prepared to exploit any opportunity which the environment provides, and be able to cope with any demand which it poses.

3. With regard to resource development, while U.S. firms tend to emphasize financial resources over others, Japanese firms place very heavy (financially-speaking) and systematic emphasis on the development of their human resources. Two general reasons for this are organizational learning and vitalization. Although other factors are surely pertinent too, a predictable consequence is that the U.S. firms are more short-run performance oriented.

4. U.S. firms characteristically face risks independently (there appear to be few government-guaranteed loans for Chrysler-like firms).

Japanese firms, while competing with each other, reduce the risks facing individual firms through interorganizational networks.

5. U.S. firms have characteristically sought to gain competitive advantage by emphasizing product strategies and implementing them in revolutionary new ways. Japanese firms have gained competitive advantage by focusing their strategies more upon operations and by attempting to continuously improve them in an incremental way.

While certain U.S. and Japanese firms depart from the contrasting approaches to strategy which have been described, our data support the hypothesis that the characterizations are reasonably typical.   The approach more typical of U.S. firms is called a "product-oriented" strategy; that typical of Japanese firms is described as an "operations-oriented" one.   In way of summary, a product-oriented strategy places greater emphasis upon new product development than operations development, on mobile resource deployment and on diversification through acquisitions (and diverstitures of businesses).   Change in response to the demands of the environment in the product-oriented firm tends to be rather discontinuous.

In contrast, the operations-oriented strategy focuses more on the incremental development of "operations," and places much emphasis on accumulating experience that contributes to the existing intra-organizational capability and "know-how." Change, therefore, tends to be incremental and more continuous.

C. Our case analyses of a number of U.S. and Japanese firms indicated the following differences in organization.

1. U.S. firms design relatively permanent hierachical structures that are thought most appropriate for their strategies. While hierarchy-dependent in a number of ways, Japanese firms employ numerous mechanisms which encourage frequent interactions horizontally and vertically. This preserves the flexibility necessary to adapt to a broad range of environmental circumstances.

2. U.S. firms effect control through relatively sophisticated and centralized systems of "objective" information flow.   In Japanese

firms, control is relatively diffused. Greater emphasis is placed upon a "loose," formally less well-defined but yet highly developed system of values and information-sharing which encourages greater self-control and more frequent interaction.

3. Capitalizing on hierarchy and the division of labor, U.S. firms emphasize individual expertise and learning. What has been learned is built into the structure and systems of the organization. Japanese firms place tremendous emphasis upon personal interaction within and between groups. This greatly facilitates information transfer and contributes to organizational learning which is retained in the organization's people.

4. U.S. efforts to cope with change are generally initiated in the form of strategy and policy at or near the top. The implementation of change then works itself down the hierarchy. In marked contrast, the top management of Japanese firms create a climate of idealism and aspiration at the top, and a certain amount of tension at lower levels by failing to provide any direction at all about how to achieve those aspirations. A high degree of intra-organizational variety is effected throughout the firm. Although oversimplified in explanation, this variety is achieved by means of frequent rotation of people through key (often unrelated) positions, imprecisely defined and overlapping roles, a high degree of shared decision-making, and by many other means. Thus, the general "mechanism" for coping with change in Japanese firms is to create a climate of tension which serves to enhance organizational vitality and to equip organizational members (through variety) to *initiate* changes themselves; the change is, therefore, from the bottom.

5. The tenure of even the highest executives of U.S. firms is relatively uncertain. The status positions of upper-level managers of Japanese firms are close to being permanent. (Jobs may be rotated but the authority of the managers remains for decision-making.) An important consequence is the continuity of policy over the long-run. Somewhat paradoxically, the hierarchy and differentiation of U.S. firms seem to rely upon a hierarchical value system of sorts. The principal underlying sources of motivation at top and bottom are assumed to be different, and the focus appears to be narrowly concentrated upon the particular functions which "are necessary" to implement a particular

strategy.   Much attention is given to values by Japanese firms,
although the focus on values, for example, as articulated through
corporate philosophy, is very broad. But there is much mutual effort
to ensure that values are shared widely.   Since basic decision
premises are shared, in Japanese organizations decisions can be made
in ambiguous situations with relative certainty that smooth
implementation will follow.

The organizing considerations discussed above are also closely related to
each other. The ensuing pattern of behavior more generally descriptive of
U.S. firms is called "bureaucratic dynamics."   That pattern more
descriptive of Japanese firms is called "group dynamics."

Bureaucratic dynamics is an organizing method that reduces environmental
variety through formalized hierarchy, rules, and planning. Group dynamics
depends for the reduction of environmental variety on much interaction
within and between groups, and the sharing of values and information.

Our research found not only differences between the two countries, but
also similarities, especially for firms with good performance.

D. The high performers in both countries shared these characteristics:

1. The high performers tended to combine a product-oriented strategy
   with group dynamics organization. This combination is best among the
   four pure types of adaptation in both countries, using average
   overall performance as a criterion.
2. At the same time, high performers had some elements of the operations
   orientation and of bureaucratic dynamics. A coexistence of elements
   from all four different strategic and organizational characteristics
   is better than any pure combination in either country.

E. Certain factors correlated with high performance differed by country:

1. Visible, active, directive leadership of executives appeared to
   contribute to corporate performance in the U.S., but did not in
   Japan. The strength of less visible indirect leadership, e.g.,

infusing values to the corporate culture and sharing visions, is associated more with high performance in Japan.

2. The synergism of efficient allocation of organizational resources contributed more to performance in the U.S. Japanese high performers tended to build resource bases with greater *slack* than Japanese low performers.

3. Organizational size contributed positively to performance in Japan. It had a negative effect on performance, especially on growth, in the U.S.

F. The choices of strategy, structure, and process are influenced by various forces.

1. A higher product orientation -- or more specifically, leadership in innovation -- exists where: human resources are emphasized; an organization faces a variable environment; and values and information are highly shared. This is true in both countries. Visible, entrepreneurial leadership and structuring of the organization is important in the U.S., while invisible leadership (or the institutionalization of values) contributes more in Japan.

2. An organization tends to be more group dynamics-oriented, when human resources are emphasized and the interpersonal skills of executives are stressed. Large size is associated with the sharing of values and information in Japan, but this is not true in the U.S.

3. Increasing environmental diversity and organizational size tend to make organizations more bureaucratic dynamics-oriented.

4. Continuous process technologies and large organizational size are associated with organizations that are more operations-oriented.

5. Finally, the socio-cultural forces of Japan make for organizations that are more group dynamics-oriented and operations-oriented. The U.S. socio-cultural background tends to foster organizations that are more bureaucratic dynamics and product-oriented.

7.2 Four Types of Environmental Adaptation

In this study, we have compared U.S. and Japanese firms along two

principal dimensions: with respect to strategy -- the operations-
orientation vs. product-orientation; and, with respect to organizing --
the group dynamics vs. bureaucratic dynamics orientation. One could say
that, in general, Japanese firms are characterized by operations-oriented
strategies and dependence on group dynamics, while U.S. firms are
characterized more by product-oriented strategies and dependence on
bureaucratic dynamics.

Figure 7-1 **Dimensions of Strategies and Organization and Interfirm
            Differences**

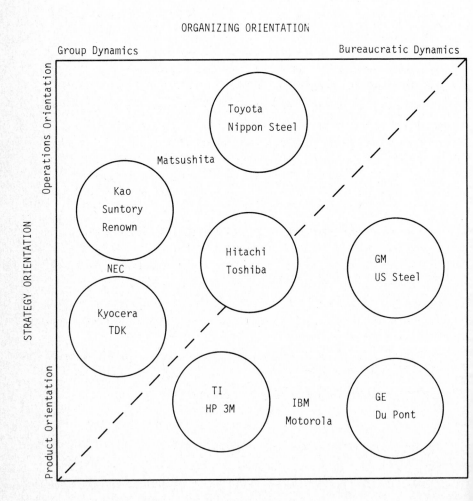

Of course, individual firms differ in their approaches to environmental adaptation within each country. As we showed in Chapter 5, these dimensions can also be used to capture the interfirm differences within a country. Figure 7-1 compares, based on the two dimensions, the approaches to environmental adaptation by the representative firms, as analyzed also in Chapter 5.

This figure illustrates not only the difference between Japanese and U.S. firms in general (Japanese firms at the upper left, and U.S. firms at the lower right) but also the differences among individual firms. Furthermore, there are among the firms, some that combine the group dynamics and product orientation (i.e., that have a mixture of typical Japanese and U.S. traits) and some that are close to a combination of bureaucratic dynamics and an operations orientation. Thus, it is necessary to differentiate four types of environmental adaptation, corresponding to the four cells of the diagram shown in Figure 7-2. We have named them the H type (upper left), the V type (lower left), the B type (upper right), and the S type (lower right).

Figure 7-2 Four Types of Adaptation to Environment

	Group Dynamics	Bureaucratic Dynamics
Operations Orientation	H Type	B Type
Product Orientation	V Type	S Type

7.2.1 The Four Types of Environmental Adaptation

In order to clarify the natures of the four types, the following
characteristics of each will be examined:
(1) Method of organizational integration and information processing,
(2) Distribution of influence and organizational form,
(3) Pattern of knowledge and information accumulation,
(4) Executive's leadership style,
(5) Response to opportunities and threats,
(6) Key to environmental adaptation and competitive strength,
(7) Information and value orientation.

The H type

The firms that are close to the H type adaptation pattern at the upper
left of Figure 7-1 are: Matsushita Electric (during its growth stage),
Toyota Motor, Suntory, Renown and Kao. The average adaptation pattern of
all Japanese firms surveyed is close to this type.   In these firms,
organizational integration is attained and information is processed
through frequent intra and intergroup interaction, the sharing of values
and information, the arousing of tension, and through interpersonal
networks.   Influence on decision making is dispersed throughout the
organization, which is of the linking-pin type. Learning activities are
carried out at various locations, including the lowest levels of the
organization.   Knowledge and information are shared through interactions,
but the relationships among groups are loose enough to permit each group's
autonomous adaptation to its environment.   Top management resemble
religious missionaries, trying to infuse the organization with ideals and
direction.   Environmental opportunities and threats are detected at the
lower levels of the organization, and adaptation to the environment tends
to be inductive and incremental. The key to environmental adaptation is
increasing the efficiency of operations and/or making small improvements
in product characteristics. The emphasis is on concerted effort and the
speed with which adjustments are made.   Importance is attached to the
information obtained at first-line production sites and through contacts
with customers. And maintaining a sense of the unity of the whole
organization is emphasized.   In such a pattern of adaptation, the *human*

factor assumes a heavy relative weight; for this reason, we have named this pattern the H type.

The V type

The firms that are close to the V type, at the lower left of Figure 7-1 are 3M and HP in the United States and Kyocera, TDK and NEC in Japan. They are the creative innovators in both countries. In this type of firm, the organizational integration is attained and information is processed through frequent interactions, the sharing of values and information, the cultivation of a commitment to technologies and products, and the formation of teams and task forces. A firm is a federation of small teams; while its top management exercises strong leadership, each team possesses a high degree of autonomy. Accumulation of knowledge and information depends on the learning activities of individuals or teams. Know-how for the purpose of creative innovation is very difficult to standardize, so such know-how is handed down by others working closely with and emulating the organization's star performers. Top management exercises entrepreneurial leadership, and internal entrepreneurs also play an important role in initiating innovations.

Responses to opportunities and threats are aggressive, and product innovation is carried out experimentally to uncover hidden niches. The key to environmental adaptation is product uniqueness, and competitive advantage is established by innovating ahead of competitors. Fresh technological or customer information is highly regarded. Risk-taking becomes a challenge and the dominant rule of behavior. New venture firms typically show this sort of adaptive response to their environments, so we have decided to call this pattern the V type of adaptation.

The B type

Firms that are close to the B type in adaptation, at the upper right corner of Figure 7-1 are Nippon Steel (before the days of the JK movement), U.S. Steel (before it became a conglomerate), and GM. Among B type firms organizational integration is attained and information is processed through rules, programs, hierarchy and the functional division of labor, and rewards are commensurate with job functions and hierarchical levels. The authority for decision-making is concentrated at the top and among an elite staff. The structure of these organizations is highly delineated along functional lines. Pivotal information and knowledge tend to be accumulated through the learning activities of an elite staff, and they are handed down in the form of systems, policies, and rules. Top leadership is "technocratic." The response to environmental opportunities and threats is passive and defensive: priority is placed on defending the status quo. The key to environmental adaptation is production efficiency, and competitive advantage is sought through reduction of costs. Much importance is attached to quantitative internal or market information; rationality, planning, and adherence to procedure become the dominant behavioral rules. Since bureaucracy plays a central role in firms with this kind of adaptation pattern, it is called the *bureaucratic* or B type of adaptation.

The S type

Some of the firms that are close to the S type adaptation pattern, indicated at the lower right corner of Figure 7-1 are GE (during the Jones era), Du Pont, and recently Motorola. The "average" U.S. firm also shows this adaptive pattern. The means to organizational integration and information processing are hierarchy, self-containedness, vertical information flow, plans and objectives, and reward for performance. The standard organizational form is multi-divisional. While decision-making authority for operations is decentralized, the authority to make resource allocation is concentrated at the top, with financial and strategy planning staffs having a strong say.

Knowledge and information are accumulated through the learning activities of the elite. The information system is designed to transmit information to the top, and knowledge and information are sometimes gained through acquisitions of other business ventures. Top management leadership is the commander type, and it pursues dynamic and consistent strategies.

Firms that have this type of adaptation pattern anticipate environmental opportunities and threats and formulate strategic plans to meet them. In this type of strategic planning, responses to changes in the environment are made deductively. One of the keys to adaptation is resource deployment. Competitive advantage is established in individual markets logically and analytically, taking into consideration the firm's own strengths and weaknesses, competitive conditions, and the missions of each business unit. Quantitative and qualitative information is collected systematically, and the consistency and systematic implementation of strategic plans become the rules of behavior. Since strategies play such an important role in this type of adaptation, we refer to it as the S type.

The four types of adaptation described (and shown in Figure 7-3) were derived empirically from a binational comparison, but they are also applicable to a comparison of firms within a country or an industry. For example, in Japan's home electric appliance industry, Sanyo and Matsushita are H type, Sony and Sharp, the V type, and Hitachi and Toshiba each have strong elements of the S type of adaptation.

Various typologies of organizations' adaptive strategies have been proposed (Mintzberg, 1973; Paine and Anderson, 1976; Miles & Snow, 1978). The typology presented here may be more generally applicable because it is derived from a broader empirical domain -- one inclusive of Japanese firms. For example, Miles and Snow's "Analyzer" corresponds to our S type; their "Defender" corresponds to our B type; and their "Prospector" corresponds to our V type. They missed H type, which is typical in Japan.

7.2.2 Types of Environmental Change and Modes of Organizational Adaptation

In chapter 6 it was concluded that the V type outperformed the others among the four pure types. Various reasons were given there, but many of them were related to the ability to creatively cope with environmental change. General characteristics of adaptive behavior in each type are discussed next.

The H type firms' adaptation to environmental changes is often passive.

Figure 7-3 Characteristics of the Types of Organizational Adaptation

H:
(1) Frequent interaction, sharing of values and information, generation of tension, very strong interpersonal networks.
(2) Loosely-coupled linking-pin form: diffusion of decision-making power throughout the organization. Priest-type leadership.
(3) Priest-type leadership.
(4) Broad learning through interaction, and sharing knowledge throughout the organization.
(5) Day-to-day operational information much through direct contact with customers and clients.
(6) Cohesion, harmony.
(7) Reactive, inductive, and incremental adaptation.
(8) Efficiency of operations, small differences in product characteristics, synergy, speed of adaptation to relatively continuous environmental change.

B:
(1) Rules, problem-reactive, hierarchy, functional division of labor, extrinsic reward system tied to job.
(2) Functional organization; concentration of power among top management and staff. Technocratic leadership.
(3) Technocratic leadership.
(4) Learning by an "elite;" transfer of knowledge through policies, manuals, and rules.
(5) Quantitative information.
(6) Adherence to policies, jobs, procedures, rules.
(7) Reactive adaptation geared toward higher quantitative output and defense of existing domain.
(8) Operating efficiency, cost-leadership.

V:
(1) Frequent interaction, sharing of values and information, emphasis on teams/task-forces; commitment to technology and product.
(2) Coalitions of small teams; diffusion of decision-making power among them. Entrepreneurial leadership.
(3) Entrepreneurial leadership.
(4) Individual and team learning/learning by modelling and observation.
(5) Fresh information concerning customers and technology.
(6) Willingness to accept risk, venture spirit.
(7) Pro-active and experimental; some-times, adaptation in major strides.
(8) Uniqueness of product, industry leader in innovation.

S:
(1) Hierarchy, vertical information channels, plans, goals, self-containment, and appraisal of performance by results.
(2) Divisional organization; concentration of power (especially for resource allocation) at the top. Military general type leadership.
(3) Military general type leadership.
(4) Learning by an "elite;" transfer of knowledge by highly institutionalized methods.
(5) Systematic forecasting.
(6) Consistency, adherence to plan, and goal-attainment.
(7) Deductive, analytical, planned adaptation.
(8) Strategic consistency.

MAJOR CHARACTERISTICS OF ADAPTATION

Each numbered item of the Table describes the dominant characteristics for organizations of the given type with respect to the following dimensions:

(1) MEANS OF ORGANIZATIONAL INTEGRATION AND INFORMATION PROCESSING.
(2) ORGANIZATIONAL FORM, AND DISTRIBUTION OF POWER.
(3) TOP MANAGEMENT LEADERSHIP.
(4) ACCUMULATION OF INFORMATION AND TRANSFER OF KNOWLEDGE.
(5) INFORMATION ORIENTATION.
(6) VALUE ORIENTATION.
(7) ADAPTIVE ORIENTATION TOWARD OPPORTUNITY AND RISK.
(8) KEY FACTORS FOR ADAPTATION AND GAINING COMPETITIVE ADVANTAGE.

At the same time, such firms have typically developed a variety of sensors enabling them to detect changes early, and they have the ability to respond quickly. For this to be possible, frequent interaction is necessary, production-site and customer information must be fed back throughout the organization swiftly, and the organizational structure must permit individual production sites to respond to change autonomously. Moreover, each autonomous group must have enough knowledge so that it can process various types of information. In order to accumulate such knowledge, continuous learning is promoted. It is to avoid conflicting adaptive efforts that values and information among the autonomous groups must be widely shared. For this reason, too, the groups must maintain a certain degree of independence and looseness in their ties with each other.

The V type firms' adaptation to environmental changes is aggressive. Perhaps it would be more appropriate to say that changes in the environment are wrought by the innovations of V type firms. Aggressive steps "to adapt" are more experimental than rational or analytical, and the research and development departments of such firms have a large degree of freedom. Knowledge can be said to be more the consequence of innovations than of steady accumulation, and the framework of knowledge is often revised. Acquiring the know-how for innovation is largely indeterminate and therefore difficult to pass on to others.

The B type organization acts in response to changes, to protect their existing industry positions, market domains, etc. They resist changes in the environment rather than respond to them. The knowledge that has been acquired is largely the result of past experience; therefore, it can only be utilized within a limited domain. Hence, the necessity of devoting themselves to protecting their existing domain.

Those in S type organizations analyze the environment, forecast the changes necessary, and formulate strategies in response. The knowledge needed to respond to changes is planned for and accumulated systematically. When swiftness is demanded, expertise may be obtained from outside the organization. Opportunities and threats that are generated by changes are perceived quickly, and resources are organized to

meet them in a way that capitalizes on the firm's strengths. Strategies
are formulated by those in the top management of each business unit and
their staffs. The efffectiveness of strategies is evaluated periodically
during implementation, and corrective measures are taken as appropriate.
The top managers are selected from among strategy planning staffs and
general managers, largely for their rational-analytical skills.

The foregoing discussion, suggests which type of adaptation is best suited
to different kinds of environmental changes.

The H type excels in responding to relatively continuous unpredictable
changes. This type of firm would occupy a superior position in an
environment in which small changes occur continuously. The V type excels
in an environment in which large unpredictable changes occur frequently.
Such firms achieve superiority by creating opportunities in fast-changing,
unpredictable environments through their innovations. B type firms are
suited to stable environments with few changes, while S type firms excel
in environments in which there occur diverse but predictable changes,
because they are able to devise strategic responses appropriate to such
changes.

As in the biology of living organisms we find a marked correlation between
the adaptive "type" that an organization is and the form of strategy that
its environment demands. And when the fit between type and environment is
appropriate, the organization's performance and chances for survival are
high.

The environment facing U.S. and Japanese organizations has become more
turbulent and is likely to be increasingly so in the future as
technological developments in various fields become more diverse and
variable. These forces have brought and will bring forth unpredictable
changes in environment. Now it is clear in general terms why the V type
outperforms the others. It is suited to the present turbulent
environment.

The four types just discussed are ideal types of organizational adaptive
forms. In reality, firms rarely strive to adapt to the environment

according to one of these ideal types. Firms cope with changes in their environments by using combinations of the four which vary in accordance with certain environmental demands. Moreover, the combination of adaptive types actually employed is also constrained by other factors. They are discussed below.

7.2.3 Factors that Determine the Combination of Adaptation Types

The combination of types of organizational adaptation that a firm pursues is influenced by the various factors discussed in Chapter 6.

The first major influence is the nature of the environmental change that a firm faces. In conditions of constant change, technological progress, new customer tastes, and varying competition, numerous opportunities and threats evolve. By coping with the one and taking advantage of the other, firms can survive and achieve good performance. As already discussed, there is a correlation between the nature of changes and the adaptation types that are suited to them. The H type of adaptation is suited to an environment in which small unpredictable changes take place continuously; the V type, to an environment in which major, unpredictable changes occur frequently; the B type, to a stable environment with few changes; and the S type, to an environment in which there occur predictable changes of diverse forms.

To generalize, as changes become greater, the V and S types, both with a strong product orientation, become more effective than the H or B types. As changes become more predictable, the B and the S types, with strong elements of bureaucratic dynamics, become more effective than the H type or the V type. This suggests that in order to cope most effectively with environmental changes, it is necessary to combine different adaptation types in accordance with the nature of those changes.

The amplitude and predictability of the environmental changes have a close relationship to the life-cycles of industries. In the beginning stage of an industry or even product, the changes in environment are large and less predictable. In this circumstance, the V type of adaptation stands to be most effective. As an industry grows, changes within it become smaller and more predictable, and elements of the H and/or S type of adaptation become increasingly necessary. Later, as an industry matures, changes become rarer and quite predictable, so the B type of adaptation becomes dominant. The life-cycle of an industry and changes in the types of adaptation dictated by the changes in life-cycle stages are depicted by a, b, and c in Figure 7-4. Other factors influence whether a, b, or c is followed and how fast the route is traveled.

Figure 7-4 Nature of Environmental Changes and Adaptation Types

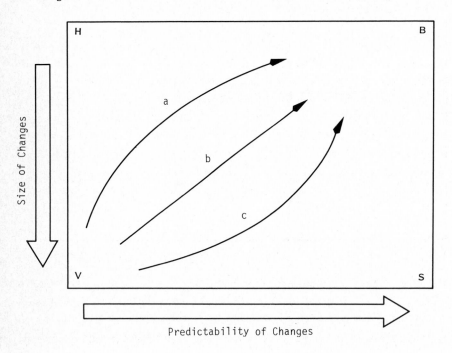

Predictability of Changes

The second factor affecting the types of adaptation pursued is the variety of products and markets faced by the firm. As stated in Chapter 5, as the diversity of product markets increases, the S type of adaptation becomes more necessary because company-wide strategic planning is required to reallocate resources among the operating divisions and to coordinate their efforts. Firms that diversify in the maturing stage of an industry, therefore, would shift, in Figure 7-4, to the right of a, b, or c with increased weight attached to S type adaptation. This is shown in Figure

7-5. Hitachi and Toshiba in Japan and GE and Du Pont in the United States are examples illustrating this shift toward the S type as they diversify.

Figure 7-5 Diversity of Product-Markets and Adaptation Types

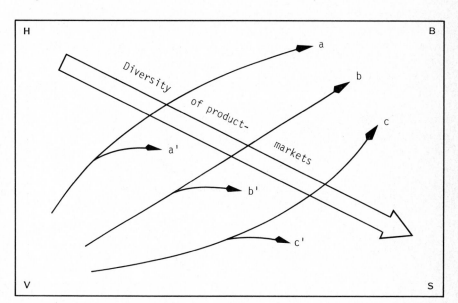

The third factor is a composite of cultural and institutional forces. As stated in Chapters 2, 3, 4, and 5, Japanese firms tend to display the H type of adaptation on the average, and U.S. firms tend to show the S type of adaptation. In terms of Figure 7-5, while Japanese firms tend to follow a or a', U. S. firms tend to take a c or c' path. This difference is the combined result of various factors. But, in general, it can be said with certainty that the cultural and institutional biases have exerted forces toward the H type of adaptation in Japan and the S type of adaptation in the United States. (see Figure 7-6.)

Factor or input markets, such as the labor and the capital markets, are heavily biased by cultural influences. As shown in Chapters 3, 4, 5, and 6, with an increase in labor market mobility, there are tendencies for the

,B and S types of adaptation, both of which rely on bureaucratic dynamics,
to be utilized more than the H or V types. When the interfirm mobility of
labor is high, the sharing of values and information is more difficult
than otherwise, and firms are compelled to rely on the formal
organizational structure, that is, on bureaucratic dynamics. In addition,
when interfirm labor mobility is high, it contributes to the ease of
deployment of resources and the adoption of a product-orientation.

Figure 7-6 Cultural Biases and Adaptation Types

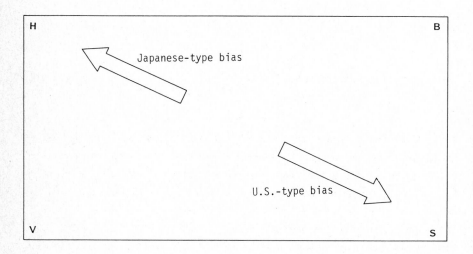

The pressure exerted by the capital markets for a quick, satisfactory
return on investment has an influence in the same direction. This is
because, in order to increase control over short-term returns on
investment, the organizational structure must be formalized to effect
rapid deployment of resources and to implement strategies with a high
product-orientation. Therefore, mobility in the labor market and pressure
from the capital markets to maximize short-term returns on investment act
together to shift the firm's adaptation pattern from the H type to the S
type. This effect of the factor markets can be seen not only in a
comparison of Japanese and the U.S. companies but also in comparisons
within each country. Figure 7-7 illustrates the point.

Figure 7-7   Factor Markets and Adaptation Types

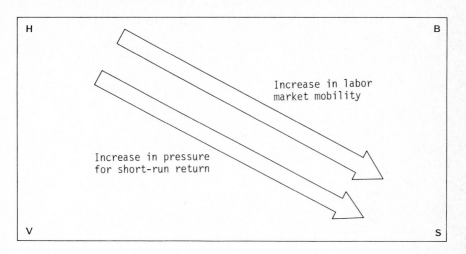

A fifth major influence on adaptation type, is the combined effect of corporate size and production technologies. As stated in Chapter 6, an increase in corporate size would result in increased reliance on the B or S type of adaptation, which emphasize bureaucratic dynamics. This is because of the difficulty of integrating the purpose and effort of a large-scale organization through group dynamics alone. In comparison, firms that are heavily dependent on capital-intensive or mass-production technologies tend to increase the relative importance that they attach to the H or B type of adaptation, both of which are strongly operations-oriented in their strategies. This is because in capital-intensive or mass-production operations, there is obviously much competitive advantage to be gained in achieving increased efficiencies in operations. Figure 7-8 shows the relationship just discussed.

It is not true that the above five factors have equal importance. The ability to cope with changes that are generated by a firm's market environment is the final determinant of the firm's necessity for internal variations and of management performance. Thus, it is most important for a firm to achieve an appropriate match of its combination of adaptation

Figure 7-8 Scale and Production Technology and Adaptation Types

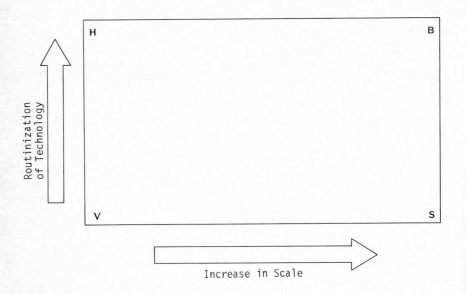

Figure 7-9 General Model of Adaptation to Environment

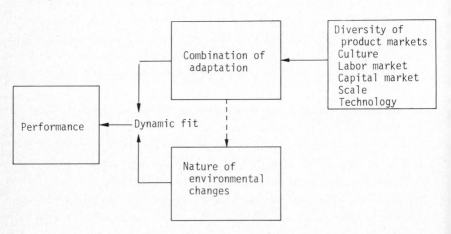

types with the environmental characteristics that it faces. Other factors can be regarded as contributing or constraining influences in this match. Figure 7-9 illustrates the above relationship in a simple way. In cases where other factors act to prevent a suitable match, it is the basic task of management to overcome such barriers. In the high performance firms, both in the United States and in Japan, discussed in Chapter 6, this has been accomplished.

Notable among firms that have overcome factors constraining adaptation are those that have grown large but still value V type adaptation. These are Kyocera and TDK in Japan and 3M, HP, and TI in the United States. As already stated, it becomes difficult to emphasize V type adaptation as an industry's life-cycle matures and when there are increases of scale and product diversity. These large corporations continued or renewed reliance upon the V type adaptation pattern -- of coping aggressively and creatively with changes. They achieve high performance through remarkable innovations and aggressive introduction of changes in their industries. The constraints to change have been overcome by the force of these firms' managers' personalities and/or by evoking a strong sense of corporate mission (Kyocera, TDK, 3M, and HP). We must note, too, that most of these firms establish operating units smaller in size than the average. This may reflect a common approach to overcoming the barriers to adaptability that frequently accompany large size.

If we examine Figure 7-1 again with the foregoing analysis in mind, we can better comprehend the reason why each firm occupies the position that it does.

7.3 Theoretical Implications -- In Search of a General Theory of Adaptation to Environment

One of the objectives of this study was to pursue a common theoretical framework which could be used to explain our quantitative and qualitative findings on management in Japan and in the U.S., and in so doing, along the way identify some of the unique characteristics of Japanese management. We have used concepts which are common to the United States and Japan so that there would be a meaningful basis for comparing the management systems and organizations of both, and concepts that are consistent with a theoretical framework which could be helpful in understanding the differences and similarities that exist. Only in so doing could we contribute to a broader framework which might be helpful in appreciating and solving the problems of organizational adaptation that all of us face.

7.3.1 Contingency Theory and the Information Processing Model

The starting theoretical framework of this study was contingency theory. Its fundamental idea is that for effectiveness, the managerial strategy and organization of a firm must fit its environment.

Contingency theory is a functionalistic analytical view rather than a single theory: it can coexist with various theoretical models. There have been attempts to explain consistently diverse empirical propositions of the contingency theory on the basis of specific theoretical models, for example, Thompson's(1967) uncertainty model and the information processing models of Nonaka (1972; 1974), Galbraith (1973), and Kagono(1980). Common to these models is the view that organizational goal achievement is made possible by the effective reduction of environmental uncertainty through systematic processing of information. The information processing models are based on cybernetics.

The fundamental hypotheses of cybernetics can be stated concisely by Ashby's "law of requisite variety," to wit: "only variety can destroy variety." Let us quote a simple example.

> In a rugby match, "the best way to control the system of fifteen men in red jerseys is to put fifteen men in white jerseys onto the field...if each red-jerseyed player is *marked* by a white-jerseyed player...then, on the average, whatever the actual play undertaken by the red team, sufficient variety can proliferate in the white team to match it." (Beer, 1966, pp.278-279)

When the law of requisite variety is applied to the relationship between a firm and its environment, it means that the firm must cope with the variety that is generated by the environment by building variety into its own organization. In cybernetics, variety is defined as "the number of possible states"; the larger the variety of temporal and special states generated by the environment, the greater the load on the organization in terms of its decision-making and information processing. In order to decrease this load, organizations must build within themselves a capability for processing diverse information. That is, in Ashby's terms, reduce environmental variety through amplification of one's own variety.[1] Accordingly, the basis of a firm's adaptation to its environment is the creation and maintenance of a dynamic equilibrium, $V_E = V_0$, between environmental variety (V_E) and the organizational variety (V_0). This is called variety engineering (Beer, 1981).

The tenets of contingency theory can be explained best by means of the information processing model. The model is also useful in designing organizational structures and systems appropriate to each organization's environment and strategy. This is possible when environments are clearly defined and strategies are clearly articulated. These requirements are observed to a considerable extent in S mode and to some extent in B mode adaptation. Therefore, the principal domain of the conventional information processing model is S and B type adaptation.

The information processing model, however, is limited in its ability to explain why the H and V modes of adaptation work. First, because it assumes the adaptation process to be a bounded-rational, goal-oriented problem-solving process (March and Simon, 1958; Thompson, 1967), it cannot explain the emergent, spontaneous adaptation of the H and V modes. In H and V type organizations, emergent actions play an important role in the adaptation process, and they are not induced by the organizatinal goals and strategies.

Second, the model assumes that inconsistencies, disequilibriums, instability, uncertainty, and ambiguity are harzardous to organizational viability (Thompson, 1967). It fails to recognize the necessity of such states for achieving those emergent leaps that are a critical element in V mode adaptation.

Third, the information processing model focuses on the formal structure of information processing networks and does not pay sufficient attention to informal, emergent interaction processes among people, which are essential aspects of H and V type adaptation. The soft aspects of organizations are more important in these adaptive modes than in the S and B modes.

According to conventional theory, the H and V types of adaptation may be thought irrational and elusive. Our findings demonstrated, however, that they are equally viable and in certain situations superior to the other types of adaptation. An alternative to the conventional view is required to explain these findings. It is submitted that any new model of organizational adaptation must explicitly treat the concept of group dynamics.

7.3.2 Theories of Group Dynamics

The H and V types of adaptation share an organizational principle in common: that of group dynamics. Group dynamics has a long intellectual tradition in organizational research in the U.S. The pioneering study of small work groups at the Hawthorne Plant in the U.S. before World War II,[2] served as impetus for many subsequent studies of small work groups. It was found that informal group norms had more impact on the behavior of group members than did formal directives. Such concepts as reference group, group cohesiveness, and group pressure[3] were born. As is well known, all of this eventually blossomed into the school of human relations. When one reads the Hawthorne experiment report, one finds a surprising resemblance between the events reported in it and those that have been recently reported in numerous studies on Japanese-style management. The foundations for group dynamics are hardly limited to Japan.

In addition, from the late 1950's to the early 1960's, Likert(1961), Argyris(1964), and others strongly advocated participatory approaches to management including enlargement and enrichment of job functions as means to make group dynamics effective. They can even be said to have proposed group dynamics as an organizing principle, although empirical research never sought to validate it at the organizational level. The bureaucratic dynamic model remained dominant both in the realm of theory and in actual practice.

There are several reasons why the organizational principle of group dynamics has not become the dominant theory in the United States:

(1) The large corporations facing environments with a high degree of variety had reasons for being concerned with the designs of their organizations, and these firms were compelled, to some extent, to rely on bureaucratic dynamics.

(2) The study of group dynamics in the United States was focused primarily at the group level. Except for the "linking pin" design proposed by Likert, there was not much attention paid to group dynamics as a principle operating at the organization level.

(3) The study of group dynamics in the United States focused on determinants of morale and motivation, and little attention was paid to the spontaneous, creative adaptability that groups were capable of; in fact, such relative autonomy was not wholly consistent with the bureaucratic dynamics model.

Nevertheless, as our data suggest, high-performing firms in the United States in reality implement organizational forms that maximize group dynamics along with bureaucratic dynamics. Only recently have there been modern studies emphasizing the organizational principle of group dynamics at the level of the firm as a whole. Ouchi's *Theory Z* (1981) and Pascale and Athos's 7S model (1981) are among these. And studies of values shared by members of a firm, behavioral norms, and corporate culture by Peters and Waterman (1982) and Deal and Kennedy (1982) have a group dynamics orientation in their discussion of group norms at the organization level.

Although any theory supported by empirical work at the organizational level has been late in coming, our data make it clear that, in actual practice, high-performing U.S. firms strongly emphasize group dynamics along wih bureaucratic dynamics.

Present theories of group dynamics explain the natural, emergent properties of organizations: shared values and norms, group cohesiveness and pressures, etc. The overall theory to date, is limited, however, in that it has focused primarily upon intra-organizational or intra-group interactions and not upon interactions between an organization and its environment. These interactions with environment are crucial for organizational adaptation. In other words, theories of group dynamics have had a *closed* natural system view. Their application to organizational theory requires an *open* natural system view (Scott, 1975).

7.3.3 Similarities and Differences between H and V Type Adaptation

The general characteristics of H and V type firms have been discussed earlier. But more must be learned about the processes which have enabled those firms to adapt so successfully to their environments. Let us, to make our analysis concrete, investigate the adaptive processes of two companies, which typify the H and V modes of adaptation, and identify their characteristics. In doing so, we seek to lay the foundation for a new model of organizational adaptation.

A typical case of H mode adaptation was exemplified by Matsushita Electric. In the 1960's and early 1970's the company had no long or middle-range strategic plans. Its "strategy" was comprised wholly of stimulating visions expressed in very general terms. Distinctive values and beliefs (Matsushita's seven principles) were articulated and widely shared among its people. The company had been building upon its strengths by continually improving its production technologies and by creating exclusive domestic distribution channels. These actions are typical of H type companies, as discussed earlier.

The key to successful adaptation to the changing environment of this industry was continuous product development and modification. These tasks were performed by divisions, subsidiaries and affiliates, all of which were highly autonomous. The company was, for reason of its many autonomous units, called "the Matsushita federation." The performance of each autonomous business unit was strictly evaluated and ranked in order in terms of sales' growth and return on sales. The same criteria were applied regardless of the maturity of product or market. All of the business units had to grow and make profits by developing new products and modifying existing ones, in order to be ranked high in performance.

Because all of Matsushita's businesses were closely related, very similar products were sometimes introduced by two or more divisions at the same time. A typical example was the radio-cassete recorder. The radio division developed a new radio set by adding a recording function to the radio. At the same time the tape-recorder division introduced a new tape recorder with a radio receiving function. There was no *ex ante* coordination but there was coordination to concentrate responsibility within one division, *ex post*, after observing the market reactions to both models. The VTR's development was another example. An internal division and Victor Co. of Japan, Ltd., a Matsushita affiliate, developed two different VTR formats. In this case also, there was no coordination in advance, but after carefully observing the market reaction to each model, the Victor format was chosen and the other format abandoned. The last case involves the development and manufacture of personal computers. At present, several different models, which are not compatible, are manufactured by different divisions, subsidiaries, and affiliates of the company. The choice of final models has not yet been made. Each division is working hard to make its model a winner, with headquarters carefully watching the market reaction and competitors' actions.

These three cases suggest that there has been much confusion, redundancy and inefficiency in Matsushita's product development process. But this has played a vital role in contributing to Matsushita's adaptability and strength. Mr. Yamashita, the president, commented:

> The superiority of a product is determined by (the manufacturing) division's efforts and market competition, not by headquarters. Each division works hard to seek market dominance. I, of course, realize that our way entails a lot of inefficiency, but this inefficiency is the inevitable cost of stimulating divisional entrepreneurship and vitality.

A typical example of a V type organization is 3M. The company has 50 thousand products. It has been a leader in much new product development and has built up its competitive position through its leadership. It also has a distinctive corporate culture with certain values widely shared by its people. These are major characteristics typical of the V type of organization.

The company's more than 40 divisions are highly autonomous profit centers. Each 3M division has an R&D department which is in charge of developing technology that is unrelated as well as related to the division's existing product lines. Division performance is evaluated in terms of return on sales, ROI, sales growth and its new product ratio. In order to achieve these targets, especially the last -- 25% of sales must be made with the products introduced in the last five years -- each division must continuously develop new products. Two or more divisions sometimes compete with each other in the same or in closely related product markets, without much coordination by the headquarters. It is a source of internal chaos but an unavoidable prerequisite for 3M's entrepreneurial creativity. 3M has a set of "rules of the game" to regulate this chaos. A 3M executive characterized his firm's state of being as "organized chaos."

Another aspect of 3M entreprenurship is its famous corporate venturing. An individual with a new product idea is permitted to apply for development funds not only to his own division but also to others, and as well to other internal sources. The existence of multiple sources raises the probability of funding a new idea. When an idea is accepted and funded, an autonomous, "mini-company" team of major functional specialists is organized. If the team proves successful, it can become a department and, then, a division. The success of a project is determined through interactions within the market place. The team members are allowed to manage the unit as if it were their own company as long as they meet certain performance criteria. The average success rate of these venturing teams is estimated to be 10 percent. The 3M approach though is to accept failures as part of the innovation process. By supporting many new ventures, despite failures, the overall absolute number of successes will increase.

The generation of new product ideas is a probablistic phenomenon. However, 3M has created various devices to increase the probability of their occurrence. The major devices are technological forums and the technological council, which enable the exchange of ordinarily unshared technical information and, thereby, raise the likelihood of new idea generation. 3M also has a "15% policy," i.e., an engineer can or should spend 15 percent of his working hours pursuing his own dream. This, too, contributes to the increased probability of new idea generation.

The two companies described above are in different industries and countries, and have different corporate cultures and distinctive competences. Their adaptive processes, however, share several characteristics in common.

First, spontaneous actions taken by an individual, team, or autonomous division, rather than the actions prescribed by a strategic plan, play a key role in the adaptation process. Each action is a chance or probabilistic phenomenon which cannot be predicted in advance -- what new idea will be generated by whom, and when, is unknown.

Second, these organizations employ devices that increase the probability of generating new ideas: autonomy is given to teams and divisions, with challenging targets assigned. Performance is carefully evaluated in terms of a limited number of criteria, achievement of which requires very significant effort. The cross-fertilization that comes from sharing heterogeneous information is, in 3M, another means of increasing the probability of new ideas.

Third, the autonomous and spontaneous actions which result often contribute to organizational chaos and instability -- an uneasy situation to unaccustomed observers. Neither systematic nor smooth, the adaptive processes of these companies include considerable fluctuations and instability.

Fourth, useful product ideas are selected through empirical testing in the market place -- more through trial and error than in accordance with a strategic analysis. To avoid too much confusion and conflict that can arise from inter-division politics, these companies articulate values and beliefs that are the foundation of distinctive corporate cultures. The cultures of these two firms, although different, both serve to regulate the fluctuations that occur, by setting the rules of the "games" operating within each company.

Fifth, the strategies of both companies appear to emerge from the adaptive process, which in large measure is dictated by the basic patterns of relationships between the organizations and their environments. Their strategies are a result of their adaptive processes rather than *ex ante* guidelines for action. If an *ex ante* guideline exists, it is articulated in general enough terms, that it may be interpreted differently by various people.

Sixth, these companies acquire new competences and new combinations of existing competences. The adaptive process involves a continuous reorganization of competences.

The two organizations discussed certainly differ in some respects. 3M has usually been a leader in product innovations, diversifying into different markets, although most innovations have been closely related to its core technology -- fine coating and bonding. Their innovations, therefore, involved some market discontinuity. In most cases, Matsushita was a follower in product innovation (e.g., in the case of VTR's, Sony was the leader), and most of its innovations were closely related to existing production technologies and markets. Therefore, its innovations were more continuous than 3M's. The interactions within Matsushita were mostly made within divisions and were more homogeneous. These differences are ones which differentiate the H and V modes of adaptation.

Reviewing related studies, the common characteristics that we have identified above may not be specific just to these two organizations but may be generalizable to many other innovative and adaptive organizations. For instance, Peters and Waterman (1982) identified eight characteristics common to well-managed U.S. companies: A bias for action; being close to the customer, autonomy and entrepreneurship; productivity through people, hands-on and value driven action, sticking to the knitting; having a simple form and lean staff; and having simultaneous loose-tight properties. Burgelman (1983) found that innovations are spontaneously initiated and championed by middle managers outside the framework of strategic plans and that some of them eventually shape a new strategic orientation for the organization. Similar findings are reported by Kanter (1983). She also notes that open communication, resource autonomy, interpersonal networks, and a distinctive corporate culture -- a "culture of pride" -- are common characteristics of innovative organizations. These findings by diverse authors suggest that the characteristics that we have identified are widely shared by many organizations. The question remains: Why do these characteristics bring forth innovation and adaptability? A new model is needed to provide an answer.

7.3.4 An Evolutionary View of Organizations -- The Self-Organizing Paradigm

A new view of organizations most pertinent to the above-mentioned characteristics is an evolutionary view that was first developed by biologists and introduced to organizational studies by Campbell (1969), Weick (1979) Aldrich (1979), McKelvey (1982), Kagono (1983), Nonaka (1983) and others. This view is closely related to an emerging new paradigm in the social sciences or science in general -- the self-organizing paradigm (Prigogine, 1980; Jantsch, 1981; Corning, 1983). Based upon the evolutionary view or self-organizing paradigm, a dynamic, stochastic, and fluctuating process of evolution is thought to be an essential aspect of an organization or social system's adaptation. According to the traditional Darwinian view, evolution is viewed as purely stochastic. In the evolutionary process of a social system, other forces may be at work: "Evolution can be viewed as a multi-leveled, dynamic process which at each level of organization combines stochastic, deterministic, and teleonomic aspects in a time-bounded matrix" (Corning, 1983; p.41). Compared to other views, essential elements of this evolutionary view are that (1) it emphasizes the dynamic stochastic aspect of the organizational change process more than a teleonomic or deterministic one (Weick, 1979); and (2) it assumes the existence of spontaneous equilibrium-breaking forces and emergent self-organizing counter-forces within organizations (Prigogine, 1980; Jantsch, 1981). Based upon this view, how are the adaptive processes of organizations to be modeled?

An organization has acquired and stored knowledge showing its members how to survive and compete in a certain environment. Organizational knowledge consists of basic units which, together, comprise routine (Nelson and

Winter, 1982) or comps (McKelvey, 1982). Routines and comps that are the
regular and predictable behavioral patterns of an organization might be
likened to genes of biological species. Fukujiro Sono, chairman of TDK
has offered this analogy. The title of this quote was 'Genes':

> I always tell the researchers at TDK two things. First I tell
> them not to imitate other people. I tell them not to come to me
> with stories of how other people have made money with this or
> that new device and try to persuade me to follow suit. TDK
> started by commercializing the Japanese invention ferrite. Our
> principal aim is to develop original technology, not to make
> money by selling it...
> I also tell our researchers not to get involved with anything
> besides magnetic and electronic materials. These are TDK's
> genes. It's our responsibility to not get involved in fields
> unrelated to the genes we've inherited.

Genes carry the knowledge and wisdom required to survive in an uncertain
environment. An organization combines inherited genes in order to
effectively acquire and utilize resources for its survival. A repertoire
of genes or a gene pool can be said to form an organization's distinctive
competence (using the terminology of the strategy researchers) or core
technology (Thompson, 1967).

As its environment changes, an organization has to acquire new genes and
replace old ones with new ones, in order to create a new gene pool
enabling the organization to cope with the new environment. Although
Thompson (1967) assumed that core technology was a fixed given, it must
continually be renewed. This process of change or renewal of the gene
pool is an evolutionary process.

Using the biological analogy, the evolutionary process of an organization
consists of three phases: variation, selection, and retention (Campbell,
1969; Weick, 1979; Aldrich, 1979).

The first phase of the evolutionary cycle is variation. Various examples
of variation are: hitting on a new product idea; discovering a new
technological or market opportunity; and finding a problem in an
organization and instituting corrective change. New variations are
equivalent to mutations in biological evolution. But variations are to a
considerable degree dependent upon individuals' cognitive processes, as is

stressed by Weick (1979). One input to variation is existing knowledge, that knowledge stored in the gene pool of an organization. The other input is the external or internal stimuli that are unpredictable and stochastic to an organization as a whole. The former is deterministic, while the latter is stochastic.

An organization generates several kinds of variation. They can be divided into two types. One is goal-oriented, teleonomic variation. Articulated strategies, plans and goals, and clearly defined responsibilities and authority generate this type of variation. Goal-oriented variations are based upon some goals or intention of an organization and are pre-selected by these means. The other type is *emergent* and *spontaneous* variation, which is generated by chance and which, using biological terminology, may be called blind variation. The individuals who initiate these variations may have the intention to do so, but their organizations may not.

Traditional theories of organization have explicitly or implicitly assumed that goal-oriented, induced variations would be more effective than haphazard variations and that behaviors based upon chance or luck are irrational. Typical S or B type organizations share these assumptions; consequently, they try to generate goal-oriented variations and reduce emergent variations. In contrast, H or V type organizations try to generate emergent as well as goal-oriented variations. These organizations are no less effective than the S or B type, as demonstrated by Matsushita and 3M. In these two organizations many innovations were not induced by detailed strategic plans formulated at the headquarters but were spontaneously proposed and championed by entrepreneurial divisions, teams or individuals. Here, variations are initiated at the micro levels. Variations at the micro level appear haphazard at the macro level. In B or S type organizations, variations are initiated at the macro level as changes in strategy and are diffused down through micro levels by means of structural design. When technologies and markets change at a high rate and future directions are difficult to predict at the macro level, it follows that variations initiated spontaneously at micro levels can be more effective than macro-induced variations. The former variations are not constrained by the existing knowledge stored at the macro level, and it is at the micro level that there is direct and broad contact with those elements of the environment that are changing, no matter how heterogeneous or complex.

It goes without saying that emergent variations in H and V type organizations do not solely rely on pure chance; that these organizations have diverse means to increase the probability of successfully emergent variations has been illustrated by examples.

Variations are the sources of organizational adaptability. Without variations, whether initiated at the macro or micro level, organizations can not acquire new competencies. Variation, however, amplifies the internal uncertainty of an organization and may bring disorder in it. Emergent variations initiated at the micro-level may especially do so, because they are not systematically wrought by a coherent strategy or plan. The confusion observed in Matsushita and 3M is the result. In order to reduce organizational uncertainty, interactions within an organization and with its environment are necessary. This gives rise to the next phase of our model.

The principal function of this selection phase is to determine the effectiveness and feasibility of new variations. Achievement comes through the interaction of various forces. It is assumed in conventional theories of organization that selection in organizations is, or should be, made systematically, based upon consistent selection criteria applied in a hierarchical structure. B and S type organizations are, indeed, based upon this assumption. The selection process of H or V type organizations, however, is different. Their selection process is not a deterministic process in which certain selection criteria are explicitly applied, but a dynamic and fluctuating process in which chance, necessity, and teleonomy work interactively (Corning, 1983). Using the terminology of March and Olsen (1976), the selection process is one in which problems and solutions held by different people are combined by chance at various choice opportunities. The process, however, is not purely random; it is to some extent, regulated and, therefore, called "organized anarchy" (March and Olsen, 1976) or "organized chaos."

One input to a selection process is existing knowledge (or existing genes). B or S type organizations rely on this input. The teleonomic forces based upon existing and coherent knowledge favor those variations that are compatible with already existing genes. This dependence upon "compatibility" with what is already known can constrain the new variations selected and, thereby, reduce organizational adaptability. Ambivalence to compatibility with existing knowledge may help new unfamiliar variations to be chosen (Weick, 1979).

Another input to the selection process is made through various internal forces. An organization is a multi-layered, multi-department system. The forms of vertical and horizontal interactions permitted and encouraged by an organization's structure determine the extent to which new unfamiliar variations are selected. The more diverse and heterogeneous the scope of interactions both vertically and horizontally, the higher the probability that unfamiliar variations will be selected, because the usefulness of superficially dissimilar but potentially advantageous variations is more likely to be recognized. In 3M one could sell a product idea not only to one's own division but also to any other division. This extends the scope of interaction and, therefore, increases the probability of selecting an unfamiliar but creative idea. In Matsushita, frequent interaction occured within each division; therefore, its innovations were more continuous -- the added variations were more like existing genes. Matsushita recently organized various cross-divisional and cross-functional teams and committees in several strategic areas to stimulate creative leaps in those areas.

Corporate culture has a tacit but strong influence upon the selection process. A culture that favors changes, innovation, experimentation, or playfulness is more likely to be tolerant of and to adopt unfamiliar ideas in its selection process. The behavior and attitudes of top management are internal inputs which are important for this reason. In some H or V organizations, top management is known to frequently walk through the plant, encouraging informality and inventiveness.

The last input to the selection process is that made through various external forces. Performance in the competitive market place is the final selection criterion for an organization as a whole or its individual

venture. When a new product venture is not accepted in the market, the
product must someday be rejected, even if it has been selected through the
interaction of internal forces. External selection forces also help to
regulate the selective process which might otherwise become chaotic. If
Matsushita had not taken market reactions into account, selection between
its competing products based upon information at lower levels of the
organization may have failed to identify that alternative optimal to the
firm as a whole. This is necessary because internal information is often
not objective. For example, according to an executive of a Japanese V
type organization:

> Formal organizational structures are so designed that even useful
> new ideas and suggestions are filtered as noise at each level of
> the hierarchy. Only top management can create a channel that is
> not inhibited by the "hierarchical noise absorbers" and which
> makes it possible to collect "useful noise."

The "useful noise" refered to here is, in the final analysis, objective
market-place information. It should be the final selection criterion for
an organization as a whole or its individual venture.

The QC circle and suggestion box systems adopted by many H type
organizations contribute to variation initiated at the shop floor. Such
variation however, is apt to be small and continuous compared to the
variation typical of V type organizations. Internal selection processes
usually favor variations that are compatible with existing ones. They are
subject to biases which are inherent to the subjective judgment of
organizational members. External selection mechanisms are not subject to
such subjective biases. The forces of the market place constitute this
kind of mechanism. Matsushita's competitive new product development
projects and 3M's trial and error approach are successful because they
ultimately rely on the unbiased reaction of the market.

The top management of some H type organizations (e.g., Suntory and Renown)
promote organizational crises so that the external selection forces become
dominant. The sense of crisis that arises from the threat perceived from
external forces facilitates the selection of new variations and the
renewal of existing genes, which are necessary for adaptation.

While organizational responses to external pressures can be most appropriate in the short-run (as stated in earlier chapters to often be true for U.S. firms), such responses can fail to "select" those variations that will be necessary in the future. Such variations must be protected from short-run external competitive pressures. A typical instance is the need to protect the people and resources devoted to basic research that may bring forth genes vital to the future. Such research must to some extent be isolated from external market pressures.

It would seem inherent to the process of selection that a variety of internal and external forces at various hierarchical levels simultaneously interact to eventually select variations or new combinations of genes. Chance, necessity, and teleonomy interact with each other in this process (Corning, 1983). Therefore, the selection process, often becomes disorderly. Perhaps, some organizations do look like "garbage cans" (March and Olsen, 1976); surely, they are subject to fluctuating processes (Prigogine, 1980). Organizations must regulate the disorder or fluctuation. Strategies, action plans, budgets, hierarchical structures, formalized reporting relationships, and control systems are visible and "hard" means of achieving regulation. Shared values and beliefs, informal peer pressures, trust, and identification with the organization are invisible, soft means. The latter are usually weaker than the former and permit more fluctuations. Traditional theories of organization place much emphasis on the usefulness of the hard means of regulation, and typical B and S type organizations depend on this idea. But, if the selection process is too closely controlled, unfamiliar but adaptive variations may not be selected, precluding adaptation. Over-reliance on soft means of regulation entails risks, too. A certain level of disorder and fluctuation is necessary for adaptation to fast-changing environments but, of course, some order of control is essential, as well.

The final phase in the process of organizational evolution is retention. It is in this process that the new genes which have been selected are added to the organization's pool, while the genes that are no longer useful are dropped. Through the processes of organizational learning and unlearning new knowledge is stored in long-term memory and obsolete knowledge is replaced (Weick, 1979). This is the final essential element of evolution, for without the learning of new responses, adaptation cannot occur.

Traditional organization theories assume that knowledge within an organization is retained mostly in sets of standard operating procedures (Cyert and March, 1963) and in formalized systems which reflect the organization's structure. Typical B or S type organizations rely heavily on such hard memories. There are also soft memories: of heroes, sagas, rituals and so on. H or V type organizations like 3M and Matsushita have an abundance of such heroes, sagas and rituals, which impart organizational knowledge, values, and ideals to the organizational members who share in them. Compared to hard memories, soft memories are more ambiguous. The important role of ambiguity in this instance is that, in leaving considerable latitude for individual involvement with the saga and for perception of its personal relevance, those who retell those sagas have greater freedom to adapt institutional culture to current circumstances. That is, organizational members have a mechanism for promulgating or modifying those genes that carry the most basic of an organization's traits -- its values.

Traditionally, it has been assumed that the major agents of organizational learning are the professional elite of the organization. They learn and communicate their knowledge to the rest of the organization via strategy, structure, and systems. But in H or V type organizations, the responsibility for learning and contributing ideas is shared by many people. QC circles and related devices observed so frequently in the typical H type organization make this kind of broad learning possible (Nonaka and Johansson, 1985). Venture projects common to the V type organization serve the same function.

Just as an individual's memory has a structure, organizational memory is also structured. The degree of structure differs, however, between organizations. When organizational memory is highly structured, it is difficult to introduce very different, novel genes to the existing gene pool; organizations tend to reject them and to retain familiar obsolete genes until they face a crisis (Hedberg, 1981). The most typical examples include the large U.S. auto firms when they faced the first oil crisis and the large Japanese steel firms in recent years. When organizational memory is loosely structured, genes may be easily replaced and new ones introduced because the loose structure tolerates a certain level of inconsistency. For example, more new and innovative options are apt to be consistent with the core values that are transmitted by rituals and sagas, than with SOP's that are designed to operationalize those values in very specific ways.

The characteristics of H and V type adaptation processes are summarized and compared with those of the B and S type in Table 7-2.

Table 7-2 Traditional vs. Evolutionary view on adaptive process

	Traditional view (B or S type)	Evolutionary view or Self-organizing paradigm (H or V type)
variation	goal-oriented; strategy-induced; planned; pre-selected; uncertainty reducing from macro to micro	haphazard; autonomous; emergent; uncertainty amplifying; from micro to macro
selection	analytical; systematic; hierarchical orderly; with pre-established and consistent criteria; deterministic	through interaction of chance, necessity and teleonomy; disordered with minimum control interaction with market; stochastic and dynamic
retention	stored in hard memories (structure and system); learning by elite; tightly structured	stored in soft memories; learning by people; loosely structured

Having outlined a model of organizational adaptation based on an evolutionary and self-organizing paradigm, we are now better equipped to answer the initial question of why H or V type organizational characteristics that may be viewed as irrational from the standpoint of traditional theory are, indeed, so effective in certain environments. The answer is that those very organizational characteristics enable organizations to generate, select, and retain new variations and, thereby, continually renew themselves. This ability is crucial to organizational viability when the environment is changing in an unpredictable manner. When an environment is static or changes in it are predictable based on existing knowledge, the traditional model would be more effective. The environments of both U.S. and Japanese companies, however, have become more and more turbulent, and it is becoming increasingly difficult to rely on such the traditional view.

As stated before, H and V type organizations differ in several respects, although they also share some key characteristics. The adaptive behavior of V type organizations is more proactive and creative. In the variation phase, variations generated in H type organizatins are smaller and more continuous than those of V type organizations. The process differences in this phase are as follows: the range of effort devoted to innovation and the cross-fertilization of ideas is broader in V type organizations; individual entrepreneurship rather than group cohesivenesses is stressed; more autonomy is given to the individual and groups; and the corporate culture stresses creativity rather than imitation, even when the latter might be more profitable in the short-run. In the selection phase, different modes of interaction are devised. QC circles and related, more conventional means for encouraging individual contributions are typically used in H type organizations. Such devices are well-suited for collecting an enormous amount of small and continuous variations, new ideas that can be easily put into practice. In contrast, the "internal venturing" of the V type organization results in discontinuous leaps of creativity, the values of which are tested through selection in the market place. In the retention phase, addition and deletion of genes is more dynamic in V type organizations. In contrast, learning takes place at the group level and is shared by more people in the H type.

7.4 Practical Implications

Finally, let us present the more important practical implications of this study with special attention to Japanese and American firms.

7.4.1 Japanese-style Management and the H Type of Adaptation

Perhaps largely for reasons of cultural biases, many Japanese firms are close to the H type mode of adaptation. Neither backward nor necessarily superior to the other type of adaptation, H type is best-suited to an environment in which numerous small changes occur continuously. The reason that Japanese firms were able to gain such strength in industries like steel, automobiles, and home appliances is that these industries were suited to H type adaptation. In contrast, the reason that many Japanese firms are facing difficulty in the aluminum and petro-chemical fields is that the H type of adaptation is not appropriate for rapid and drastic changes. Moreover, that phenomenal high technology breakthroughs are infrequent in Japan indicates a limitation of H type adaptation. To summarize, the H type has the following advantages:

(1) Being suited for adaptation to continuous but incremental changes;
(2) Making possible the subtle combination and concerted efforts of various organizational elements;
(3) Very broadly stimulating the accumulation of experience and knowledge, and enhancing sensitivity toward information;
(4) Revitalizing the organization because of strong adherence to widely shared value.

At the same time, however, H type adaptation suffers from the following disadvantages:

(1) There is much slack, and inefficient resource allocation results;
(2) Responses to sudden and drastic structural changes are weak;
(3) Because resource allocation tends to be cumulative throughout the organization, there is greater danger of being saddled with unprofitable ventures;
(4) And because relationships between major parts of the organization are loose, there are instances where organizational confusion emerges.

In order to strengthen these advantages and compensate for the ntages, the firms in Japan that are high performers show stregthened S type adaptation mechanism. This, however, has not fully mitigated the disadvantages of H type adaptation.

A most serious short-coming typical in Japan, is that the H mode is not sufficiently understood and not a systematic management approach. Many corporate managers and executives in Japan stated in our interviews: "We made steady efforts at each stage of our activities; it seems that, before we were aware of it, our firm had come to occupy an important position in the world market." This statement truly indicates the essence of Japanese-style H type adaptation. The system and process have, themselves, spontaneously emerged, but because it is not a well-articulated, systematic approach to management, H type adaptation is difficult to change in a methodical and substantial way and to implement internationally. Our study suggests these principles of management of H type organization:

1. To form groups in which the members can interact frequently and intensively.
2. To make the group as much as possible self-contained so that it can identify problems and spontaneously take measures to solve them.
3. To educate people (on-the-job, and off-the-job) so that they can work on non-routine problems.
4. To create a need for improvement by setting a challenging goal, facilitating competition between groups, occasionally enacting organizational crises, building organizational tension and so on.
5. To give people positive rewards when successful; it will reinforce people's willingness to participate
6. To make information available so that each group can adopt a wide-ranging perspective.
7. To reduce the active interventions of top executives and staff; their help must be invisible.
8. To intensify intra-organizational learning so that knowledge can be shared among employees.
9. To specify the focus of organizational learning through visionary statements so that knowledge will be accumulated.

One should not underestimate the role of QC circles and related programs that involve group dynamics at the work sites in raising productivity in Japan. However, as long as the system of thorough reexamination of daily work activities constitutes the core of environmental adaptation, it will be difficult to promote great innovative leaps, those "paradigm changes" that are responsible for truly great progress. We submit, therefore, that a serious re-thinking of H type adaptation is essential if great progress is desired in the future. Hints for this re-direction, are suggested in our qualitative study.

A typical move from H type to V type is exemplified by NEC. NEC, which was once thought a very conservative, traditional Japanese company, has taken measures which from our perspective have shifted it towards the V type mode.[4] These measures, a sort of "cultural revolution," were instituted by former president Kobayashi. They indicate one way to manage an H to V type transition process. His actions included the following:

(1) Suggesting and articulating a future domain, "Computers and Communications (C&C)," as a stimulating vision.
(2) Popularizing the phrase "Stability is instability and instability is stability" (the meaning intended is that a company in a stable state becomes too conservative and thus is actually in a vary dangerous state, while a company with a certain degree of disequilibrium is more stable because its people are always alert and quick to act creatively).
(3) Actually creating disequilibrium by divesting the atomic energy business (it was not compatible with the "C&C" vision) and by investing a significant amount of money in semiconductors. The semiconductor investment was a strategic trigger that initiated a series of creative variations.
(4) Fostering small successes in the new product area (e.g., the PC-8000 personal computer) which became symbols or models for new patterns of action within the company. These also have became "cores" of growth in the desired direction, and the development of follow-up products using similar technologies has stimulated more variation.
(5) Rotating a number of key people to accelerate the cross-fertilization of ideas and expertise.

These actions brought forth a chain of large innovative variations in NEC over a period of 7 to 8 years. Some of the variations were intended but many were not. One variation induced another variation, which in turn induced others. As this spontaneous reactive chain accumulated, the company "mutated" from its past state of strategic equilibrium as a dominant supplier to NTT, to a new state as a diversified electornics company active in computers, communications, and electronic devices.

We believe that a transition from H to V type must be brought forth in this way. The transition of NEC did not rely on strategic planning or the typical evolutionary pattern employed by many Japanese companies -- QC or TQC. A disequilibrium was caused by unusual actions initiated by top management. A series of emergent variations followed, and thus goal-oriented actions from top-down and emergent variations from bottom-up became synchronized. Managing transition, then is basically involves a synchronization process.

7.4.2 S Type Adaptation and the American Firm

As the most successful U.S. organizations have grown, they have come to adopt increasingly S types of adaptation. The high degree of professionalism of managers, the training of MBA's, and corporate jargon with its emphasis upon strategic planning, takeover, diversification, ROI, etc. both reflect and contribute to the further rationalization of corporate America. The consequence is wholly consistent with the logic of the S type of adaptation which is a very rational approach to change. S type adaptation has the following advantages:

(1) Because much importance is attached to prediction and resource reallocation based upon such prediction, the S type is capable of rapid, major change in response to changes in the environment.
(2) The mobility of resources in the environments of American S type firms makes very efficient resource allocation possible.
(3) Major product innovations are more likely because of the S type's high product orientation.
(4) A large volume of information can be processed.
(5) The firm is able to integrate effort within the organization as a

whole.

GE and its sophisticated strategic planning system with its focus on strategic business units (SBU's) is the epitome of a firm with S type adaptation. But, as the organization becomes very big, the cost of maintaining these advantages becomes increasingly great; the S type of adaptation also has potential weaknesses, among them the following:

(1) Because the S type of adaptation, with its tendency toward major reallocation of resources, seeks key "strategic advantages," it often overlooks small changes in customer and environmental demands. It is, therefore, susceptible to considerable encroachment by competitors into unexploited niches.

(2) Its logical approach to building upon product concepts in order to gain or maintain competitive advantage leads, at times, to dogmatic strategies.

(3) As organizations with S type adaptation become taller and more stratified, it becomes increasingly more difficult for lower-level parts of the organization to act autonomously.

(4) Other "ills of bureaucracy" -- overly complex systems, excessive red-tape, confusing means with ends, suboptimization, etc., become more prevalent.

Recently GE's new chairman, Jack Welch, reemphasized in his company, the importance of having an entrepreneurial spirit.[5] In essence, he was arguing that GE must neither be lulled into assuming a defensive B type strategy nor succumb to the weaknesses which often accrue to S type firms. Instead, it should strive for the innovativeness of V type adaptation.

The sophisticated planning system, which was established by the former chairman Jones, is thought to have become a straitjacket on divisions, (or SBUs), discouraging their entrepreneurial innovativeness. This new dysfunction of bureaucracy called "paralysis through analysis syndrome" was described by Peters and Waterman (1982). The current reorganization started by Welch is a typical process designed to encourage V type adaptation in an S type organization. It is a pursuit to create a hybrid

of S and V type adaptation and demands a well-organized coexistence of
intended variations (strategic actions at the top) with emergent,
spontaneous variations (creative innovation at the division level).

7.4.3 Toward a Symbiosis of Heterogeneous Types of Adaptation

It is clear that the environments surrounding corporations in both Japan
and the United States are undergoing drastic change. Technological
revolutions in electronics, information processing, communication,
biological engineering, and other fields are expected to bring very
fundamental change not only to related industries but to the entire
economic and social structure. Such change is certainly threatening to
many firms, but it also creates tremendous opportunities. Change of this
magnitude does not occur spontaneously, but is a cumulative result of
innovations by many firms. The firms most likely to contribute
significantly to such innovation and change are firms with V type
adaptation. Moreover, in order to survive the drastic changes anticipated
for the future, today's firms must adopt elements of V type adaptation.

New ventures, filled with the entrepreneurial spirit of their founders,
are without doubt the purest V type firms, but the V type of adaptation is
also most characteristic of a number of very large and well-established
firms in both the United States and Japan, for example, 3M, HP, TI,
Kyocera, and TDK. Firms like GE which are not primarily V type have also
sought to increase their emphasis of V type characteristics. U.S. authors
also have suggested that innovative U.S. firms share a significant number
of characteristics which are described in this study as being V type
(Peters and Waterman, 1982; Kanter, 1983).

Closer to the V type of adaptation than the S type of the "average" U.S.
firm, the "excellent" organization might be described as being one which
is striving for a balance between our S and V types of adaptation. It
should be noted that market and social conditions in the United States,
with their emphasis on individuality, innovation, entrepreneurship, and
the availability of venture capital, contribute to a general climate that
is favorable to V type adaptation.

The pure V type organizations, however, have inherent instability, because they rely on the creative inventions of internal entrepreneurs which are probabilistic phenomena. When a company relies solely on probabilistic phenomena, chance determines its variability and growth. This vulnerability is exemplified by the fact that some V type organizations face trouble when one new product does not perform well. Some teleonomic interventions are needed to compensate for this vulnerability. As interventions discourage creativity of an organization when they occur too frequently, a subtle balance of emergent V type adaptation and the teleonomic S type must be maintained.

Incorporating S type into V type is exemplified in recent reorganizations by 3M and HP.[6] The underlying intention common to the two companies is to strengthen the macro level strategic functions. These reorganizations will hopefully enable the companies to generate intended macro variations (strategic actions) that are synchronized with spontaneous micro variations (creative innovations), thereby decreasing vulnerability. Although GE is moving in the contrary direction (from S to V), it too is pursuing a balance of V and S types. As shown in Chapter 6, this hybrid outperforms any pure type of adaptation. The key to its management is to synchronize macro induced and micro induced variations so that synergism between the two kinds of variations is maximized.

In Japan, a hybrid between the typical H type of adaption and the V type is needed; it would undoubtedly be different from the hybrids in the United States. Because H type adaptation is already somewhat self-organizing, the major elements needed are strategic direction and stimulation from the top that are compatible with the creative potentials of groups at the micro level (Imai et al., 1984). Some Japanese companies have successfully incorporated such direction. One example is NEC. Another is Matsushita, a company which was a typical traditional H type organization, but which today is in a transition process to a symbiotic form.

As typical H type organizations rely on shared values and information (corporate culture) rather than on formal structures and systems in integrating people's efforts, the transition process necessarily includes a "cultural revolution" as a critical element. A cultural revolution (the change of shared values, norms and beliefs) is more difficult than the change of formal structures and systems. The measures taken by NEC suggest how to manage the transition process. An important facet is to articulate a new vision and, based upon it, to create a significant disequilibrium which can be reduced by a creative leap by a small group of people. Matsushita, for example, set "new media" as a new vision on its domain and invested heavily in the semiconductor business (over 100 billion yen).[7] Such investment creates a large disequilibrium but it induces creative leaps by internal entrepreneurs. When these leaps (large variations) are synchronized with traditional small incremental variations, Matsushita will have achieved a new strategic equilibrium.

Both in the U.S. and Japan, successful organizations seek to establish hybrids of different modes of adaptation, although the "mix" may differ by country and perhaps by industry. The common key is a synchronization of different types of variations -- emergent vs. intended variations and small incremental vs. large discontinuous variations. The management of this synchronization is today's challenge. Those companies solving it will survive and grow into the next century; those that don't will stagnate and fall behind. We would be the first, though, to acknowledge that the creation and maintenance of coexistence among antagonistic elements in one organization may be difficult. How it is being done needs to be examined more closely, and general but detailed analyses of successful cases would help us to explore how to manage the process. Such a study would be beneficial to business people everywhere in the world. We also hope that the topic will receive further attention from scholars both here in Japan and in the U.S.

Notes

1. In terms of information theory, this is equivalent to Shannon's tenth theorem: The capacity of a channel is not large enough to erase the ambiguity of signals that are transmitted. Needless to say, variety is manipulated by entropy.

2. See Mayo (1933), Whitehead (1938), Roethlisberyer & Dickson (1939).

3. See Homans (1950), Cartwright & Zander (1960)

4. Nonaka, I., "Nippon Denki" (NEC), Written in Japanese, *Will*, January 1984, pp.80-87.

5. General Electric--Business Development, ICCH 4-382-092, 1982.

6. Smith, L., "3M: the Lures and Limits of Innovation," *Fortune*, October 20, 1980; "Can John Young Redesign Hewlett-Packard?", *Business Week*, December 6, 1982.

7. Nonaka, I. and T. Kagono, "Matsushita Denki" (Matsushita Electric), Written in Japanese, *Will*, January 1985, pp.106-113.

References

Aldrich, H., *Organizations and Environments*, Englewood Cliffs, N.J.: Prentice-Hall, 1979.

Argyris, C., *Integrating the Individual and the Organization*, New York: John Wiley, 1964.

Argyris, C. and D. A. Shon, *Organizational Learning, A Theory of Action Perspective*, Reading, Mass.: Addison Wesley, 1978.

Beer, S., *Decision and Control*, London: John Wiley, 1966.

Burgelman, R. A., "A Process Model of Internal Corporate Venturing in the Diversified Major Firm," *Administrative Science Quarterly* 28, 1983, pp.223-244.

Burns, T. and G. M. Stalker, *The Management of Innovation*, London: Tavistock, 1961.

Campbell, D. T., "Variation and Selective Retention in Sociocultural Evolution," *General Systems*, 14, 1969, pp.69-83.

Cartwright, D. and A. Zander (eds.), *Group Dynamics and Theory*, Evanston, Ill.: Row Peterson, 1960.

Child, J., "Organization Structure, Environment and Performance: The Role of Strategic Choice," *Sociology*, 6-1, 1972, pp.1-22.

Corning, P. A., *The Synergism Hypothesis: A Theory of Progressive Evolution*, New York: McGraw-Hill, 1983.

Cyert, R. M. and J. G. March, *A Behavioral Theory of the Firm*, Englewood Cliffs, N.J.: Prentice-Hall, 1963.

Deal, T. and A. W. Kennedy, *Corporate Culture*, Reading, Mass.: Addison-Wesley, 1982.

Galbraith, J., *Designing Complex Organizations*, Reading, Mass.: Addison-Wesley, 1973.

Hedberg, B., "How Organizations Learn and Unlearn," in P. Nystrom and W. Starbuck (eds.), *Handbook of Organizational Design, Vol. 1: Adapting Organizations to Their Environments*, Oxford, Oxford University Press, 1981.

Homans, G. C., *The Human Group*, New York: Harcourt, 1950.

Imai, K., I. Nonaka and H. Takeuchi, "Managing the New Product Development Process: How Japanese Companies Learn and Unlearn," paper presented at the Harvard Business School 75th Anniversary Colloquium on Productivity and Technology, March 28-29, 1984.

Jantsch, E., "Unifying Principles of Evolution," in E. Jantsch (ed.), *Evolutionary Vision*, Boulder, Col.: Westview Press, 1981.

Kagono, T., *Keiei Soshiki no Kankyo Tekio* (Environmental Adaptation of Business Organizations), Tokyo: Hakuto Shobo, 1980.

Kagono, T., "*Bunkashinka no Purosesumoderu to Soshikiriron* (Process Model of Cultural Evolution and Organization Theory)," Written in Japanese, *Soshiki Kagaku (Organizational Science)*, 17-3, 1983, pp.2-15.

Kanter, R. M., *The Change Masters*, New York: Simon and Schuster, 1983.

Lawrence, P. R. and J. W. Lorsch, *Organization and Environment*, Boston: Harvard Business School, Division of Research, 1967.

Likert, R., *New Pattern of Management*, New York: McGraw-Hill, 1961.

March, J. G. and Olsen, *Ambiguity and Organizations*, Bergen: Universitetsforlaget, 1976.

Mayo, E., *The Human Problems of an Industrial Civilization*, New York: Macmillan, 1933.

McKelvey, B., *Organizational Systematics: Taxonomy, Evolution, Classification*, Berkeley, Calif.: University of California Press, 1982.

Miles, R. E. and C. C. Snow, *Organizational Strategy, Structure, and Process*, New York: McGraw-Hill, 1978.

Mintzberg, H., "Strategy Making in Three Modes," *California Management Review*, 16, 1973, pp.44-58.

Nelson, R. and S. G. Winter, *An Evolutionary Theory of Economic Change*, Cambridge, Mass.: Belknap-Harvard, 1982.

Nonaka, I., *Organization and Market: Exploratory Study of Centralization vs. Decentralization*, Unpublished Ph.D. Dissertation, Graduate School of Business Administration, University of California Berkeley, 1972.

Nonaka, I., *Soshiki to Shijo* (Organizations and Markets), Written in Japanese, Tokyo: Chikura Shobo, 1974.

Nonaka, I., *"Shinkateki Senryaku to Kigyo Bunka* (Evolutionary Strategy and Corporate Culture)," Written in Japanese, *Soshiki Kagaku (Organizational Science)*, 17-3, 1983, pp.47-58.

Nonaka, I. and J. K. Johansson, "Japanese Management: What about the "Hard" Skills?," *Academy of Management Review*, forthcoming.

Ouchi, W. G., *Theory Z*, Reading, Mass.: Addison-Wesley, 1981.

Paine, F. T and C. R. Anderson, "Contingencies Affecting Strategy Formulation and Effectiveness," *Journal of Management Studies*, 13, 1976, pp.147-158.

Pascale, R. T. and A. G. Athos, *The Art of Japanese Management*, New York: Simon and Schuster, 1981.

Peters, T. J., "Management Systems: The Language of Organizational Character and Competence," *Organizational Dynamics*, 9, 1980, pp.3-26.

Peters, T. J. and R. H. Waterman, Jr., *In Search of Excellence*, New York: Harper & Row, 1982.

Prigogine, I., *From Being to Becoming*, San Francisco: W. M. Freeman, 1980.

Roethlisberger, F. J. and W. J. Dickson, *Management and the Worker*, Cambridge, Mass.: Harvard University Press, 1939.

Schumpeter, J. A., *The Theory of Economic Development*, Cambridge, Mass.: Harvard university Press, 1934.

Scott, W.R., "Organizational Structure," in A. Inkeles (ed.), *Annual Review of Sociology, vol. 1*, Palo Alto, Calif.: Annual Reviews, 1975.

Thompson J., *Organization in Action*, New York: McGraw Hill, 1967.

Weick, K., *The Social Psychology of Organizing, 2nd Edition*, Reading, Mass.: Addison Wesley, 1979.

Whitehead, T. N., *The Industrial Worker*, Cambridge, Mass.: Harvard University Press, 1938.

Woodward, J., *Industrial Organization: Theory and Practice*, London: Oxford University Press, 1965.

Appendix A Questionnaire -- Japanese Version

経営システムの国際比較に関する質問調査票

| ご回答にあたって

(1) この調査の目的は，日本とアメリカの企業の経営システムの間にいかなる相違があるかを明らかにすることにあります.

(2) 質問票は，貴社の経営環境，目標，戦略，経営システムなどからなっています．ご回答は，こうした点について貴社を代表してお答えいただける方にご記入いただきたく，お願いいたします.

2 ご返送のお願い

(1) ご記入いただきました調査票は，添付の封筒にてご返送いただきますようお願いいたします.

(2) ご返送は恐れいりますが，5 月 31 日までにご投函くださいますようお願い申しあげます.

貴 社 名			
		TEL　（　　）ー（　　）	
記 入 者 御 氏 名		役 職	

問 |　貴社の外部環境をどのように特徴づけることができるでしようか．それぞれの項目について，両極に示した記述を参考にしながら，貴社の外部環境を示すと思われる数字に ○ 印をご記入ください.

(1) 貴社の製品市場はどの程度の多様性をもっていますか.

(2) 貴社の生産・販売活動は地理的にどの程度のひろがりをもっていますか.

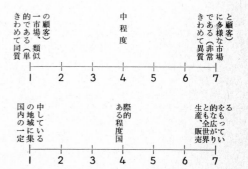

(3) 貴社の販売促進手段はどの程度多岐にわたっていますか.

(4) 顧客に製品の詳細な技術データを提供する必要がありますか.

(5) 貴社の市場は一般にどの程度競争的ですか.

(6) 一般に貴社は市場環境や競争条件にどの程度影響を与え変化させることができますか.

(7) 貴社の市場における新製品や新技術の頻度は一般にどの程度ですか.

(8) 貴社の市場において予測できない需要変動の発生頻度はどの程度ですか.

(9) 貴社と銀行，大株主とのこれまでの関係は，将来計画の策定にあたって，

(10) 貴社と主要な流通業者，大口顧客とのこれまでの関係は，将来計画の策定にあたって，

(11) 貴社と原材料供給業者，部品供給会社，外注会社とのこれまでの関係は，将来計画の策定にあたって，

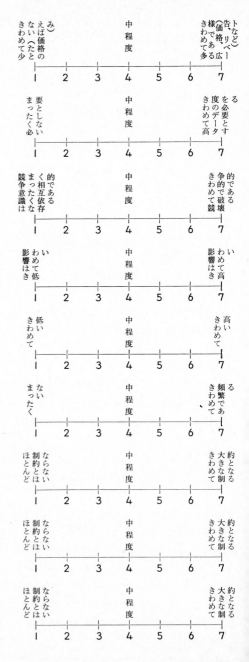

(12) 政府・監督機関とのこれまでの関係は，将来計画の策定にあたって，

ほとんど制約とはならない　中程度　きわめて大きな制約となる

| 1 | 2 | 3 | 4 | 5 | 6 | 7 |

(13) 貴社の業界では，共同研究開発や共同市場開拓など企業間の協力はどの程度頻繁に行なわれていますか．

きわめて稀である　中程度　きわめて頻繁に行なわれている

| 1 | 2 | 3 | 4 | 5 | 6 | 7 |

(14) 貴社の業界における管理者の流動性はどの程度ですか．

きわめて固定的である　中程度　会社間の移動がきわめて多い

| 1 | 2 | 3 | 4 | 5 | 6 | 7 |

(15) 貴社の業界における専門技術者の流動性はどの程度ですか．

きわめて固定的である　中程度　会社間の移動がきわめて多い

| 1 | 2 | 3 | 4 | 5 | 6 | 7 |

(16) 貴社の主要市場（最大の売上比率をもつ市場）の収益性はどの程度ですか．

きわめて低い半が赤字の企業（大業）　中程度　きわめて高い半が高収益の企業（大業）

| 1 | 2 | 3 | 4 | 5 | 6 | 7 |

(17) その市場に対する新規参入の困難度はどの程度ですか．

きわめて容易である　中程度　きわめて困難である

| 1 | 2 | 3 | 4 | 5 | 6 | 7 |

問2　次の表は製品の市場占有率と製品市場の成長性を基準に製品を4つのグループに分けたものです．それぞれの製品グループの貴社における売上構成比の概要をお知らせください．

市 場 占 有 率

	高い（業界首位または2位）	低い（業界3位以下）
市場成長率　高い　10%	約 _____ %	約 _____ %
低い	約 _____ %	約 _____ %

問 3　次のそれぞれの生産方法で生産される製品の比率はどの程度ですか. 各生産方法を用いて生産される製品の生産
構成比の概要をお知らせください.

個別受注生産（注文服, 特殊装置のように顧客の注文に応じて単品あるい
　　は少量で生産される製品）　　　　　　　　　　　　　　　　　　　　約　　　　　　　%

小ロット生産（工作機, 染料, 高級婦人服のように類似の製品が小さな
　　バッチ, ロットで生産される製品）　　　　　　　　　　　　　　　　約　　　　　　　%

大ロット生産（化学薬品, 部品, カン, ボトル, 原糸など, 大ロット,
　　大バッチで生産される製品）　　　　　　　　　　　　　　　　　　　約　　　　　　　%

組立ラインによる大量生産（自動車, 家電製品のように組立ラインによっ
　　て生産される製品）　　　　　　　　　　　　　　　　　　　　　　　約　　　　　　　%

連続的な装置生産（石油精製のように, バッチやシフトではなく連続的か
　　つ自動的に生産される製品）　　　　　　　　　　　　　　　　　　　約　　　　　　　%

　　　　　　　　　　　　　　　　　　　　　　　　　　　　　　　　　　計　　100　%

問 4　以下の文章は, 経営戦略およびその基礎にある経営理念を記述したものです. それぞれの文章は貴社の経営戦略
の特色にどの程度妥当するでしょうか. 該当する数字に〇印を記入してお答えください.

	そのとおりまったく	どちらかといえば正しい	どちらともいえない	どちらかといえばちがう	まったくちがう
1. あらゆる市場において一貫して高シェアを志向し, コスト効率の利点を追求する.	1	2	3	4	5
2. 新製品, 新市場開発のリスクを回避し, フォロアーの利点を追求する.	1	2	3	4	5
3. 少数の重点市場セグメントに経営資源を集中する.	1	2	3	4	5
4. 株主の利益を追求することこそ, 最も重要な社会的責任である.	1	2	3	4	5
5. 競合者と同一市場で正面から対決する.	1	2	3	4	5
6. 問題事業分野からの撤退についても積極的である.	1	2	3	4	5
7. 新しい製品ラインの追加は, 既存の技術基盤と強いつながりのあるものに限定される.	1	2	3	4	5

		そのとおりまったく	どちらかといえば正しい	どちらともいえない	どちらかといえばちがう	まったくちがう
8.	自社に有利な市場セグメントを見つけ，競合者との共存をめざす．	1	2	3	4	5
9.	海外市場の開拓に積極的である．	1	2	3	4	5
10.	経営戦略の策定にあたっては，精緻な分析手法と体系的な調査データを重視する．	1	2	3	4	5
11.	常に新製品，新市場開発のリスクを積極的に負うイノベーターである．	1	2	3	4	5
12.	新規事業の進出のための吸収・合併を積極的に行なう．	1	2	3	4	5
13.	管理職や専門職の人材確保は，即戦力よりも長期人事計画に基づいて行なわれる．	1	2	3	4	5
14.	新しい製品ラインの追加は，既存のマーケティング能力をいかせる分野に限定される．	1	2	3	4	5
15.	未知の市場に対しても，広範な情報収集活動を展開する．	1	2	3	4	5
16.	高付加価値・高品質製品を志向して，非価格のマーケティング戦略を追求する．	1	2	3	4	5
17.	既存技術ノウハウの企業化よりも，多様な技術ノウハウの蓄積を重視する．	1	2	3	4	5
18.	経営の基本戦略は現在の社長，会長，あるいは創業者のユニークな理念と不可分である．	1	2	3	4	5
19.	社会的責任の遂行は，経営政策の中に明確に組み込まれている．	1	2	3	4	5
20.	海外生産子会社への投資に積極的である．	1	2	3	4	5
21.	経営者は現場の管理者や専門家の自発的な提案を頻繁に採用・実施する．	1	2	3	4	5
22.	経営戦略の策定にあたっては，経験に富んだ経営者の直観が重視される．	1	2	3	4	5

問5　貴社のなかで最大の売上比率を占める事業分野において収益を獲得するためには，次の戦略はそれぞれどの程度
　　　の重要性を占めるでしょうか．過去5年間ならびに将来5年間の重要性を評価し，順位をつけてください．

	過去5年	将来5年
製品戦略（製品計画，新製品の市場調査，研究開発など）	（　　）	（　　）
販売促進戦略（販売管理と人的販売，広告，マーケティング・コミュニケーションなど）	（　　）	（　　）
流通戦略（流通チヤネルの選択，配送，在庫プログラムなど）	（　　）	（　　）
価格戦略（価格政策，価格決定など）	（　　）	（　　）
生産戦略（量産効果，コスト・ダウン，システムの弾力化など）	（　　）	（　　）

問6　貴社の研究開発活動についておたずねします．

(1)　貴社の昨年度の総売上高に占める研究開発費の比率は約何%でしょうか．　　　　　　　　_____ %

(2)　1973年の石油ショック以後に新たに追加された製品ラインの昨年度の売
　　上高に占める比率は約何%でしょうか．　　　　　　　　　　　　　　　　_____ %

(3)　研究開発においては以下の項目をそれぞれどの程度重視しておられます
　　か．合計が100点になるように，それぞれの重要性に応じた得点を与えて
　　ください．
　　　　新技術についての基礎研究
　　　　既存製品の改善のための，モデル・チェンジ，デザイン，流行の研究
　　　　新製品の開発
　　　　新しい製造方法の開発，工程の改善

計　100点

問7　貴社では以下の経営管理システムを利用されていますか．利用されているシステムのすべてに ○ 印をつけてください．　（いくつでも）

1	職務規程	15	広告・宣伝計画システム
2	標準原価計算システム	16	短期経営計画システム
3	弾力的予算統制システム	17	中期経営計画システム
4	業績評価システム	18	戦略的計画システム
5	月次業務報告制度	19	資金繰り計画
6	目標管理制度 (MBO)	20	資本予算システム
7	客観的人事昇進基準	21	財務投資分析システム
8	管理者の社内教育プログラム	22	PPBS
9	公式賃金・給与算定システム	23	コンティンジェンシー・プランニング・システム
10	設備投資分析システム	24	戦略事業単位 (SBU)
11	需要予測システム	25	プロジェクト・マネジャー制
12	売上調査分析システム	26	プロダクト・マネジャー制 (ブランド・マネジャー制)
13	セールスマン業績評価システム	27	マトリクス組織
14	競争要因分析システム	28	経営情報システム (MIS)

問8　貴社の組織は製品別あるいは地域別の事業ユニット(たとえば製品事業部，地域事業部)に細分されていますか．

1　はい　　　——下の問 (1)〜(6) にお答えください．

2　いいえ　　——**問9** にお進みください．

(1)　どの程度の数の事業ユニットあるいは事業部に分けられていますか．業務運営上の決定に関してある程度の自立性をもっている事業ユニットの数をお答えください．

1	2〜5	5	31〜50
2	6〜10	6	51〜100
3	11〜20	7	101〜200
4	21〜30	8	201以上

(2)　各事業ユニットの業績はどのようにして評価されていますか．もっとも近い文章の数字に ○ 印をご記入ください．

1　各事業ユニットの業績を単一の共通基準で評価する．

2　各事業ユニットの業績を複数の共通基準で評価し，基準のウエイトもほぼ共通である．

3　各事業ユニットの業績を複数の共通基準で評価するが，基準のウエイトは事業ユニットによって異なる．

4　各事業ユニットの業績をまったく異なった基準で評価する．

(3) 事業ユニットは一般にどの程度の自立性をもっていますか. もっとも近い文章の数字に ○ 印をご記入ください.

   1 あらゆる決定にきびしい制約がある.

   2 資本支出上の決定にきびしい制約があるが, 業務上の決定には部分的な制約しかない.

   3 資本支出上の決定にきびしい制約があるが, 業務上の決定はほぼ自由に下しうる.

   4 あらゆる決定をほぼ自由に下しうる.

(4) 典型的な事業ユニットはどのような職能をもっていますか. 以下の職能のうち, 事業ユニットによって遂行されている職能に ○ 印をご記入ください. （いくつでも）

   1 生 産   6 財 務

   2 販 売   7 基礎研究

   3 マーケティング計画   8 応用研究と開発

   4 人 事   9 購 買

   5 会計・コントロール

(5) 次のような制度が採用されていますか. 採用されている制度すべてに ○ 印をご記入ください. （いくつでも）

   1 複数の事業ユニットを統轄し, 社長に直属する事業グループ重役

   2 事業グループ重役を補佐するジェネラル・スタッフ

   3 複数の事業ユニットに共通の問題の解決にあたる臨時グループ（タスク・フォース）

   4 複数の事業ユニットに共通の問題の解決にあたる常設グループ（チーム）

   5 複数の事業ユニットに共通の問題について, ユニット相互の協力促進をめざす専任の調整担当者

(6) 事業ユニットの業績は, 事業ユニットの責任者のボーナスや給与に反映されますか. もっとも近い文章の数字に ○ 印をご記入ください.

   1 まったく反映されない, 業績データは計画目的のみに使われる

   2 名目的に反映される, 業績データは主として計画目的に使われる

   3 実質的な差が生じる, 個々の責任者への報酬は上司によって個別に決定される

   4 実質的な差が生じる, 個々の責任者への報酬は客観的な算定基準によって決定される

問9 以下の文章は，組織や経営者，管理者，一般成員の行動を記述したものです．貴社の組織の現状にもっとも妥当すると思われる程度を，該当する数字に ◯ 印を記入してお答えください．

	そのとおりまったく	いえばほぼ正しどちらかと	いえないどちらとも	いえばちがどちらかと	がうまったくち
(1) 経営者と管理者の責任・権限が，明確かつ具体的に規定されている．	1	2	3	4	5
(2) 人材育成手段として，多様な職種を経験するような計画的ローテーションが重視されている．	1	2	3	4	5
(3) 経営者は問題解決の基本的考え方を示すだけで，具体的解決策は担当部門に委任される．	1	2	3	4	5
(4) 経営者のポリシーが組織の末端にまで浸透している．	1	2	3	4	5
(5) 仕事のうえでは，人間関係の調和よりも個人のイニシアチブが奨励される．	1	2	3	4	5
(6) 管理職に対応する専門職の昇進体系が明確に規定されている．	1	2	3	4	5
(7) 集団のコンセンサスによる意思決定や行為が支持される傾向がある．	1	2	3	4	5
(8) 対立は，上司の権限によってすみやかに解決される．	1	2	3	4	5
(9) 経営者や管理者の職務規程は抽象的であり，きわめて弾力的に運営されている．	1	2	3	4	5
(10) 経営者，管理者，部下の間で，多くの情報が共有されている．	1	2	3	4	5
(11) 成員の会社に対する一体感が強い．	1	2	3	4	5
(12) 組織は，特定の経営者や管理者を配慮して編成されている．	1	2	3	4	5
(13) 経営者は，管理者間，部門間の競争を奨励する．	1	2	3	4	5
(14) 経営者は，ラインの管理者や監督者と公式，非公式の会合を頻繁にもつ．	1	2	3	4	5
(15) 経営者の経営理念，哲学，主義信条が組織の諸制度に反映されている．	1	2	3	4	5
(16) 自己統制と仕事に対する関心が管理システムの基礎になっている．	1	2	3	4	5
(17) 経営者は，従業員の会社との一体感を高めるように気を配る．	1	2	3	4	5

		まったくそのとおり	いどちらかといえば正しと	いどちらともえない	いどちらかといえばちがう	がまったくちう
(18)	管理者の業績は，あくまで結果で評価される．	1	2	3	4	5
(19)	経営者や管理者は，公式の場で意見の対立が表面化しないように，事前に意見・情報の交換を行なう．	1	2	3	4	5
(20)	会社の一員であることに，成員は魅力や誇りを感じている．	1	2	3	4	5
(21)	経営者は，経営管理後継者群に常に気を配っている．	1	2	3	4	5
(22)	経営者，管理者，一般従業員の退職年令は明確に規定されている．	1	2	3	4	5
(23)	組織風土は，経営者の個人的パーソナリティと切離して考えられない．	1	2	3	4	5
(24)	経営者は積極的に問題を発見し，率先垂範して解決法を指示する．	1	2	3	4	5
(25)	経営者や管理者は会社の外でも親交をもっている．	1	2	3	4	5
(26)	経営者は，「何を知りたいか」という情報要求を関連部門に常に明示する．	1	2	3	4	5
(27)	多くの経営者，管理者は，仮にポストや収入面でもっと良い就職の機会があっても，会社を移らない．	1	2	3	4	5
(28)	経営者は，公式の情報ルート以外に信頼できる組織内外の情報源を常に開拓しようとする．	1	2	3	4	5
(29)	管理者の業績は，その人のもっているポテンシャルを考慮できるように長い眼で評価される．	1	2	3	4	5
(30)	重要な情報は，通常経営者や管理者の間で非公式にやりとりされる．	1	2	3	4	5
(31)	意見や見解の相違がある場合には，経営者や管理者は，根本的な解決を先に延ばしても，まず一時的な妥協点を設定する．	1	2	3	4	5
(32)	経営者や管理者の多くは，現在の会社以外での職歴をもっていない．	1	2	3	4	5
(33)	経営者は，組織の内外で起った出来事や第一線の実態についての情報を自ら積極的に収集する．	1	2	3	4	5
(34)	成員の行動は規則と上司によって厳格に管理されている．	1	2	3	4	5

	そのとおりまったくそ	いえば正しどちらかと	いえないどちらとも	どちらかがいえばちう	がうまったくち
㉟ 経営者の多くは会社の「生え抜き」である.	1	2	3	4	5
㊱ 一般に変化を追求し，変化に挑戦する組織風土がある.	1	2	3	4	5
㊲ 経営者は常に信賞必罰を徹底する.	1	2	3	4	5
㊳ 経営者や管理者は，意見や見解の対立点について時間がかかっても徹底的に話し合う.	1	2	3	4	5

問10-1 新しい製品ラインの選択や主要設備の更新について，以下の階層はそれぞれどの程度の発言力や影響力をもっていると思われますか.

	ほとんどあるいは全く影響力をもたない	やや影響力をもつ	かなり影響力をもつ	多くの影響力をもつ	きわめて多くの影響力をもつ
社 長	1	2	3	4	5
役員会議	1	2	3	4	5
事業本部長*	1	2	3	4	5
事業部長*	1	2	3	4	5
担当部長（たとえば営業部長，生産部長）	1	2	3	4	5
担当部門内の会議	1	2	3	4	5

　＊ これらの制度を採用されていない場合には，その行を空白にしておいてください.

問10-2 一般に次の部門は貴社全体の業績に影響を与える事柄について，それぞれどの程度の発言力や影響力をもっていると思われますか.

	ほとんどあるいは全く影響力をもたない	やや影響力をもつ	かなり影響力をもつ	多くの影響力をもつ	きわめて多くの影響力をもつ
販売・マーケティング	1	2	3	4	5
研究開発	1	2	3	4	5
製 造	1	2	3	4	5
財務・会計	1	2	3	4	5
総務・人事・労務	1	2	3	4	5
社長室・企画	1	2	3	4	5
資材・購買	1	2	3	4	5

問11 貴社における組織改革のプロセスについておうかがいいたします.

A. 過去5年間に,貴社において全社規模の組織改革が行なわれましたか.

      1　行なわれた————下のBの問にお答えください.

      2　行なわれない——**問12** にお進みください.

B. 以下の文章は,組織改革ないし組織変更のプロセスを記述したものです.最近の組織改革を主に念頭において,貴社の組織改革の特色にもっとも妥当すると思われる程度を,該当する数字に ○ 印を記入してお答えください.

	そのとおりまったく	どちらかといえば正しい	どちらともいえない	どちらかといえばちがう	まったくちがう
(1)　組織改革は経営者の交替をともなった.	1	2	3	4	5
(2)　組織改革は漸進的に行なわれた.	1	2	3	4	5
(3)　組織改革のねらいは,内部効率の改善にあった.	1	2	3	4	5
(4)　組織改革は,経営意思の方向を伝達する機会として利用された.	1	2	3	4	5
(5)　組織改革のために,徹底した組織とタスクの分析が行なわれた.	1	2	3	4	5
(6)　組織改革はほぼ一定期間ごとに実施されてきた.	1	2	3	4	5
(7)　組織改革のねらいは,市場での競争に対処するために組織の機動性を強化することにあった.	1	2	3	4	5
(8)　組織改革には,様々な階層の経営者・管理者の意見が反映された.	1	2	3	4	5
(9)　組織改革の要諦は急激な変化をねらわないことであるという考えのもとに改革が実行された.	1	2	3	4	5
(10)　組織改革については,常設の機関で常に検討されていた.	1	2	3	4	5
(11)　組織改革は,将来の事業展開の布石として行なわれた.	1	2	3	4	5
(12)　組織改革はいっきょに行なわれた.	1	2	3	4	5
(13)　組織改革は,メンバーの志気の高揚をめざしたものであった.	1	2	3	4	5
(14)　組織改革は,経営者の発意でトップ・ダウンに進められた.	1	2	3	4	5

	そのとおり	どちらかといえば正しい	どちらともいえない	どちらかといえばちがう	まったくちがう
(15) 組織改革は, 社外のコンサルタントを含むプロジェクト・チームにより企画・導入された.	1	2	3	4	5
(16) 競争会社の組織については常日頃研究している.	1	2	3	4	5
(17) 組織改革の1つの目的は, タテマエと実態との乖離を埋めることにあった.	1	2	3	4	5

問12 次にあげた上級経営担当者の要件はそれぞれどの程度重要であるとお考えでしょうか. 貴社にとっての重要性を評価し, 該当する数字に ○ 印をご記入ください.

	絶対不可欠	重要	あれば望ましい	無関係	ないほうが望ましい
(1) 一定の分野についての深い専門知識	1	2	3	4	5
(2) 会社と事業についての広汎な知識	1	2	3	4	5
(3) アイデアの斬新さ, 新しいアイデアへの許容力	1	2	3	4	5
(4) 強固な理念・哲学	1	2	3	4	5
(5) 冒険心, リスク志向	1	2	3	4	5
(6) 緻密な計画力	1	2	3	4	5
(7) 組織づくりと統率力	1	2	3	4	5
(8) 会社への忠誠心	1	2	3	4	5
(9) 他の経営者との協調性	1	2	3	4	5
(10) 公平さ	1	2	3	4	5
(11) 実 績	1	2	3	4	5
(12) 社外経験	1	2	3	4	5
(13) 多様な情報を処理・統合する能力	1	2	3	4	5
(14) 株主や金融機関への信用	1	2	3	4	5
(15) 社内での人望	1	2	3	4	5

問13-1 現在の貴社における戦略的に重要な目標はどのようなものでしょうか．上位3項目を選び順位をつけてください．

順　位

ROI（投下資本利益率）

市場占有率の向上

新製品比率

株主のキヤピタル・ゲイン（株価の上昇）

生産・物流システムの合理化

自己資本比率

製品ポートフォリオの改善

作業条件の改善

会社の社会的イメージの上昇

問13-2 貴社の経営者は次にあげる目標の達成度に関して，いかなる態度を表明しておられますか．それぞれの目標に対するその評価をお知らせください．

	非常に不満足	不満足	どちらともいえない	満足	非常に満足
(1) 売上高成長率	1	2	3	4	5
(2) 主要製品の市場占有率	1	2	3	4	5
(3) 新製品比率	1	2	3	4	5
(4) 収益伸び率	1	2	3	4	5
(5) 投下資本収益率	1	2	3	4	5
(6) 株主のキヤピタル・ゲイン（株価の上昇）	1	2	3	4	5
(7) 製品品質の改善	1	2	3	4	5
(8) 生産・物流システムの合理化	1	2	3	4	5
(9) マーケティング能力の強化	1	2	3	4	5
(10) 研究開発能力の強化	1	2	3	4	5
(11) 製品ポートフォリオの改善	1	2	3	4	5
(12) 資産の流動性（流動資産比率，自己資本比率など）	1	2	3	4	5
(13) 従業員のモラールの改善	1	2	3	4	5
(14) 従業員福祉の改善（給与上昇，職場・昇進機会の確保，休業条件の改善など）	1	2	3	4	5
(15) 人材開発	1	2	3	4	5
(16) 従業員の定着率	1	2	3	4	5

問14-1 '80年代の経営課題は何であるとお考えでしょうか．貴社のお考えをご自由にお聞かせください．

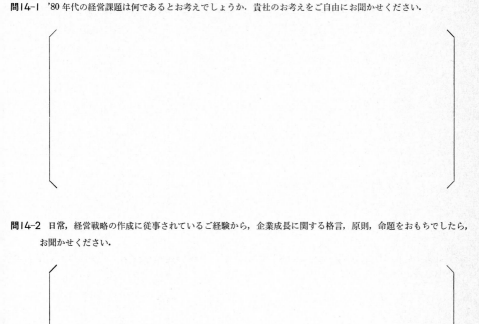

問14-2 日常，経営戦略の作成に従事されているご経験から，企業成長に関する格言，原則，命題をおもちでしたら，お聞かせください．

貴重なご意見をご回答いただきまして誠にありがとうございました．
（記入もれ，記入間違いがないかどうか再度ご確認のうえご返送ください．）

INTERNATIONAL COMPARISON OF MANAGEMENT SYSTEMS

Questionnaire

We hope you are willing to participate in this research study by filling out this questionnaire. Although the completion of this questionnaire in its entirety will be very much appreciated, if you find it impossible to fill it out, even the selective completion of this questionnaire will be appreciated as well because we need a sufficient number of responses in order to analyze general characteristics of U.S. firms.   If you cannot answer some specific questions for any reasons, please leave them blank and proceed to the next questions.

Most of the questions do not require detailed figures or data and are not difficult to answer, although some questions require your subjective judgment.   We would like to know your judgment on *"how things actually are"* rather than on *"how things ought to be."* Please respond to each question, reflecting the way it is in your company.

We understand that some of the information is confidential and are taking every precaution to protect you and your company.   All responses are entered in the data file in coded form with company identities known only to the members of the project.   The responses of any individual company will not be disclosed in any external report except for the restatement of responses sent back to each respondent.

If possible, please return this questionnaire with:
(1)   a copy of organizational chart showing basic structure of your company, and
(2)   a copy of the most recent annual report.

Thank you in advance for your cooperation.

Your name [please print]_____

Your position_____

The address to which a summary report should be mailed:

Street _____   City _____

State _____   Zip Code _____

1. **How would you characterize the *business environment* of your company? Please circle the number on the scale that best represents your judgment about each aspect of the environment. In question (1), for example, please circle 1 if your product-markets are very homogeneous, circle 7 if they are very heterogeneous. If neither extreme represents your judgment, circle an appropriate number in between, considering the distances from the descriptions at both extremes and, if any, at midpoint, 4.**

(1)   The markets that you serve are...

very homogeneous (e.g., a single undifferentiated market and very similar customers) **1 2 3 4 5 6 7** very heterogeneous (e.g., a great diversity of markets, types of customers, etc.)
↑
mixed

(2)   The production and marketing operations of your company are geographically...

very concentrated (e.g., in a single region of the U.S.) **1 2 3 4 5 6 7** very widely dispersed (e.g., global both in production and marketing)
↑
mixed (e.g., somewhat international)

(3)   The promotional strategy your company utilizes is generally....

very limited (e.g., pricing only) **1 2 3 4 5 6 7** very diverse (e.g., pricing, advertising, rebates, etc., are all utilized)

(4)   Providing customers with detailed technical informations about your products is generally....

unnecessary **1 2 3 4 5 6 7** indispensable (i.e., very detailed informations are needed)

(5)   The markets that you serve are generally....

not competitive (i.e., competitors live in peaceful coexistence) **1 2 3 4 5 6 7** very competitive and hostile

(6)   In the markets that you serve, your company is generally....

unable to affect the competitive situation **1 2 3 4 5 6 7** able to control the competitive situation

(7)   In the markets that you serve, the frequency of new product introductions and technological innovations is generally....

very low **1 2 3 4 5 6 7** very high

(8)   In the markets that you serve, the frequency of unpredictable changes in demand is....

very low **1 2 3 4 5 6 7** very high

(9)   Existing relationships with banks and major stockholders impose....

very minor constraints on future plans **1 2 3 4 5 6 7** very restrictive constraints on future plans

(10)   Existing relationships with major distributors and customers impose....

very minor constraints on future plans **1 2 3 4 5 6 7** very restrictive constraints on future plans

(11)   Existing relationships with major suppliers and subcontractors impose....

very minor constraints on future plans **1 2 3 4 5 6 7** very restrictive constraints on future plans

(12) Existing relationships with regulatory bodies and government impose . . . .

very minor constraints on future plans   **1 2 3 4 5 6 7**   very restrictive constraints on future plans

(13) Joint efforts (e.g., joint R&D projects, joint marketing, etc.) among firms in your industry are . . . .

very rare   **1 2 3 4 5 6 7**   very frequent

(14) The mobility of managers among firms in your industry is . . . .

very low (e.g., very low turnover of managers)   **1 2 3 4 5 6 7**   very high (e.g., managers frequently change their companies)

(15) The mobility of technological experts among firms in your industry is . . . .

very low (e.g., very low turnover of technological experts)   **1 2 3 4 5 6 7**   very high (e.g., technological experts frequently change their companies)

(16) The average profitability of firms in the market that accounts for the largest percentage of your sales (i.e., your primary market) is . . . .

very low (e.g., most of the firms in the industry are losing money)   **1 2 3 4 5 6 7**   very high (e.g., most of the firms make a lot of money)

(17) Entry barriers in **your primary market** are . . . .

very low (e.g., many new competitors have entered or may potentially do so)   **1 2 3 4 5 6 7**   very high (e.g., no new entry in a long time)

2. **The following table is a simplified version of the well-known Product Portfolio Matrix in which products are classified into four groups based on the growth rate of market and competitive position in the market. How would you characterize the product portfolio of your company? Please roughly apportion the total sales of your company among the four groups.**

Competitive position

		Strong (First or second in market share)	Weak (Third or lower in market share)
Growth rate of market	High (10% or higher)	(Stars) _____%	(Question Marks) _____%
	Low (lower than 10%)	(Cash Cow) _____%	(Dogs) _____%

Total 100%

3. **Listed below are different *production technologies or methods* available. To what extent is each technology utilized in your company? Please indicate rough percentage of output of each technology to total production.**

   •**Custom technology** (production or fabrication of a single unit or few units of products to customer specifications or needs, such as made-to-order dresses, specialized equipment, etc.) _____ %

   •**Small batch, jop shop technology** (creation of a small batch of similar units, such as fashionable dresses, tools and dies, etc.) _____ %

   •**Large batch technology** (e.g., used in manufacturing large batches of drugs and chemicals, parts, cans and bottles, yarns, etc.) _____ %

   •**Mass production technology** (e.g., used in mass production of autos, appliances, etc.) _____ %

   •**Continuous process technology** (e.g., used in oil refineries and other automated industries, in which output is produced continuously rather than in batch or shift) _____ %

                                                              Total   **100%**

4. **To what extent does each statement listed below correctly describe your company's strategies and underlying value and belief? Please circle the appropriate number:**

   1- "definitely true"
   2- "somewhat true"
   3- "can not say one way or the other"
   4- "somewhat incorrect"
   5- "definitely incorrect"

	definitely true				definitely incorrect
1. Your company consistently seeks high market share and tries to take advantage of cost efficiencies in every market.	1	2	3	4	5
2. Your company exploits the advantage of being a "follower" and tries to reduce risks on the development of new products and/or markets.	1	2	3	4	5
3. Your company concentrates resources in a few strategic market segments.	1	2	3	4	5
4. The pursuit of stockholder benefits is thought to be the most important social responsibility of your company.	1	2	3	4	5
5. Your company competes head-on with competitors.	1	2	3	4	5
6. Your company does not hesitate to divest from questionable businesses.	1	2	3	4	5
7. The diversification targets are restricted to those product lines which have close commonality with the existing technological base.	1	2	3	4	5
8. Your company selects the market segments in which it has advantages and pursues coexistence with competitors.	1	2	3	4	5
9. Your company has been actively developing foreign markets.	1	2	3	4	5

		definitely true				definitely incorrect
10.	Strategy formulation in your company is based upon systematic research data and sophisticated analytical methods.	1	2	3	4	5
11.	Your company is always an innovator which actively takes risks on the development of new product and/or market.	1	2	3	4	5
12.	Your company has actively acquired new businesses.	1	2	3	4	5
13.	The recruitment of managerial personnel and technological experts are based upon long-range personnel planning rather than immediate needs.	1	2	3	4	5
14.	The diversification targets are restricted to those product lines in which existing strengths in marketing can be applied.	1	2	3	4	5
15.	Information is sought extensively even on markets unrelated to present businesses.	1	2	3	4	5
16.	Your company aims to produce high quality products with high value added and to rely on non-price marketing strategies.	1	2	3	4	5
17.	Your company emphasizes accumulating diverse base of know-how more than making better use of existing know-how.	1	2	3	4	5
18.	The basic strategy of your company is inseparable from the unique value and belief of the present C.E.O. or the original founder.	1	2	3	4	5
19.	The fulfillment of various social responsibilities is clearly built into the corporate strategy of your company.	1	2	3	4	5
20.	Your company has been actively investing in foreign production subsidiaries.	1	2	3	4	5
21.	Voluntary recommendations made by lower-level managers are frequently followed by senior executives.	1	2	3	4	5
22.	The intuitive judgment of experienced executives plays a major role in formulating strategy.	1	2	3	4	5

5. **How important are the following strategies in the business that account for the largest percentage of your sales (i.e., your primary business)? Please rank the strategies in order of present and future importance: 1- most important to 5- least important.**

	Last five years	Next five years
•**Product strategy** (product planning, market research for new products, R&D, etc.)	( )	( )
•**Promotional strategy** (sales management and personal selling, advertising, and other marketing communication strategies)	( )	( )
•**Distribution strategy** (choice of distribution channel, distribution and inventory program, etc.)	( )	( )
•**Pricing strategy** (price policy, pricing decision, etc.)	( )	( )
•**Production strategy** (economy of scale, cost reduction, flexibility of production system, etc.)	( )	( )

6. The following questions relate to your company's *R&D activities* :

(1)   How much did your company spend in R&D last year? Please state
the approximate percentage of R&D expenditures to total sales in the
last year.   _____ %

(2)   What percentage of last year's sales was accounted by new product
lines introduced since 1973 (year of the first oil crisis)? Please state
the approximate percentage of new product line sales to total sales.   _____ %

(3)   How important are the following kinds of R&D activities to your
company? Please indicate the relative importance of each item by
percentage points, the sum of which totals 100%.

•Basic research on new technologies

•Research on improving and updating existing products

•Development of new products

•Development of new production methods and processes

Total   100%

**7. Are any of the following *management or planning systems or organizational devices* cur-
rently being utilized in your company? Please circle the numbers of those items that are
being utilized. (*multiple answers*)**

1 Formalized job description

2 Standard cost accounting system

3 Flexible budgetary control system

4 Performance evaluation system

5 Monthly operation reporting system

6 Management by objectives (MBO)

7 Objective promotion criteria

8 Internal training program for managers

9 Objective formula for wage/salary determination

10 Fixed assets investment analysis system

11 Sales forecasting system

12 Sales review and analysis system

13 Sales force performance appraisal system

14 Competition analysis system

15 Planning system for PR and advertisement

16 Short-range planning system

17 Middle-range planning system

18 Strategic planning system

19 Cash-flow planning system

20 Capital budgeting system

21 Financial investment analysis system

22 Planning-programming-budgeting system (PPBS)

23 Contingency planning system

24 Strategic business unit system

25 Project management system

26 Product or brand manager system

27 Matrix organization

28 Management information system (MIS)

**8. Is your company's organization divided into autonomous business units on geographic and/or
product bases (i.e., geographic divisions, product divisions, etc.)?**

1 **YES**——Please answer question (1) to (6) below.

2 **NO** ——Please proceed to question 9.

(1)   How many business units or divisions are identified in your company? Please re-
strict your calculation to basic business units that have some degree of autonomy in
operating decisions. Please circle the appropriate number.

1	2 — 5 units	5	31 — 50 units
2	6 — 10 units	6	51 — 100 units
3	11 — 20 units	7	101 — 200 units
4	21 — 30 units	8	more than 201 units

(2) How are the performances of the business units evaluated? Please circle the number of the most appropriate description.

1 The performance of each unit is evaluated by one common criterion.

2 The performance of each unit is evaluated by several common criteria and the weights attached to the criteria are nearly the same for each unit.

3 The performance of each unit is evaluated by several common criteria but the weights attached to the criteria are differentiated from unit to unit.

4 The performance of each unit is evaluated by criteria specific to it.

(3) How autonomous are the business units in making decisions? Please circle the number of the most appropriate description.

1 Severe constraints are imposed on all kinds of decisions.

2 Some constraints are imposed on operating decisions and severe constraints on capital expenditure decisions.

3 None or very few constraints are imposed on operating decisions but severe constraints on capital expenditure decisions.

4 None or very few constraints are imposed on any decisions.

(4) What kinds of function are performed by typical business units? Please circle the numbers of functions that are performed by these business units. (*multiple answers*)

1 production
2 sales
3 marketing planning
4 personnel
5 control
6 finance
7 basic research
8 applied research and development
9 purchasing

(5) Does your company employ the following organizational systems? Please circle the numbers if the systems are in use. (*multiple answers*)

1 Group executives who are responsible for several business units and report to the chief executive officer.

2 General staff which supports the group executives.

3 Task forces that are *temporarily* organized to solve functional problems common to several business units.

4 Teams which are *permanently* organized to solve functional problems common to several business units.

5 Functional coordinator whose primary task is to facilitate collaboration among several business units on functional problems common to them.

(6) Is the performance of each business unit reflected in the bonus and/or salary of its general manager? Please circle the number of the most appropriate description.

1 Not reflected at all; performance figures used *only* for planning purposes.

2 Reflected only nominally; performance figures used *mainly* for planning purposes.

3 Reflected substantially, with financial remuneration for each manager being determined individually by his superior.

4 Reflected substantially, with financial remuneration for each manager being determined by objective formulas.

9. **To what extent does each statement listed below correctly describe the characteristics of your company's organization? Please circle the 5-point scale appropriately:**

    1- "definitely true"
    2- "somewhat true"
    3- "can not say one way or the other"
    4- "somewhat incorrect"
    5- "definitely incorrect"

		definitely true			definitely incorrect	
(1)	The authority and responsibility of every executive or manager are clearly and concretely defined in your company.	1	2	3	4	5
(2)	Planned job rotation of managers is emphasized as a device for developing their capabilities.	1	2	3	4	5
(3)	In your company the function of senior executives is thought to set the way of thinking about problems, therefore, the actual problem-solving is delegated to their subordinates.	1	2	3	4	5
(4)	Even the first-line employees have intimate knowledge about the basic policy of your company.	1	2	3	4	5
(5)	In your company individual managers' initiative is valued more than the harmony of human relations.	1	2	3	4	5
(6)	Career paths for specialists as well as for managerial personnel are clearly defined.	1	2	3	4	5
(7)	Consensus is heavily emphasized in the decisions and actions of each decision unit.	1	2	3	4	5
(8)	The conflict among executives and managers are promptly resolved based upon superiors' authority.	1	2	3	4	5
(9)	The job descriptions for executives and managers are general and, therefore, applied very flexibly.	1	2	3	4	5
(10)	Executives, managers, and employees in your company share a considerable amount of common information.	1	2	3	4	5
(11)	Employees and managers have a strong sense of identification with your company.	1	2	3	4	5
(12)	The organization of your company is designed with some specific executives and/or managers in mind.	1	2	3	4	5
(13)	Senior executives always encourage competition among managers or among divisions.	1	2	3	4	5
(14)	Senior executives have frequent formal and/or informal meetings with line managers and supervisors.	1	2	3	4	5
(15)	The value and belief of the chief executive officer is reflected in every system in your organization.	1	2	3	4	5
(16)	Your company's control system is based on employees' self-discipline and commitment to work.	1	2	3	4	5
(17)	Senior executives strive to promote sense of identification with the company among employees.	1	2	3	4	5
(18)	The performance of each manager is evaluated by the end results of his/her efforts rather than by the amount of the effort itself.	1	2	3	4	5

		definitely true				definitely incorrect

(19) Executives and managers exchange information in advance of a formal meeting so that differences in opinion and judgment are not brought up at the meeting.   1 2 3 4 5

(20) Employees and managers are proud of being members of your company.   1 2 3 4 5

(21) Senior executives are constantly conscious of developing capability of their potential successors.   1 2 3 4 5

(22) Retirement ages of workers, managers, and executives are clearly defined.   1 2 3 4 5

(23) The organization's climate is inseparable from the unique value and belief of the chief executive officer.   1 2 3 4 5

(24) Senior executives actively search for problems within your company and take the leadership in solving them.   1 2 3 4 5

(25) Executives and managers also have close social relationships outside of work.   1 2 3 4 5

(26) Senior executives always clarify information requests (i.e., what needs to be known) about each division or department.   1 2 3 4 5

(27) Most executives and managers will not leave this company even if a higher pay or a higher position is offered by another company.   1 2 3 4 5

(28) Senior executives always try to develop reliable sources of information aside from formal channels of information already available.   1 2 3 4 5

(29) The performance of each manager is evaluated over 5 to 10 years term so that his/her potential capabilities can be taken into account.   1 2 3 4 5

(30) Important information is usually exchanged informally among executives and managers.   1 2 3 4 5

(31) When there is a difference in opinion and judgment among executives and managers, they always seek to find a temporary compromise rather than to impose a final decision.   1 2 3 4 5

(32) Most executives and managers have no prior job experience outside this company.   1 2 3 4 5

(33) Senior executives actively gather information by themselves about relevant events in and out of your company and about situations on the line.   1 2 3 4 5

(34) Employees' and managers' actions are strictly controlled by rules and by their superiors.   1 2 3 4 5

(35) Most senior executives have been promoted from within.   1 2 3 4 5

(36) The organization's climate is to pursue and challenge any change.   1 2 3 4 5

(37) Senior executives are strict in applying rewards and punishments.   1 2 3 4 5

(38) Executives and managers thoroughly discuss differences in opinion and judgment among themselves even though such discussions are time consuming.   1 2 3 4 5

10-1. How much influence has each of the following persons or groups on making decisions relating to the acquisitions and/or development of new product lines, the divestment of existing product lines, the renewal of major facilities, etc.?

	little or no influence	some influence	quite a bit of influence	a great deal of influence	a very great deal of influence
·Chief executive officer	1	2	3	4	5
·Committee of corporate senior executives	1	2	3	4	5
·General managers of business group*	1	2	3	4	5
·General managers of business unit*	1	2	3	4	5
·Chief functional managers (e.g., production managers, marketing managers, etc.)	1	2	3	4	5
·Committees in functional department	1	2	3	4	5

* If your company is not organized around divisions, these lines can be left blank.

10-2. How much influence has each of the following departments when making joint decisions that may determine the overall performance of your company? Please circle the number which best represents the amount of influence of each department.

	little or no influence	some influence	quite a bit of influence	a great deal of influence	a very great deal of influence
(1) Sales and marketing	1	2	3	4	5
(2) R&D	1	2	3	4	5
(3) Production	1	2	3	4	5
(4) Control and finance	1	2	3	4	5
(5) Personnel, labor relations	1	2	3	4	5
(6) Corporate planning staff	1	2	3	4	5
(7) Purchasing, procurement	1	2	3	4	5

11. The following questions address the process of major reorganization.

A. Has your company made corporate-wide reorganizations during the last 5 years?

    1 YES——Please proceed to question B.

    2 NO ——Please proceed to question 12.

B. To what extent does each statement listed below correctly describe the characteristics of *the most recent reorganization* in your company? Please circle the appropriate number:

    1- "definitely true"

    2- "somewhat true"

    3- "can not say one way or the other"

    4- "somewhat incorrect"

    5- "definitely incorrect"

	definitely true				definitely incorrect
(1) The reorganization was accompanied by the replacement of one or more senior executives.	1	2	3	4	5
(2) The reorganization was implemented incrementally.	1	2	3	4	5
(3) The primary purpose of the reorganization was to improve internal efficiency.	1	2	3	4	5
(4) The reorganization was utilized as an opportunity to inform employees of the intention of senior executives.	1	2	3	4	5

		definitely true				definitely incorrect
(5)	Extensive organization and task analyses were made prior to the reorganization.	1	2	3	4	5
(6)	The organization of your company has been reorganized periodically.	1	2	3	4	5
(7)	The primary purpose of the reorganization was to strengthen the flexibility of the organization to cope with competition.	1	2	3	4	5
(8)	The opinions of executives and managers at various levels are reflected in the reorganization.	1	2	3	4	5
(9)	The reorganization was based on the idea that the key to successful reorganization was not to seek radical change.	1	2	3	4	5
(10)	The organization is continually reviewed by a department in charge of organizational design.	1	2	3	4	5
(11)	The reorganization provided for future business extension.	1	2	3	4	5
(12)	The reorganization was implemented all at once.	1	2	3	4	5
(13)	One purpose of the reorganization was to raise the *esprit de corps* of managers and employees.	1	2	3	4	5
(14)	The reorganization was initiated by the chief executive officer and implemented "top-down".	1	2	3	4	5
(15)	The reorganization was planned by a task force that included external consultants.	1	2	3	4	5
(16)	Organizations of competing companies were extensively studied.	1	2	3	4	5
(17)	One purpose of reorganization was to eliminate discrepancy between "what ought to be" and "what actually is".	1	2	3	4	5

12. **How important are the following personal traits and capability for senior executives of your company? Please evaluate the importance of each on the following scale by circling the appropriate number :**

   1- "indispensable"
   2- "important"
   3- "desirable"
   4- "not important"
   5- "undesirable"

		indispensable				undesirable
(1)	Depth of professional knowledge in a specific field	1	2	3	4	5
(2)	General knowledge of the company and its business	1	2	3	4	5
(3)	Ability to produce and accept new and creative ideas	1	2	3	4	5
(4)	Sound and consistent value and belief	1	2	3	4	5
(5)	Willingness to take risk	1	2	3	4	5
(6)	Ability to formulate detailed plans	1	2	3	4	5
(7)	Ability to organize and lead	1	2	3	4	5
(8)	Commitment to and identification with the company	1	2	3	4	5
(9)	Ability to promote harmony and collaboration among executives	1	2	3	4	5
(10)	Sense of equity and fairness	1	2	3	4	5
(11)	Past record of high performance	1	2	3	4	5
(12)	Experience in other companies	1	2	3	4	5
(13)	Ability to integrate diverse information	1	2	3	4	5
(14)	Credibility with stockholders and banks	1	2	3	4	5
(15)	Popularity and credibility with the subordinates	1	2	3	4	5

13-1. How important are the following goals for your company? Please select three important goals and rank them in order of importance: 1- the most important to 3- the third most important.

ranking

- Return on investment
- Increase in market share
- New product ratio
- Capital gain for stockholder (i.e., increase in share price)
- Efficiency of production and physical distribution
- Equity/debt ratio
- Improvement of product portfolio
- Improvement in quality of working conditions
- Improvement in public image of the company

13-2. What levels of satisfaction or dissatisfaction are your senior executives expressing regarding how well the company achieved its goals? Please indicate their level of satisfaction by circling the appropriate number:

> **1-** "great dissatisfaction"
> **2-** "dissatisfaction"
> **3-** "neither dissatisfaction nor satisfaction"
> **4-** "satisfaction"
> **5-** "great satisfaction"

		great dissatis- faction				great satis- faction
(1)	Sales growth	1	2	3	4	5
(2)	Increase in market share (of major products)	1	2	3	4	5
(3)	New product ratio	1	2	3	4	5
(4)	Growth of earnings	1	2	3	4	5
(5)	Return on investment	1	2	3	4	5
(6)	Capital gain for stockholders (i.e., increase in share price)	1	2	3	4	5
(7)	Improvement in product quality	1	2	3	4	5
(8)	Improvement in efficiency of production and physical distribution	1	2	3	4	5
(9)	Strengthening of marketing capability	1	2	3	4	5
(10)	Strengthening of R&D capability	1	2	3	4	5
(11)	Improvement of product portfolio	1	2	3	4	5
(12)	Liquidity of assets (e.g., liquidity ratio, equity ratio, etc.)	1	2	3	4	5
(13)	Improvement in morale of employees	1	2	3	4	5
(14)	Improvement in employees' welfare (e.g., increase in pay, job security, and opportunity for promotion from within, improvement of work environment)	1	2	3	4	5
(15)	Development of human resources	1	2	3	4	5
(16)	Reduction of labor turnover	1	2	3	4	5

14-1. What do you think will be the management problems that your company will face in 1980's? Please write your judgment in the space provided below.

_____

_____

_____

_____

_____

_____

_____

14-2. What rule, maxim, and theory of corporate growth and development do you have? Please write them in the space provided below.

_____

_____

_____

_____

_____

_____

_____

THANK YOU VERY MUCH FOR YOUR THOUGHTFUL COOPERATION!

Appendix C: Japanese Company Descriptions

The following are the brief descriptions of the 19 Japanese companies selected for our intensive case study. The descriptions are based upon readily available published materials as of 1982 (exchange rate of 1 dollar = 249 yen).

Toray Industries, Inc.

Chairman: Tsuguhide Fujiyoshi   President: Yoshikazu Ito
Sales: 2,271 (million dollars)   Employees: 13,979

Toray is Japan's largest manufacturer of synthetic fibers. The company also produces plastics and chemicals, and it has interests abroad in synthetic fiber production, mostly in Southeast Asia.

Toray was established as Toyo Rayon Co. by Mitsui & Co., one of the major Zaibatsus, in 1926 to manufacture rayon. The company expanded into nylon production in 1951 under a license agreement from Du Pont. Toray integrated backward into petrochemicals in the late 1960s and forward into knitted textiles in the early 1970s. In the 1970s, Toray also developed a number of new products and materials, such as the suede-like *Ecsaine* in 1970, *Torayca* carbon fiber in 1971, and ultra-fine vicuna-like *Toraylina* in 1976. Rayon production, the company's original business, had been progressively phased out and by 1975 Toray had completely withdrawn from the business.

Toray has four major lines of business. *The synthetic fiber business* accounted for 69% of Toray's sales in fiscal 1982. *Plastics* constituted 22% of sales in the same year and consisted mainly of polyester film, polypropylene film and ABS resin. *Chemicals*, which accounted for 6% of sales, were mainly raw materials and intermediates for synthetic fiber production, such as cyclohexane, caprolactam, para-xylene and ortho-xylene. *Other products* represented 3% of sales and included amino acids, carbon fiber, elastomeric fiber, and printing plates.

Historically, Toray has had a strong orientation towards R&D.   Many
Japanese think of it as a technological leader.

NEC Corporation

    Chairman: Koji Kobayashi   President: Tadahiro Sekimoto
    Sales: 5,034 (million dollars)   Employees: 36,057

NEC is Japan's leading producer of communications equipment, the world's
leading supplier of satellite communication earth stations, among Japan's
largest computer mainframe makers, and one of the largest producers of
integrated circuits in the world.

According to the company's annual report of 1981, the policy of NEC "is to
make continued progress in 'C&C', or the integration of computers and
communications.   In the coming years, 'C&C'-based information systems will
alter the fabric of modern society.   And NEC is well-positioned to play a
major role in this rapidly growing market."

NEC was incorporated in 1899 as a joint venture between Japanese investors
and Western Electric Co. (USA) to manufacture telephones.   The size of the
company grew with the expansion of the telephone system and became a major
supplier to the government-owned telephone company (NTT).   After the war,
the company expanded into home appliances and electronics.   The extension
into electronics was coupled with diversification moves to lessen
dependence on NTT, which in the 1950s and 1960s had accounted for more
than half of sales.   In the 1970s, the company began producing computers
and integrated backward into the manufacture of integrated circuits and
other components.

Communications accounted for 39% of NEC's revenues in fiscal 1982,
computers for 28%, electron devices for 25%, and home electronics for
8%.   The company has built enviable positions in some of these industries,
including a Japanese personal computer market share of more than 50%.

Hitachi, Ltd.

Chairman: Hirokichi Yoshiyama   President: Katsushige Mita

Sales: 9,370 (million dollars)   Employees: 74,942

Hitachi is the largest manufacturer of electrical equipment in Japan and one of the largest in the world. The company manufactures a broad range of industrial and consumer products, including computers, communications, home appliances, heavy industrial equipment, and electrical machinery.

Hitachi, which was incorporated in 1920, had its origins in the machinery repair shop of a mining company in 1910 in the town of Hitachi. Originally a manufacturer of mechanical equipment, the company branched out into production of vacuum tubes and light bulbs in the 1940s. After the war, Hitachi began mass-producing refrigerators and radios. Most of the firm's products were developed internally. In the mid-1950s, it launched an automatic telephone exchange. Another milestone was the development of the company's first computer, the HITAC 8000, in 1965. In the 1960s, production of color TV sets and electronic calculators brought substantial growth. In 1967, the company began producing its own integrated circuits. Major growth in the 1970s came from computers and other electronic equipment, while the original industrial machinery and the transport equipment businesses declined in importance.

Hitachi now has five major lines of product. *Communications and electronic equipment*, including measuring instruments, accounted for 30% of total sales in fiscal 1982. Some of the important products in this category are telephone exchanges, facsimile equipment, and computers. *Electric utility apparatus and electrical equipment* represented 24% of 1982 sales and included a complete range of heavy machinery for electric power generation and distribution. *Consumer products* accounted for 22% of sales and consisted of home appliances. *Transportation equipment* made up 11% of sales and included electric and diesel locomotives and passenger railcars. Finally *industrial machinery*, the remaining 13%, encompassed a wide range of products, including compressors, pumps, construction machinery, and elevators.

Toshiba Corporation
    Chairman: Kazuo Iwata   President: Shoichi Saba
    Sales: 8,077 (million dollars)   Employees: 65,690

Toshiba is the third largest manufacturer of electrical equipment in
Japan, after Matsushita and Hitachi. Toshiba has three major lines of
business. *Home electric appliances* accounted for 32% of Toshiba's sales
in fiscal 1982, *heavy electric machinery* for 37% and *electronic components
and industrial electronics* for the remaining 31%.

Toshiba had its origins in two long-established electrical companies,
Shibaura Seisaku-sho and Tokyo Denki, which merged in 1939 to form Tokyo
Shibaura Electric. (The company changed its name to Toshiba Corporation
in 1984.) The original Shibaura Seisaku-sho was founded in 1875 as Tanaka
Seizo-sha by Mr. H. Tanaka, who is considered the 'Edison of Japan', to
produce telegraph equipment. This company gradually expanded into heavier
electrical equipment such as generators (first waterwheel generator in
Japan in 1894), electric motors and transformers and into consumer
products, such as electric fans and refrigerators. Lasting links were
forged with GE of the USA in 1895, when technicians and managers were sent
to the USA for a study. At one point, namely 1939, GE held 30% of the
equity. (GE now owns 10% of Toshiba's stock.) Tokyo Denki was founded in
1890 by Dr. I. Fujioka as Hakunetsu-sha to manufacture the first
incandescent lamps in Japan. This company expanded into vacuum tubes,
meters, radio sets (first produced in Japan in 1924) and radio
communications equipment.

After the merger of the two companies in 1939, Toshiba expanded both its
consumer product and industrial equipment lines. In the consumer product
area, Toshiba began mass producing TV sets in 1949, added a range of home
appliances in the 1950s and 1960s, and launched the first color TV sets
with predominantly electronic circuits in 1971. Recently, video tape
recorders have been added. In the industrial equipment area, the company
has had a number of "firsts." In 1955, it produced the world's largest
hydrogen-cooled synchronous condenser. It manufactured the first radar
(1962) and space communications equipment (1963) in Japan, the world's
first electrostatic ticket processing machine (1968), and also the world's

largest water turbines (1972) and electronic engine control modules (1977). In its more than 100 years of operation, the company has established a solid reputation for technological innovation.

Fujitsu, Ltd.

Chairman: Taiyu Kobayashi   President: Takuma Yamamoto
Sales: 3,240 (million dollars) Employees: 37,272

Fujitsu is Japan's largest mainframe computer manufacturer, Japan's second largest manufacturer of telecommunications systems and equipment, and among the major producers of semiconductors and other electronic components.

Fujitsu was founded in 1935 as a spin-off from Fuji Electric to manufacture automatic telephone exchanges, telephone sets, and related equipment. In 1937, the company began to produce carrier transmission equipment. After World War II, Fujitsu began developing data processing equipment and introduced the first Japanese-made computer, the FACOM 100, in 1954. Since then, the company has developed a full range of computer systems, from one-chip microcomputers to extremely large-scale systems, while the original businesses have diminished in importance.

Computers and data processing systems made up 66% of total sales in fiscal 1982. Other important products included communications systems, accounting for 19% of 1982 sales and semiconductors and electronic components (15%). The focus of the company's research and development is placed upon computer and computer-related areas. The past success in developing the high electron mobility transistor(HEMT), which is expected to be a key device in next-generation computers, reflects the company's aggressive commitment to R&D.

In contrast to NEC, Fujitsu's computers are compatible with IBM, which is also the case with Hitachi. Fujitsu supplies products and technology to ICL in Britain, Siemens in West Germany, and Amdahl in the U.S. In March, 1984, Fujitsu increased its equity stake in Amdahl from 30% to 49.5%.

Ajinomoto Co., Inc.

    Chairman: Saburosuke Suzuki   President: Katsuhiro Utada
    Sales: 1,640 (million dollars)   Employees: 5,556

Ajinomoto is the leading manufacturer of monosodium glutamate, or M.S.G., in the world. This crystalline flavor enhancer -- discovered in seaweed by K. Ikeda, a chemist, and now made from cane molasses -- formed the basis for what has become a very international corporation. The company has 35 domestic and 17 overseas affiliates and employs approximately 20,000 employees worldwide.

Ajinomoto started as Suzuki Pharmaceutical Works, which was set up by S. Suzuki in 1907, to exploit the patents for monosodium glutamate on a commercial scale. In 1908, the new seasoning was launched under the *Ajinomoto* label. The company expanded rapidly in Japan and abroad, giving a license to an American company for production in the United States in the 1920s and setting up a plant in Manchuria in 1936. In the mid-1950s, Ajinomoto developed the expertise for producing amino acids.

Seasonings under the *Ajinomoto* brand name accounted for 24% of the company's total sales in 1982, *oils and fats* for 22%, *processed foodstuffs* for 36%, *amino acids* for 11% and *other products* for 7%. Total sales were ten times that of 1962; the company grew at a rate of 12% a year in the intervening two decades. There are many explanations for this achievement, but three in particular should be mentioned: (1) the broad diversification made possible by further developing the skills and experience the company acquired with *Ajinomoto* seasoning; (2) the active development of joint ventures with overseas companies; and (3) the extensive investment in facilities and resources abroad whcich began early in the company's history.

Ajinomoto has broadened its domestic marketing base through cooperative ventures with major overseas companies. They include CPC International (soup, mayonnaise and margarine), General Foods (coffee and protein foods), the Charles River Co. (axenic laboratory animals) of the United States, and Gelbe-Danon (fresh dairy products) of France.

The chemical research that has made Ajinomoto Japan's best-known food additive company has led the company to undertake aggressive expansion into biotechnology, drug development, and cancer research, although the company is still heavily dependent on internationally marketed food additives, mostly M.S.G., and domestically marketed foods (like soups and low-calorie mayonnaise).

Toyota Motor Corporation

Chairman: Masaya Hanai   President: Eiji Toyoda

Sales: 19,649 (million dollars)   Employees: 51,034

Toyota is the largest automobile manufacturer in Japan and the second largest in the world. In addition to passenger cars and commercial vehicles (trucks and buses), Toyota produces prefabricated houses. The company has 17 assembly plants abroad, mainly in Australia, Southeast Asia, and Latin America.

In fiscal 1978-79, Toyota produced 2.03 million passenger cars (including jeeps), 39% of which were sold overseas. During the same period, Toyota captured a share of almost 32% of the total Japanese market, including commercial vehicles. If Toyota's affiliates -- Hino and Daihatsu -- were added, this share reached 39%. For the same year, the company produced 828,000 trucks and buses, of which 51% were sold overseas.

Passenger cars and commercial vehicles accounted for 57% and 19% of total sales in fiscal 1982, respectively. Other products represented 24% of total sales.

In Japan, Toyota has integrated backward into the production of steel and automobile components through a network of affiliates. Major members of the Toyota group included Toyoda Automatic Loom Works (19.3% owned), Toyota Auto body (38.8% owned), Kanto Auto Works (24.8% owned), Aisin Seiki (20.3% owned), Nippondenso (22.0% owned), and Aichi Steel Works (20.9% owned).

Toyota was founded by K. Toyoda, who set up an automobile division in the

Toyoda Automatic Loom Works in 1933. Toyota Motor was incorporated as a separate company in 1937 and completed its first plant to mass produce passenger cars one year later. After the war, Toyota modernized its production facilities and attained rapid growth in the 1950s with the expansion of domestic demand. The *Crown*, the first totally Japanese-made passenger car, was introduced in 1955. In the late 1950s and early 1960s, the company instituted a comprehensive quality control system and expanded capacity with the opening of the *Motomachi* plant in 1959. In 1962, cumulative production reached one million units. Annual unit production exceeded the one-million marked, in 1968 and the two-million mark in 1972. Foreign assembly operations began in the 1960s in Southeast Asia and later expanded to Australia and Latin America.

The company's success is attributed to an efficient mass production system, continuous cost reduction and quality improvement efforts (including a highly successful employee suggestion system), and strong domestic and international marketing networks. The company recently put a more active sales policy into operation to attain its target of selling "2 million cars in the domestic market." In the long run, Toyota hopes to acquire 10% of the global market.

Kao Corporation

Chairman: Kazuo Arai   President: Yoshio Maruta
Sales: 1,227 (million dollars)   Employees: 4,783

Kao Corporation, established in 1887, is Japan's largest manufacturer of soaps, detergents, laundry finishing agents, and hair care products. The company's name *Kao*, which was the name of the first toilet soap the company put on the market, means "queen of the flowers." Its key corporate value is *seiketsu*, meaning cleanliness or purity. The company is developing new products to *help people make themselves and their surroundings cleaner*, and its success has made the firm's smiling crescent moon trademark one of the most familiar in Japan.

Today, Kao is a leading chemical manufacturer, with some 200 household products and over 1,000 industrial products. The company's sales have quadrupled to 1,227 million dollars in fiscal 1982. Of this total, household products contributed 1,043 million dollars (85% of sales) and products used in industry, 184 million dollars (15% of sales).

The company has stressed integrated research and development. Its initial major breakthrough came in 1928, when it developed Japan's first modified edible fat specifically for confectionary and bread-baking use. Following this success, Kao embarked on efforts to improve its hydrogenation and splitting technology for oil and fat and to establish its own technology for high-pressure hydrogenation. The research results led to expanded activities into new areas, such as synthetic detergents and shampoos. Its technologies have been put to use in an extensive range of industrial chemicals.

The consumer distribution network is comprised of Kao's exclusive *hanshas*, the distribution companies that handle only its products within individual marketing areas. Some 79 such *hanshas* work in close cooperation with the parent company, maintaining a strong sense of identity. By setting up the *hansha*, Kao has succeeded in building its own distribution channel, therefore eliminating the complexity and inefficiency of multiple marketing channels. The operations of these *hanshas* have been systematically improved over the years through such marketing efforts as planned shipments to retail stores, effective shelf layouts, and advice in retail store management. The company thinks the depth of this cooperation is possible because the company's exclusive *hanshas* handle only Kao's consumer products.

Renown, Inc.

Chairman: Yasue Ito   President: Hiromichi Inagawa
Sales: 874 (million dollars)   Employees: 4,085

Renown is one of the leading companies in the apparel industry in Japan. It is primarily engaged in distributing a wide variety of clothing, mostly produced by sub-contractors but some directly, throughout Japan.

Merchandise sold by Renown is divided into nine categories: women's ready-to-wear (18.6% of total sales in fiscal 1982), women's outerwear (16.7%), children's outerwear (10.4%), men's outerwear (25.0%), women's underwear (4.2%), men's and children's underwear (8.2%), hosiery (10.4%), infants' clothing (5.5%) and miscellaneous (1.0%).

Most of the goods marketed by the company are based on designs supplied by the company, although the company also uses designs licensed from fashion houses in Europe and the United States. The company employs approximately 200 designers.

Sub-contractors supplied approximately 71% of the goods sold in 1983. Most of the 380 sub-contractors are small and dependent on Renown and has had long-standing business relationships. No single sub-contractor accounted for more than 2% of goods sold in 1983. Each sub-contractor makes a specific type of product for Renown at an agreed price. In 1983, approximately 30% of the goods purchased by Renown from sub-contractors was purchased through trading companies, which provided, in effect, financing to sub-contractors by purchasing their stock and holding it in their name until delivery to Renown.

Renown supplies its goods directly to retail outlets rather than through wholesalers, who still today often act as intermediaries between manufactures and retailers in the clothing industry in Japan. This policy not only increases profitability, but also enables Renown, by frequent contact with retailers, to monitor fashion trends directly and to react quickly to changes in consumer demand.

Takeda Chemical Industries, Ltd.
    Chairman: Shinbei Konishi   President: Ikushiro Kurabayashi
    Sales: 1,883 (million dollars)   Employees: 11,100

Takeda is Japan's largest manufacturer of pharmaceuticals. Its other products include basic and agricultural chemicals and foodstuffs. Abroad, the company has manufacturing operations in Southeast Asia and Mexico. While these overseas investments are appreciable, they are not of major strategic importance to the firm.

The company, which was founded by the Takeda family in Osaka in 1781, originated as a drug wholesaler. Beginning in the Meiji era, Takeda began importing Western medicines. The first plant was opened in 1895, and by 1910 the company had expanded into fine chemicals production. After its incorporation in 1925, Takeda began systematic research and development and succeeded in synthesizing Vitamin C in 1937 and Vitamin B_1 in 1938. After World War II, Takeda began a period of rapid growth with the discovery of the synthesis of Alinamin, a thiamine derivative, which is now Takeda's leading product. In the late 1950s, the company expanded into the food industry through its flavoring agents, centralized its research and development, and set up its first overseas plant in Mexico. In the 1960s, it established joint ventures in Southeast Asia and enlarged its domestic capacity substantially. Takeda also diversified further into agricultural chemicals and, in a more limited way, into cosmetics.

In fiscal 1982, pharmaceuticals accounted for 62% of total sales. Bulk vitamins and antibiotics were among the most important products. The company's other principal products were foodstuffs, mainly flavor enhancing agents, which accounted for 12% of sales in 1982, industrial chemicals and chemical products (14% of 1982 sales) with main products being TDI, polyurethane resins, and latex; and agricultural chemicals and cosmetics, which together accounted for the remaining 12% of sales.

Takeda's share of the Japanese pharmaceutical market is approximately 5%, and the firm is bolstering its position through various joint ventures with foreign companies, such as Roussel Uclaf and Abbott Laboratories.

Sumitomo Electric Industries, Ltd.

Chairman: Masao Kamei   President: Tetsuro Kawakami

Sales: 1,677 (million dollars)   Employees: 11,897

Sumitomo Electric is Japan's largest manufacturer of electrical wire and cable. The company also produces tungsten carbide tools and disc brakes, and is engaged in electric power construction. Further, it is Japan's biggest manufacturer of optical fibers and compound semiconductors.

Abroad, it has manufacturing facilities in Korea and Southeast Asia. The company is setting up an optical laboratory in North Carolina in the United States which will be completed in early 1985. This laboratory will be the first genuine research facility to be set up in the U.S. by any Japanese company.

Sumitomo Electric Wire & Cable Works, the direct predecessor of the present company, was established as a separate firm in 1911. In the early 1920s, the company laid the longest underwater power cable in the world at the time in Japan's Inland Sea. In the 1930s, Sumitomo Electric added special wires, such as piano wires, to its product lines and began manufacturing carbide tools. During the war, the company started to produce rubber products, such as vibration absorbers. After the war, rapid expansion was fostered by the reconstruction of the country and capacity was added accordingly. In the early 1960s, the company started making plastic to cover its wire and cables and diversified into non-electrical automotive components when it began to produce disc brakes. The expansion was aided by a number of agreements with foreign firms, including Western Electric and Ford.

Today, Sumitomo Electric is well known for its strong orientation toward R&D activities and as a highly diversified high-tech firm. Electrical wires and cables represented 58% of total sales in fiscal 1982. They are produced for a wide variety of applications, including electronics. The government-owned telephone company, NTT, is its major customer in this business. Other principal products included powdered alloys (9% of 1982 sales); special wires (7%); and others, including electrical engineering and construction works (26%).

Amada Co., Ltd.

President: Isamu Amada

Sales: 340 (million dollars)　　　Employees: 1,325

Amada is Japan's largest manufacturer of metal processing machinery. The company's products include bandsaws, electric discharge machines, machining centers, punch and power presses, shearing machines, laser cutting machines, punches and dies. Amada is also a world-class manufacturer of automated flexible manufacturing systems, or FMS, and is moving into the three dimensional measuring equipment and industrial robotic fields.

The company began business in 1946 by reconditioning lathes and marketing them in the cost-conscious post-war days. In 1955 the company constructed its first contour bandsaw and soon became a leading manufacturer in the bandsaw field in Japan. In the mid-1960s, Amada began diversifying its business line in reaction to the recession. For example, an arrangement with U.S. Industry, Inc. of the U.S. was concluded, and the manufacture and sale of Torc-Pac presses were started. Similar arrangements with Promecam Sisson Lehman S.A., of France were made, and the manufacture and sale of press brakes were begun. In 1971, U.S. Amada, Ltd. was established as a technical development company in Seattle. In 1977, the company opened a large exhibition hall in the suburbs of Tokyo, intended as a display area for the total system it supplied and as an area for discussing the problems of developing new products.

The large exhibition hall is called *Amada Machine Tool Plaza*. It allows the company to come into direct contact with the users, listen to their needs, and to serve them better. Both parties can informally discuss their problems and exchange ideas on the development of further machining techniques and system plans. Visitors can inspect all products the company produces, and about 80,000 people visit the Plaza each year. Orders received here account for approximately 80% of net sales.

Suntory, Ltd.
      President: Keizo Saji
      Sales: 3,226 (million dollars)   Employees: 4,507

Suntory is the largest manufacturer of wine and spirits in Japan. The company was established in 1899 by S. Torii, the father of the present chairman, K. Saji. The company's first product was a sweet wine -- called *Akadama* -- which is still a popular label in liquor stores and supermarkets in Japan. Suntory itself is currently the nation's oldest and largest distiller of whisky and a major producer of wine and beer.

The firm has strong orientations toward growth and diversification, and its pioneering efforts in the Japanese beverage industry have led to the development of more than 200 different beverage products -- a number which is growing constantly. Suntory is, however, more than just a producer of whisky, wine and beer. The company's products cover the entire spectrum of spirits, ranging from gin and tequila to ready-to-drink cocktails and of exotic liqueurs. Suntory also produces non-alcoholic beverages, such as natural fruit juices, carbonated and non-carbonated fruit drinks, and tonic and mineral water. Recently, it launched a new line of snack foods as an expansion into the packaged food sector. These products are handled separately from the company's main lines. All foods and non-alcoholic beverages are marketed by Suntory Foods, Ltd., a wholly-owned subsidiary established in 1972 to facilitate continuing deversification.

The company now has six divisions: wine & spirits, beer, soft drinks and food, restaurants and fast food, pharmaceuticals, and international.

The launching of the new type of beer by the company in 1963 is a prototypical story. In the early 1960's, K. Saji, then Managing Director of Suntory, brought his own dream to his father, chairman Torii. Young Saji was confident that there was a market in Japan for a new genre of beer featuring a different taste. Torii's unwavering entrepreneurial spirit prompted his reply of "yatte minahare" -- which can loosely be translated as "You'll never know unless you try." It was this willingness to test the unkown -- a spirit that pervades all of Suntory's business endeavors -- that allowed Saji to perfect and launch Suntory's light, Danish-style beer in 1963.

Recently, the company has emphasized research and development activities. For example, Suntory's Institute for Biomedical Research was established in 1979 upon the company's entry into the pharmaceutical field. This Institute consists of seven laboratories: Chemistry, Experimental Pharmacology, Clinical Pharmacology, Pharmaceutics, Genetic Technology, and Bio-Engineering. In addition to the pharmacological screening of synthetic compounds, researchers are involved in the practical application of recent biotechnological advances, such as genetic engineering, to the development of new peptide medicines. In 1981, this laboratory succeeded in using synthetic genes to produce an opioid peptide, alphaneoendorphin and also some immune interferons found in bacteria and yeast for the first time in the world.

西武

Seibu Group
Chairman: Seiji Tsutsumi
Sales: 8,967 (million dollars)   Employees: 67,500

The Seibu Group, composed of 95 companies, is Japan's leading merchandise conglomerate. Sales of the Group's flagship store in Ikebukuro (the largest department store in Japan) were more than $1 billion in 1982.

The Group has a strong orientation toward diversification and presently has eight divisions: Department Stores, Superstores, Real Estate/Leisure, Manufacturing, Credit/Finance, Restaurants/Food Services, Transportation /Aero-Survey, and Insurance. Of these, the first two are the largest and most important.

The Department Store Division, led by Seibu Department Stores, Ltd., includes specialty stores, shopping centers, and companies importing products for the Group through tie-ups with overseas enterprises. The companies in this division, centered in the Tokyo and Osaka areas but extending throughout Japan, together contribute approximately 45% of the sales for the Seibu Group. They have a reputation for developing both innovative retailing concepts and new employee programs. For example, although many traditional department stores in Japan still depend heavily on wholesalers for the selection and purchase of goods, Seibu stores have their own in-house buyers. Seibu Department Stores was also the first Japanese retail organization to institute professional specialization, creating for its employees a separate job ladder within which job advancement is based on merit.

The Superstores Division includes 255 Seiyu supermarkets and 310 FamilyMart convenience stores. The FamilyMart Co., Ltd., has operations nationwide. These mostly franchised outlets are rooted in their neighborhoods and occupy a strategic position among the Group's retail companies. They provide daily foods and other products virtually at the doorsteps of consumers, keeping the firm's supplier's happy and its positive image before the public.

Seiyu is committed to providing high quality daily-life products and has constantly redefined the superstore concept. Today, it is moving beyond its traditional retailing range to offer insurance, consumer finance, adult education, and many leisure-oriented services, in cooperation with other divisions in the Seibu Group.

Historically, the Seibu Group has had a good relationship with Sears, Roebuck & Co., establishing joint ventures such as the Seibu All state Life Insurance Co.

Komatsu, Ltd.
 Chairman: Ryoichi Kawai   President: Shoji Nogawa
 Sales: 2,621 (million dollars)   Employees: 17,002

Komatsu is the world's second largest manufacturer of construction machinery. It owns 31% of Kamatsu Forklift, Japan's second largest manufacturer of forklift trucks; and 52% of Komatsu Construction, a civil engineering contracting firm. It also produces a line of industrial presses. Despite the local nature of construction, this company is very international, with exports accounting for 64% of total 1982 sales.

Construction machinery accounted for 87% of the company's sales in 1982. Main products included bulldozers, for which Komatsu has a market share of about 60% in Japan; crawler tractors; dozer and power shovels; cranes and excavators; pipelayers; and graders and scrapers.

The company was incorporated in 1921 as a manufacturer of mining equipment. In the 1930s, Kamotsu expanded into crawler-type farm machinery and steel castings and, in 1940, added the production of large hydraulic presses. In 1942, Komatsu began manufacturing bulldozers and dozer attachments, now its most important product line. Soon after World War II, it started making its own diesel engines and expanded into fork lift truck production. In the 1950s, Komatsu entered a period of rapid growth, paralleling the reconstruction of Japan. Growth came from a combination of products, some developed internally and others made under license from foreign firms. Several new products were introduced in 1960s. They included the Komatsu-Cummins engine in 1961; power cranes and excavators in 1962; Komatsu-Robbins tunnel boring machines in 1963; the Payloader four-wheel drive shovel loader in 1965; the world's first remote-control amphibious bulldozer in 1969; and an underwater bulldozer in 1972. Along with new product development, Komatsu has emphasized quality improvement activities an a company-wide basis. The company is now well known for its excellent mechanisms related to quality control.

Nippon Steel Corporation

Chairman: Eishiro Saito   President: Yutaka Takeda
Sales: 10,941 (million dollars)   Employees: 69,043

Nippon Steel is the world's leading steel producer in terms of capacity, with an annual productive capability of approximately 45 million tons. In a typical year, it provides roughly a third of Japan's total iron and steel production.

Steel and steel products accounted for 87% of the corporation's sales in 1982. Important products were steel plate and sheets; steel bars and shapes; special steels; fabricated goods, mainly pipes; and pig iron and steel ingot. Other products and engineering services made up the remaining 13% of sales. Exports accounted for 37% of total sales, China was a large customer for the company.

Nippon Steel traces its history back to Japan's first western-style melting furnace, which started operating at Kamaishi in 1857. The resulting Kamaishi Iron Works and a number of other steel companies, including Yawata Steel, Wanishi Steel, Fuji Iron & Steel, Mitsubishi Steel, Kyushu Iron & Steel, and Toyo Steel were integrated as Nippon Steel Co. under government auspices in 1934. After World war II, the company

was split up under the Excessive Economic Power Deconcentration Law into
Yawata Iron & Steel, Fuji Iron & Steel, Nittetsu Steamship, and Harima
Refractories. The present company was formed through the merger of Yawata
amd Fuji in 1970. After its formation, the firm entered into a limited
number of joint ventures overseas, mainly in Southeast Asia.

Although the principal focus of Nippon Steel has been the operation of its
Steel Division, which embraces almost every facet of iron- and steel-
making, the company has been expanding its engineering services in order
to become less dependent on the cyclical steel market. The company's
engineering activities have involved the design, manufacture, and
engineering of numerous types of steel-making plants and equipment. They
also involve computerized management controls for iron- and steel-making
processes.

Kyocera Corporation
    President: Kazuo Inamori
    Sales: 535 (million dollars)   Employees: 7,884

Kyocera corporation is the world's largest manufacturer of ceramic
packaging for semiconductors. The Kyoto-based company makes about 70% of
the world's ceramic packages and generally records an excellent financial
performance. For the years 1976-1981, the annual revenue growth rate has
averaged 29%, with an average return on sales rate of 12%.

The company produces over 3,000 items, an extremely wide variety of
products for its size. They can be categorized into five groups: (1)
semiconductor ceramic packages (50% of total sales in fiscal 1982); (2)
electronic parts, such as chip condensors and quartz oscillators (17.5%);
(3) ceramic parts for industrial machinery (10%); (4) ceramic materials,
such as alumina substrate (7%); and (5) other products, including
artificial jewel (*Crescentvert*), solar cells and solar water heaters, and
Bioceram, a material suitable for medical and dental implants.

Kyocera was established in 1959 by president K. Inamori and seven "kindred
spirits," who worked together at Shofu Kogyo Co., a producer of high

voltage cable glass. Conflicts with superiors led them to resign and start their own firm. Inamori is an especially effective leader, who is known for his ability to inspire employees. Employee effort is a central concept in the "Kyocera Philosophy," which calls for the development of mutual trust and faith among managers and workers, and demands the recruitment of people willing to work two or three times harder than anyone else.

Organizationally, the company is divided into as many as 300 groups of 3 to 50 employees that are called "amoeba organizations." An "amoeba" is the smallest unit (average number of people, about 20) with self-supporting accounting systems subdivided according to the product type or production process. The idea is "to break the sections producing added value into small units." Based on this idea, all the departments except three -- General Affairs, Accounting and R&D -- are subdivided into amoebas and the management of one amoeba is left in the hands of its leader. To judge the productivity of each amoeba and to check if it is really self-supporting financially, a concept of "hourly productivity" had been adopted. It is a coefficient to indicate the added value per hour per member. As a result of this system, everyone knows how much money has been generated by expenditures in various areas, and they tend to maximize their own efforts. Kyocera workers are said to run rather than walk.

Although it is still basically a ceramic materials company, Kyocera is rapidly moving into new product areas, including copying machines, stereos, and hand-held computers. The company is also moving into telecommunications. It is a major partner in a corporation which will compete directly with the soon-to-be-private Japanese telecommunications giant, NTT.

TDK Corporation
President: Fukujiro Sono
Sales: 1,047 (million dollars)   Employees: 7,091

TDK Corporation is the world's largest manufacturer of magnetic recording tapes and ferrite products and a major producer of coil and ceramic components. To most people, TDK means tape. The Tokyo-based company's reputation for high-quality sound and image reproduction has made TDK a household name worldwide.

TDK Corporation was founded in 1935 to undertake the first commercial production of ferrite, a ferromagnetic material invented in 1933 by two Japanese professors at Tokyo Institute of Technology, Drs. Y. Kato and T. Takei.

TDK has grown along with ferrite, and half a century later, it is still the world's leading manufacturer of this essential magnetic material. It makes a broad range of electronic components using ferrite. Drawing on its wealth of knowledge of electronic materials and production technology, the company expanded into ceramic capacitors and magnetic recording tapes in the early 1950s and into ferrite magnets and coil components in the early 1960s. More recently, TDK has further broadened its product development programs by building up expertise in semiconductor technology, new recording media, and new types of magnetic recording heads. TDK's products are used in a wide variety of consumer goods, such as VTRs, audio equipment, and TVs, as well as in office automation, telecommunications equipment, and in many industrial applications.

Traditionally, the company emphasized R&D activities as the basis for growth. To achieve maximum returns on R&D investment, the company has narrowed the scope of its activities to match the principal developments in the electronics industry at large. The company is targeting its resources in three areas -- new recording media, semiconductor applied products, and magnetic heads. It is also beginning to internationalize research activities. A product development facility in Los Angeles, California, was established in 1984 to design and manufacture prototypes of promising transformers, noise filters, power supplies, and other component parts.

In a separate thrust towards new growth, TDK is also now putting emphasis on tie-ups with companies outside of the electronics industry to explore new applications for TDK technology. At present, TDK has collaborative projects with more than 10 companies, both domestic and foreign, the majority of which are in the chemical industry.

Matsushita Electric Industrial Co., Ltd.

Chairman: Masaharu Matsushita   President: Toshihiko Yamashita

Sales: 9,933 (million dollars)   Employees: 38,037

Matsushita is the world's largest maker of consumer electronic products and second to Hitachi as the largest company in the Japanese electrical industry.   The company's products are sold under such brand names as National, Panasonic, Technics, Quasar, Victor, and JVC.   It supplies IBM Japan with personal computers on an OEM basis.

Founded in 1918 to manufacture electrical plugs and sockets, Matsushita was incorporated in 1935.   The company now has seven major lines of business: video equipment (31% of total sales in fiscal 1982), audio equipment (12%), home appliances (21%), communications and industrial equipment (15%) and others (21%).   The last category includes such items as phonograph records, pre-recorded tapes, electric pencil sharpners, bicycles, and photographic products.

Three factors played a substantial role in the company's expansion: licensing agreements, forward integration, and expansion abroad.   In 1952, Matsushita concluded a licensing agreement with Philips, gaining access to most of Philips's technology (lamps, cathode ray and electron tubes, semiconductors).   Similar   agreements   with   Western   Electric (semiconductors, thin-film equipment) and RCA (TVs, radios, tape recorders) followed.   In the late 1950s, the company strengthened its competitive position by assuming most of its own wholesaling functions. Beginning in the late 1950s, a string of manufacturing subsidiaries and joint ventures were set up, mainly in Southeast Asia, North and Latin America and, to a lesser extent, in Europe.   The North American operations were expanded with the aquisition in 1974 of Motorola's TV production interests in the U.S.A. and Canada.

Although Matsushita had been considered a technological follower in the past, the company has been putting a major emphasis in developing its own

R&D since the early 1960s.   It operates 23 principal research
laboratories, including the Central Research Laboratories which are
engaged in all phases of the basic research and development work pertinent
to the company's products.   Internal research has led to the development
of a range of remarkable new products, such as color video tapes
/recorders, color facsimile equipment, and paper-thin batteries.

Matsushita has been at the leading edge of organizational innovation.   In
the 1930s, when the number of employees of the company was then only
1,600, the founder, Konosuke Matsushita, already conceived of divisional
organization as a means of keeping things small and manageable.   Since
then, this principle has not changed.   Matsushita's divisions are largely
autonomous profit centers that are encouraged to compete with one another.